Street Smart
Real Estate Investing
Allen Cymrot's Strategies
for Increasing Your Net Worth

Street Smart Real Estate Investing

Allen Cymrot's Strategies for Increasing Your Net Worth

Allen Cymrot

with

Anita Goldwasser

Dow-Jones Irwin
Homewood, Illinois 60430

This publication is designed to provide accurate and
authoritative information in regard to the subject matter
covered. It is sold with the understanding that neither the
author nor the publisher is engaged in rendering legal, accounting,
or other professional service. If legal advice or other expert
assistance is required, the services of a competent
professional person should be sought.

*From a Declaration of Principles jointly adopted by a Committee
of the American Bar Association and a Committee of Publishers.*

Acquisitions editor: Richard A. Luecke
Project editor: Jane Lightell
Production manager: Stephen K. Emry
Compositor: Carlisle Communications Limited
Typeface: 11/13 Times Roman
Printer: Arcata Graphics/Kingsport

ISBN 1-55623-075-3

Library of Congress Catalog Card No. 87–73241

Printed in the United States of America

2 3 4 5 6 7 8 9 0 K 5 4 3 2 1 0 9 8

TO BARBARA
For your patience, understanding, support, and love

PREFACE

Why do the rich get richer? Have you marveled at friends who take frequent vacations, live in luxurious homes and enjoy an upscale lifestyle—when they earn the same money you do? What's their secret? They work at it.

These people understand the concept of net worth (personal wealth) and know how to increase the value of their assets. Successful investing isn't a matter of luck; it requires planning and know-how. This book helps you meet the challenge—by providing you with the necessary perspective, knowledge, and tools. We'll focus on real estate, the investment vehicle with a proven track record for increasing net worth on an accelerating basis. You'll learn why it's never a bad time to buy—if you buy right, the street-smart way.

My book goes beyond the conventional "cookbook" instructions for real estate investing. This is not a get-rich-quick book that utilizes the old, hackneyed approaches such as pyramiding ten transactions in order to achieve wealth, risky no-money-down techniques, or vague admonitions to buy low and sell high. This book treats real estate as a business, using the sound principles of a business. In addition to showing you step-by-step procedures for buying, managing and selling, this volume explains WHY these strategies work successfully. These insights build your skill and confidence, enabling you to increase your net worth over a lifetime of investing.

I felt compelled to write this book after talking to thousands of investors like you—at seminars for professional people, business groups, and retirement organizations, in addition to lectures before graduate students at the University of Chicago and Stanford University. I found one obvious common denominator; all human beings have some aspect of success, in their business life, social life, or their involvement with charitable organizations. But the vast majority of people haven't carried that success into their investment life. There seems to be a bridge that is missing. This book can serve as that bridge—connecting those principles that reflect your success in other aspects of your life with the investment side of your life.

Many people assert that the United States is the greatest country in the world, citing its many freedoms and opportunities. Yet they don't take advantage of the opportunities to achieve financial freedom. My book will show you how to succeed.

Are you thinking of starting modestly—purchasing your first home, or investing in a duplex? Perhaps you're ready to invest in an apartment house, office buildings, or even a $20 million dollar shopping center. Whatever your investment choice, this book shows how to achieve success. Using my exclusive Economic Valuation System, you'll be able to screen prospective purchases for seven major physical and financial factors that make or break a deal. The sound business principles you'll apply worked in the past, they're effective today, and they'll work in the future—for novice investors as well as sophisticates.

I guarantee to sweep away the mystique of real estate investing without resorting to a confusing jumble of numbers and charts. Whether you choose to invest (and manage) actively or passively, this book will pave the way for your profits.

I wish to thank Anita Goldwasser for her skilled help in transforming my ideas and thoughts into a meaningful book. Her contributions to the team effort are much appreciated. William H. Oliver, my agent, has earned a special acknowledgment of gratitude. He suggested that I write this book and was a welcome source of encouragement as I worked on it. At this time, I would also like to recognize the many people associated with me in the real estate field through the years; they have enriched my life. Finally, I want to express my thanks to the editors at Dow-Jones Irwin for their enthusiasm, patience, and understanding.

ALLEN CYMROT

CONTENTS

Weekends. Evaluating the Location. *Hilltop Locations: The Aesthetics Are Nice, but the Problems Aren't.* Tips to Remember.

The Good News and Bad News About Repairs. The Perils of Ignoring "Minor" Repairs. First Steps in Verifying Structural Integrity. *Visual Inspection. Look at Recent Work Orders. Talk to Clients/Tenants. Interview the Staff. Interview the Potential Seller.* Hiring the Right Professional. The Structural Integrity Worksheet. Tips to Remember.

The Empty Box. A Tale of Two Buildings. Style. Amenities for Today and Tomorrow. The Amenities Worksheet. Tips to Remember.

A Quantitative Look at Capitalization Ratios. *Small Changes in the Capitalization Rate Lead to Major Changes in the Bottom Line.* A Qualitative Look at Capitalization Ratios. *Analyzing Income. Analyzing Expenses.* Tips to Remember.

The Lender's Point of View. Your Role as a Corporate Treasurer. How to Obtain the Best Possible Mortgage. Seven Keys to a Good Mortgage. *1. Initial Cost of Mortgage. 2. Mortgage Costs Along the Way.*

Which Should You Choose: Fixed or Variable?
Taking Advantage of Interest Rate Changes.
Impounds. 3. When Must the Mortgage Be Paid
Back? 4. Lock-in and Prepayment Considerations. 5.
Assumptions of a Mortgage. 6. Can the Lender Attach
Your Personal Assets? 7. How Committed Is the
Lending Institution? Beware of Participation
Mortgages. Tips to Remember.

The Upside and Downside of Borrowed Money. Risk.
Achieving Perfect Balance. Negative and Positive
Borrowing Costs. *What Leverage Is Appropriate for*
You? Special Buying Opportunities. Avoid
Overextending Yourself. Keeping Leverage Flexible.
Increasing Your Leverage. Decreasing Your Leverage.
Final Thoughts on Leverage. Tips to Remember.

The Buck Stops with You. The Buck Stops with Your
Property Manager. Generating Income. Expenses:
Keeping Them Under Control. Selection of a
Property Management Company. Property
Management: People versus Things. Tips to
Remember.

Income Stops Growing. Rising Capital Expenditures.
Anticipating the Turning Point. *Area. Location.*
Structural Integrity. Capitalization Ratio. Steps in
Selling. *Setting a Price and Terms. Cleaning Up*
Your Act. Marketing Your Real Estate. While You're
Waiting for a Buyer. What Next? Tips to Remember.

CHAPTER 1

STARTING ON SQUARE ONE

Most people know how to earn money, but not how to make it grow. They choose a career, learn how to excel in it, and receive a good salary. But then what happens to their personal financial growth? For too many individuals, nothing happens. Their bank accounts remain anemic. In school, we're never taught how to take the next step—that of increasing our net worth. Many individuals don't even know that this term refers to the value of their overall assets—their personal wealth. How can they reach for something they don't understand?

Your net worth is a living, dynamic figure—a statement of your financial accomplishment. Successful people keep frequent tabs on this figure. But you rarely hear average people ask one another, "What are you doing to increase your net worth?" When was the last time YOU used the term "net worth" in the context of increasing your personal wealth? You can't take steps to increase your net worth unless you understand the concept, think about it, talk about it, and *do* something about it. If you think, "I'd like to get rich," you can't achieve this goal unless you know what "rich" is. "Rich" is an increased net worth—but you aren't going to increase your net worth unless you have reasons for doing so. You're unlikely to make a strong effort until you specifically identify WHY you want to be rich. Take the time to think about what you want in life. After clarifying your goals and motivating yourself, you're ready to start making plans to become financially rich.

How can you increase your net worth? Putting money in the bank is a conservative approach. Other investments bring greater financial rewards. This book will help you develop a long-term philosophy and strategy for investing. Historically, sensible investments in real estate have been one of the best ways to increase net worth on an accelerating basis.

This book isn't designed for people who want to make day trades on the stock market, or in-and-out real estate transactions within a month to keep pace with new legislative changes. If you apply sound business principles to real estate investing, you will be positioned for a longer term holding period—*and greater amounts of appreciation.* This long-term approach is probably one of the major reasons why real estate investing has been more successful than most other forms of investment; it doesn't rely on "in-and-out" transactions. Short-term investment strategies saddle you with hefty commission costs; they also considerably reduce the probability of success.

The greater your net worth, the easier it is to enjoy "the good life." What does "the good life" mean to you? This is an appropriate time to stop and define this concept for yourself.

We spend a great deal of time planning our leisure-time activities, but a disproportionately small amount of time developing a strategy to increase our net worth. The average couple planning to go out on Saturday night discusses a wide range of choices: Where should we have dinner? What show should we see afterward? Who should we go with? What will we wear? Who will baby-sit the children? What time should we pick up the sitter?

But when a broker or friend comes up with a hot "get-rich-quick" tip, people tend to open their wallets without asking key questions. Does the investment make sense from a business point of view? They don't bother to find out about the bottom line. Yet people train themselves to ask questions about most other things they're interested in. If your hobby is tennis and a friend says, "Here's a great tennis racquet you should buy," you would ask a series of questions about the weight, how it is strung, the guarantee, and a host of other factors. Because you're familiar with tennis, you aren't going to buy a racquet without asking qualifying questions.

Why don't people do this before investing? Because they haven't trained themselves. This book will be your bridge to investment success, developing your ability to ask the right questions.

ASKING THE RIGHT QUESTIONS

Do you have friends with similar backgrounds and earnings who enjoy a richer lifestyle? How do they accomplish this? They probably spend time evaluating where they are financially, where they want to be in a few years, and how to get there. They do their homework, evaluating potential investments carefully. They plan their financial future in a businesslike manner. You might think of this approach in terms of taking an automobile trip from point A to point B—only, in this case, you'll be reflecting on a financial destination. What are your goals? How can you achieve them? What path will you follow? Do you have the discipline to carry through? Your rewards are the goals that you set. They can be whatever you dictate—perhaps a month-long trip around the world, an expensive home and car, or a comfortable retirement before you're 50.

Throughout this book, we'll introduce you to a number of "laws" that emphasize the basics of real estate investing. Here's the first:

CYMROT'S LAW NUMBER 1:
Introspection Is a Must

Before making any investment decisions, you must understand yourself and your financial picture. Research yourself before analyzing prospective real estate investments. Evaluate the security of your job or business, the amount of time you can commit to investment research, and your preference for active versus passive investing.

John Smith = A Business

Before making any investment decisions, develop the habit of thinking in business terms. Take the first step by following the same practices used by owners of successful companies. These people evaluate their firm's success by focusing on balance sheets and profit and loss statements. We'll explain these accounting terms shortly. As long as we live in a capitalistic society where money is the means of exchange and a measure of wealth, you should treat your financial picture just as if you are a business. Consider that your personal business is John Smith, Inc., with you as the president, chief executive officer, and treasurer, in charge of long-term planning. Then apply business principles to your financial picture. Prepare your own profit and loss statements and balance sheets periodically. Once you regard yourself as a business entity, it will be easier to relate to the business aspects of real estate investing—or any other type of investing.

THE "GOOD LIFE"

Recognizing that there's more to life than financial statements, let's look at the broad picture before discussing real estate investments. Figure 1-1 highlights the three key essentials composing the triangle of life. You need to dedicate a reasonable time to each one if you want a productive, satisfying life.

   This triangle represents the sum of everything that contributes toward "the good life" for you and your family. When you enjoy good health, outstanding personal relationships with family, friends, and business associates, plus a great deal of discretionary income (financial security), the quality of your life is enhanced. If one of these three elements is diminished or missing, it's more difficult for you to be productive and make positive contributions to your personal and family well-being.

FIGURE 1–1
Your Personal Triangle of Life

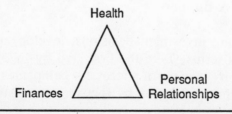

Since this book isn't about health or personal relationships, let's move to the finances side of the triangle. There are two ways to evaluate the financial success of a company or an individual. The first is a profit and loss statement. The second is a balance sheet. These comprise the essence of your whole financial picture.

CYMROT'S LAW NUMBER 2:
You Increase Net Worth by Understanding Business

So that all readers have a complete understanding of profit and loss statements and balance sheets, we'll examine them now.

PROFIT AND LOSS STATEMENTS

A profit and loss statement (often referred to as a P&L statement) is an accounting record that shows net profit or loss over a cumulative period of time. It consists of two parts: income and expenses. Although the time frame is generally one year, some businesses prepare P&L statements quarterly, monthly, or even weekly. The P&L statement is a cumulative total of all income that was taken in from business transactions during a fiscal period, minus all of the expenses for the same cumulative time. These expenses include tax liability and interest on debt. Anything left over is profit.

Business Profit and Loss Statement

Figure 1–2 shows a greatly simplified profit and loss statement for a real estate business.

Personal Profit and Loss Statement

A personal profit and loss statement (see Figure 1–3) shows whether you are spending too much or not earning enough. Have you ever prepared one of these statements by adding up your expenses during a particular time frame and subtracting them from your income? When

FIGURE 1–2
Profit and Loss Statement for Idyllic Real Estate,
January 1, 1987–December 31, 1987

Income:	$10,000
Expenses	−(4,000)
Net Operating Income (NOI)	$ 6,000

Explanation: Net Operating Income is defined as Income
minus Expenses.

Net Operating Income:	$ 6,000
Debt Service:	−(4,500)
Profit (Operating Cash Flow)	$ 1,500
Profit Margin:	15%

Explanation: Debt Service includes mortgage payments and
other debts.

The "bottom line" is your operating cash flow.

$$\text{Profit margin} = \frac{\text{Operating Cash Flow}}{\text{Income}} \times 100$$

A discussion of profit margins appears later in this chapter.

was the last time you did so? Have you analyzed the results? Did you
have money left over? How much? What did you do with those funds?
If you used them wisely, they could boost your net worth.

Later in this chapter, we'll analyze the financial statements of
three individuals.

FIGURE 1–3
Personal Profit and Loss Statement for John Jones,
January 1, 1988–December 31, 1988

Income:	
Earnings	$30,000
Interest and Dividends	1,000
Total Income:	$31,000
Expenses:	
Food, Clothing, Entertainment	12,000
Housing	9,000
Interest & Principal on Loans	1,000
Insurance	1,000
Taxes	6,000
Total Expenses:	$29,000
Profits (money left over):	$ 2,000
Profit Margin:	6.5%

If we think of ourselves as a business, we must keep records of our expenses. Some people divide their expenses into too many categories and this complicates matters. Keep your list simple; include all expenses, but restrict the subject headings to major categories. Like any business, you can't evaluate your expenses or fine-tune them unless you add them up and analyze them. Then, compare them to your income.

BALANCE SHEETS

A balance sheet is a statement showing the assets and liabilities of a business at a particular point in time. The bottom line indicates net worth—what you would have left if you liquidated all your assets. It represents a summary that is true at a single point in time.

You can't have a balance sheet without a profit and loss statement first. What is the impact of a P&L statement? It increases or decreases the net worth on your balance sheet, depending upon the extent of profits (cash flow) that make up the bottom line.

Businesses prepare balance sheets quarterly and annually. By comparing the results at various times, they can see whether their net worth is growing or shrinking. Financial experts measure a company's success by its balance sheet, not by its earnings.

Figure 1–4 is a sample balance sheet for a typical business.

FIGURE 1–4
Balance Sheet for Idyllic Real Estate, January 1, 1988

Assets:		
Land	$ 100,000	
Building	900,000	
Cash	10,000	
Appliances	20,000	
Equipment	5,000	
Total Assets:	$1,035,000	
Liabilities:		
Mortgage	$ 600,000	
Debt on Equipment	10,000	
Total Liabilities:	$ 610,000	
Equity in Investment:	$ 425,000	= Net Worth

Personal Balance Sheet

A personal balance sheet shows the assets you own—anything that has value. Estimate the monetary value of your home, car, stocks, bonds, and savings; and your personal possessions such as furniture, books, clothing, jewelry. From that total, subtract money you owe, such as your mortgage, credit card debt, and money owed on your car. What does your personal balance sheet tell you? If you sold everything you own and paid off all your debts, the money left would be your net worth at the moment.

A negative net worth signifies impending or actual bankruptcy. You cannot have a negative net worth and survive in the business world. If your net worth stays the same from one year to the next, you're not going anywhere. If your net worth has increased, how can you use that money effectively?

Figure 1–5 shows typical entries in a personal balance sheet. Although magazine articles frequently print sample balance sheets that encourage you to break down your assets into numerous categories, it's not necessary to go into great detail for your personal balance sheet. You're not working on a budget analysis, but an overall picture. For example, it's not necessary to list the individual

FIGURE 1–5
Personal Balance Sheet for Susan Jackson, January 1, 1988

Assets:	
Vehicles	$ 15,000
Personal	5,000
Cash	3,000
Furniture	6,000
House	80,000
Stocks, bonds	5,000
Total Assets:	$114,000
Liabilities:	
Debt on car, furniture	$ 20,000
Mortgage	60,000
Total Liabilities:	$ 80,000
Net Worth:	$ 34,000

(Net Worth = Total Assets minus Total Liabilities = Personal Wealth)

values of your first car, second car, RV, and boat when one total figure for all vehicles will suffice.

A WINNING PROGRESSION

- Convert excess earnings from your profit and loss statement to good investments.
- Use part of that money to invest in real estate; this moves tangible assets to your balance sheet.
- As your investments increase in value, your net worth increases.

FINANCIAL STATEMENTS: WHAT DO THOSE NUMBERS MEAN FOR YOU?

What role do these financial statements play in your life? They represent one of the key essentials in the Triangle of Life. Your P&L statement represents income available to pay for such items as food, clothing, and entertainment. Your current earnings finance these expenditures.

Your balance sheet represents assets. When you buy a home, a car, a boat, or finance your child's education, the money for these and other major capital expenditures comes from your balance sheet—your net worth—not from your current earnings. These expenditures are financed by the strength of your balance sheet. Your income may make the monthly payments, but your balance sheet provides funds for the down payment.

Income buys daily necessities and little frills; ASSETS BUY OTHER ASSETS. You can replace one asset with another—buying a larger home by selling your first home, or buying a new car by selling your older one.

A balance sheet reflects how well you manage your income. Each year you try to add more and more to the bottom line. When you compare your balance sheets at yearly or half-yearly intervals, you'll know whether your net worth is growing or shrinking. How well are you managing your income? This trend over a period of time will answer that question. That's why it's important to prepare these statements periodically.

Important Point. A person is much better off with a strong balance sheet and very little income than with a large income and a sick balance sheet.

As an example, consider the financial picture of the following two individuals. Which one is likely to have a greater net worth?

Harry Executive, president of his own company, earns $150,000 a year. He drives a $30,000 Mercedes, lives in a home worth $500,000, has an extensive wardrobe, and takes frequent vacations. There's a mortgage of $400,000 on his home, and he owes $20,000 on his car.

Pamela Pennypincher, a widow, lives in a modest house worth $80,000. The mortgage has been paid off. Her only income is a $500 monthly Social Security check plus income and dividends from stocks, bonds, and certificates of deposit with a market value of $300,000.

Now, read between the lines of these simplistic vignettes. Although Harry Executive earns a hefty income, he's a big spender with a lavish lifestyle. Chances are that Pamela Pennypincher has a healthier balance sheet and a greater net worth. These are extreme cases that are totally the opposite of each other. Harry probably spends too much and Pamela too little. Harry's net worth stays static and Pamela's goes up. Net worth has value to you only when you use it. Make your net worth grow; then use it and enjoy it!

WHAT'S THE VALUE OF A BUSINESS MENTALITY?

We've talked about using a businesslike approach to increasing your net worth—but how should we define the term business? It is an entity that attempts to produce profits from the sale and/or leasing of goods and/or services. A business is an activity involving many different types of decisions. These include the hiring and training of personnel, obtaining clients and servicing them, managing income and expenses so there will be more income and less expenses, firing of personnel, and the preparation of manuals and working procedures. A business involves conformance to various laws and mores within society. In other words, it's a breathing, living activity with significant interrelations between people and society.

A corporation can be an entity; so can a person who produces goods or services by working. How does real estate fit into the picture? **Real estate is a business that buys, sells or leases square feet.**

Why are profits so important? Since we use money as the medium of exchange for all goods and services, the more money you can generate, the greater its value. If you, as an individual, develop skills that can generate money, people will hire and pay you. If a business generates money, people will be willing to buy that business for a higher price. If you buy good real estate, maintain it well, and have the ability to attract clients willing to pay higher rents, you've increased the value of that building. You'll be able to sell it at a profit.

PROFITS

Profits refer to the financial gain from a transaction. Put simply, we might express it as:

Sales price − (cost + expenses) = profits.

What's the difference between profits and profit margin? Prior to the ultimate sale of real estate you own, one of the key measurements in determining how much profit you can sell the real estate (or any business) for is the profit margin. The profit margin is the relationship between the money you have left after paying all your expenses and the amount of money you've taken in along the way. It can be expressed in the following formula:

$$\frac{\$ \text{ left after paying expenses and taxes}}{\text{Sales or income taken in}} = \text{Profit margin}$$

Suppose your income is $100. After paying expenses and taxes, you have $1 left. That's a 1 percent profit margin. Such a small profit margin doesn't leave much room for error. If your income doesn't increase, you must manage expenses very carefully.

Refer to Figure 1–2 for a sample profit and loss statement.

What do profit margins tell you? They are a continuing measurement within the P&L statement of the relationship between income and expenses. You must always analyze income and expenses on a separate basis, but it is equally as important to measure the relationship between the two. Profit margins indicate trends over a period of time. Businesspeople watch out for the danger signal of deteriorating profit margins, which means that income isn't going up fast enough while expenses are going up too fast. Or, expenses may be going up while income is going down or staying the same. Ideally, you want to widen the gap between income and expenses. You can achieve this in two ways:

1. Income increases while expenses decrease.

2. Income increases at a faster rate than expenses.

Corporations pay accountants a fortune to analyze profit and loss statements. Keep tabs on your financial health regularly. If your P&L statement for last year shows that you had 2 percent of your income left over after all expenses, and you have 4 percent left over this year, you're moving in the right direction. Your profit margin is a key ingredient in determining the relation of your income to your expenses. You *must* be aware of this figure before you can ask yourself questions such as, "Am I spending too much money on entertainment? Have I borrowed too much, with high interest due? Am I paying too much in taxes?"

Interpreting Personal Financial Statements

What messages do P&L statements and balance sheets reveal? We'll examine financial statements for three individuals. The first person is twenty-five years old, owns a car, and rents an apartment. The second person is forty years old and owns two cars and a house. The third person, a fifty-year-old, owns three cars, the house he lives in, and has invested in additional real estate.

Person A, the twenty-five-year-old, has a total income of $31,000 and expenses of $29,000. That leaves $2,000, for a profit margin of 6.5 percent.

Person B, the forty-year-old, has an income of $42,000 and expenses of $37,000. His profit margin is 11.9 percent, almost twice the bottom line of Person A.

FIGURE 1–6
Secrets Revealed in Personal Financial Statements

Profit and Loss Statements

	Person A Age 25	Person B Age 40	Person C Age 50
INCOME:			
Earnings	$ 30,000	$ 40,000	$ 55,000
Interest & Dividends	1,000	2,000	5,000
Total Income	31,000	42,000	60,000
EXPENSES:			
Food, clothing, entertainment	12,000	13,000	15,000
Housing	9,000	11,000	20,000
Interest & Principal on Loans	1,000	2,000	3,000
Insurance	1,000	1,000	3,000
Taxes	6,000	10,000	12,000
Total Expenses	29,000	37,000	53,000
Net Earnings (Profit)	2,000	5,000	7,000
Profit Margin	6.5%	11.9%	11.7%

Balance Sheets

	Person A	Person B	Person C
ASSETS:			
Cars	$ 15,000*	25,000**	30,000***
Personal	5,000	10,000	20,000
Cash	3,000	20,000	50,000
Furniture	6,000	15,000	25,000
Stocks and Bonds	17,000	40,000	60,000
House	—	150,000	200,000
Other Real Estate	—	—	100,000
Total Assets	46,000	260,000	485,000
LIABILITIES:			
Debt (cars, furniture, stock margin account)	20,000	40,000	60,000
Home mortgage	—	100,000	75,000
Mortgages on other real estate	—	—	75,000
Total Liabilities	20,000	140,000	210,000
Net worth (Assets minus Liabilities)	26,000	120,000	275,000

* One car
** Two cars
*** Three cars

Person C, the fifty-year-old, has the highest income ($60,000) but his profit margin is 11.7 percent, a fraction less than Person B.

All of these people are in reasonably good health financially. If you were lending money to one of these people, which one would you choose? Which one has a better ability to save money? Which one appears to be managing his or her affairs best? Earnings don't tell the entire story. To determine who is the best manager, look at the profit margins.

Now let's evaluate their balance sheets. These simplified statements ignore potential tax liabilities. If Person A sold everything he owned and paid off his debts, he would have a net worth of $26,000. Person B has a net worth of $120,000. Person C has amassed a net worth of $275,000. Observe that his assets also include investment real estate worth $100,000. At retirement time, this individual can augment his income from investment real estate with earnings from an IRA, a pension plan, and Social Security.

Important Point.   If you take control and manage your affairs well when you're young, you won't have to let the tide carry you along.

If Person B owned investment real estate, his net worth might be closer to that of Person C, but he would have achieved his goal ten years earlier on the time scale. Take charge now, and you might be in the position of Person C long before you reach fifty.

PROFITS AND LOSSES IN THE REAL WORLD

"How high can it go?" That's the first question most people ask before they invest. They're overly optimistic, with visions of making bundles of money. But when someone recommends an investment, it's smarter to ask, "How low can it go?" If an investment doesn't work out, you face an uphill battle waiting for the value to struggle back to its original amount. Recovering a loss is much more difficult than most people realize.

Business is a matter of percentages. Figure 1–7 demonstrates how difficult it is to get back to where you've started.

If you invest $100 and the value of the investment declines to $50, you lose 50 percent of your money. What percentage does it

FIGURE 1–7
The Sad Truth about Losses

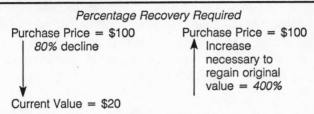

Percentage Recovery Required

Purchase Price = $100
  80% decline

Current Value = $20

Purchase Price = $100
Increase
necessary to
regain original
value = 400%

have to increase to get your money back? A hefty 100 percent, since the value must double.

Let's see how continuing losses work against you geometrically. (We use this term because losses involve a situation that expands and continues to worsen.) The gap widens as the value keeps dropping. Suppose you continue to lose money—another $30 this time—and your investment is now worth only $20. That's a total decline of 80 percent. In this case, a 100 percent increase

---

CYMROT'S LAW NUMBER 3:
Compromise Is Essential

Look for somewhat less appreciation to make sure you're protected on the downside. People are attracted to big returns, but it's often wiser—and safer—to make a tradeoff. Using a stock market analogy, you might be better off with a lower-yielding AAA bond instead of a higher-yielding non-rated bond. The high-risk bond might go up 50 percent if you choose well, but it could decline 40 percent if you've made a wrong decision. The safer choice might be a AAA bond with an upward potential of 20 percent and a downside risk of 5 percent. Always be aware of the risk-versus-return element in your investments. If you settle for a lesser upward movement, this compromise might mean the difference between big profits and sleepless nights. The choice is yours. There is nothing wrong with attempting to achieve high gains, but understand that this is accompanied by high risk. You need to understand the perils of high risk; therefore, let risky investments represent an intelligent percentage of your overall assets.

would only bring the value up to $40. To climb back to its original value, your investment would now have to increase 400 percent.

If you invest in something that declines 20 percent a year for a period of four years, it will require an unrealistically high annual percentage increase to bring you back to your starting point. Remember this if you lose money in the stock market and wait for the stock to regain its original value.

Great But Unrealistic Expectations

Real estate investing is a long-term proposition. We'll see why in later chapters. If you want short-term profits, try the stock market. But even there, be realistic. Suppose you want to trade in stocks and ask your broker, "Can you recommend a stock selling for around $20 a share that could go up $2 per share in a week?" That's only a 10 percent increase. But put it in perspective. A return of 10 percent per week works out to a 520 percent simple not compounded annual return. That's totally unrealistic. In assessing risk and return for any investment, avoid blind greed and blind faith.

Many "how-to" books and real estate seminars suggest that anyone can accumulate a fortune almost overnight—but the "get rich quick" mentality inevitably has flaws. You can't substitute gimmicks for value-oriented investing. Later in this book, you'll learn how to use the exclusive Economic Value System to make long-term profits in real estate.

TIPS FOR INVESTORS

- Think of yourself as a business.
- Prepare profit and loss statements and balance sheets regularly.
- Use your net worth, not your earnings, as a measure of your financial accomplishments.
- Look for trends in your financial statements.
- Analyze risk versus reward. Be prepared to spend time researching potential investments.
- Be realistic. Don't look for the elusive "fast buck."

CHAPTER 2

USING REAL ESTATE TO INCREASE YOUR NET WORTH

Now that you've begun to "think business," we're ready to move forward. This chapter explains why real estate is one of the best tools available to increase your personal wealth and shows how to capitalize on its unique strengths.

Webster's dictionary defines real estate as "improvements on land." We'll view this term in a more practical manner, separating it into two components:

1. Real estate is a business.
2. This business buys, sells, or leases square feet.

Real estate values have been judged or created by a host of measurements. Some are gimmicks, such as tax benefits, and some are merely convenient indicators, such as gross rent multipliers. That's fine if you wish to subject your hard-earned money to fashions and current vogues. Such an approach is all right for buying clothes, but not for investing large sums of money. So let's use a consistent and dependable method, one that applies to all businesses. We can judge the success of a real estate business by the balance sheet, and, more importantly, by the profit and loss statement. The success of any business is judged by these same criteria.

Our definition of real estate refers to income-producing property. This narrows the field down to any real estate that has a profit and loss statement associated with it. In other words, it has clients. Those clients create income and expenses, and therefore we have the same ingredients as any business.

What types of real estate have no profit and loss statements? This category includes raw land, your own private home or a condominium you live in. None of these produce income. A private house doesn't have a profit and loss statement; the person who owns it does. Whether an office building is owned by an individual or a company, that building has its own income and expenses, hence its own profit and loss statement.

We've restricted our definition of real estate to land with improvements. An improvement can be defined as buildings that exist on the land. For our purposes, we don't consider roads, water, or electrical infrastructure as improvements. Raw land has no improvements. It is highly speculative and doesn't fit into our definition. Land doesn't generate a profit and loss statement, it isn't a business, and it doesn't have a structure on it.

Land can be of value in three ways. The first two are commercial and the third is personal.

1. You've purchased the land and you intend to add improvements of a commercial nature, constructing income-producing real estate.
2. Land you've purchased is in the path of progress. You intend to sell it as soon as development continues close enough to the land to warrant a sufficiently high selling price.
3. You purchased the land to build something for personal use that you intend to enjoy. This might range from a second home to a hunting lodge.

Except for those three reasons, don't purchase raw land, because there will be no value to what you've put your money into. In this book, we'll focus on income-producing real estate.

Every business either has a tangible product or provides a service. Supermarkets sell groceries. Lawyers sell their legal services. The product in real estate is square feet. How that square footage is packaged determines what it is called. It could be packaged as a hotel, or packaged another way and called an office building. The packaging depends upon its function. But boiled down to the simplest terms, the "package" is square feet that will be leased or sold. We'll concentrate on the three investments that offer the best opportunities to increase your net worth: housing, office buildings, and shopping centers.

Suppose you're currently in the market for a house or condominium to live in. Is it necessary to read a book like this? Absolutely.

The principles that make income-producing property successful are mostly the same as those that make the owner of a private home or condo successful.

By making a smart purchase initially, you'll be in a better position to make a profit later if you decide to sell or lease your property.

To recap the message from Chapter 1, if you develop a personal P&L statement that shows a profit margin, you can invest part or all of that money in real estate. This investment then becomes an asset that moves on to your balance sheet. You observed in our sample balance sheets for individuals that the fifty-year-old individual who owned investment real estate increased his net worth dramatically. That's the path you can also follow.

CYMROT'S LAW NUMBER 4:
The Only Proper Use of Real Estate Is to Increase Net Worth

The strength of real estate as an investment is no different from any other investment—and that is its ability to make money. As a business, real estate has some unique features which give it certain advantages, but it is no different than any other business. When it generates more dollars on the bottom line, it creates more value. When you sell, the money received boosts your net worth.

WHAT MAKES REAL ESTATE UNIQUE?

Why are housing, office buildings, and shopping centers excellent investments? In the past, they've satisfied basic human needs essential to our society, and, in the future, they'll continue in that role. They provide places where people live, work, and shop—all nondiscretionary, long-term activities. These functions are essential in our daily lives. Many other businesses sell goods and services that are discretionary. You don't *need* a stock or bond, but you do need shelter, a place to work, and stores to shop in. You may not need to buy three new suits this year; one might be enough. But the extras in your wardrobe would be nice to have. That's a discretionary choice. Are you thinking of purchasing a zoom lens for your camera? Unless you're a professional photographer, that decision isn't vital. Again it's a matter of choice. But you absolutely need a place to live, work, and shop. At night you return to a place you own or rent. The next day, you go to work in order to earn an income. On weekends you shop for food. Thus real estate associated with places where people live, work, and shop will be an economically sound investment—if you follow sound real estate principles. They will bring you closer to your goal of increasing net worth than raw land, hotels, and warehouses, all things being equal.

Another unique characteristic of real estate as a business is that it doesn't disappear, even though it may fail to be a money-making venture. When a restaurant or appliance store fails, the business vanishes without a trace. But have you ever seen an apartment house disappear? This characteristic is both good news and bad news.

The good news is that a building has staying power. Assuming that the structure isn't sinking in the middle of Everglades swampland, the owner will have future opportunities to make money with it. The bad news is that other types of businesses can move into areas that offer more opportunities. If the neighborhood deteriorates, a shopkeeper can move to a better area. As the owner of a building, you're stuck.

Like many businesses, real estate is cyclical. Continuing with the real estate-shopkeeper analogy, both can have inventory problems. If a retailer has too many widgets in stock, he can reduce his inventory with a sale, or even give them away to charity. But, if real estate is overbuilt in your area, your inventory of square feet remains fixed. If your apartment house has 200 units, you can't change the amount of your inventory whether the demand is for 100 or 400 units. If the vacancy rate is high, you can't reduce your inventory to match the demand.

Real estate is an industry that creates excesses and shortages for many reasons. During periods of high demand, there isn't enough building space to go around. Prices are high and the boom is on. New construction abounds. This is inevitably followed by an oversupply. Then competition for buyers and tenants heats up. We've lived through the repeated cycles of scarcity and glut in the oil, electronics and automobile industries; we accept these swings as inevitable in any industry that manufactures a commodity. The same holds true in real estate. In a later chapter you'll learn how to take advantage of real estate cycles.

WHAT MAKES A BUSINESS INCREASE IN VALUE?

As long as we're not living in a bartering society, the key ingredient in the business world is money. It's the medium of exchange for buying all goods and services. If you own a business—such as real estate—that has the capability to generate more and more money, it has more value. Figure 2–1 demonstrates this point graphically. In it, we're assuming that you purchased three companies—X, Y, and Z—paying $1,000 for each. At the time of purchase, each had annual earnings of $100.

Now, five years later, Company X is still earning $100 per year. Chances are that it will sell for approximately $1,000 (with a slight adjustment for inflation). So you're right back where you started. There has been no capital appreciation, hence no increase in value. In other words, you can't sell it at a profit.

Company Y now has earnings of $300 per year. Since the earnings have tripled, you might expect to sell it for $3,000, but you're in for a pleasant surprise. When a business is growing, people are willing to pay a little bit out into the future because this growth is intact. The upward trend in earnings encourages buyers to pay a premium price. Adjusting for inflation, you could probably sell Company Y for $3,600. The extra $600 represents a 20 percent premium (.20 × $3,000).

Since earnings in Company Z have gone up six times, a buyer would be willing to pay further into the future. Instead of selling for $6,000 dollars (six times the original price), you might expect a 40 percent premium, making the selling price $8,400, again adjusting for inflation.

The premiums used in this illustration are examples of what a premium could do and are not based on any specific formula.

FIGURE 2–1
A Tale of Three Companies

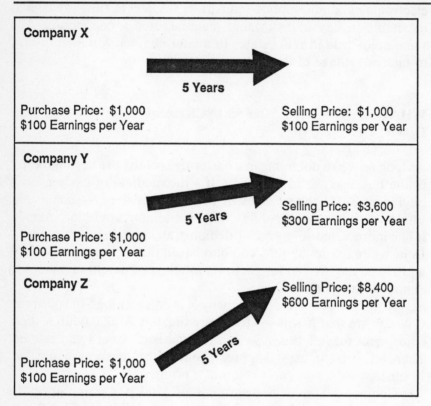

Company X

5 Years

Purchase Price: $1,000
$100 Earnings per Year

Selling Price: $1,000
$100 Earnings per Year

Company Y

5 Years

Purchase Price: $1,000
$100 Earnings per Year

Selling Price: $3,600
$300 Earnings per Year

Company Z

5 Years

Purchase Price: $1,000
$100 Earnings per Year

Selling Price; $8,400
$600 Earnings per Year

Steady growth in earnings attracts buyers willing to pay a premium price. When earnings are flat, people won't pay a premium since there's no growth.

You see this same price action in the stock market where investors look at the price/earnings ratio (p/e ratio). This is defined as the price of a company's stock divided by its earnings. The higher the ratio, the greater the optimism about continued growth in company earnings. For example, if a company earns $1 per share and the stock sells for $10 per share, the p/e ratio is ten. That might be considered average. If the stock is selling for $20 or $30 a share, this higher price reflects greater buyer optimism. As the probability of growth increases, investors attach a premium to the stock and pay a higher price per share. Stock in high-flying companies might sell for more than fifty times earnings if investors feel that the probability of earnings growth will continue.

In real estate or in the stock market, *the more a business grows, the greater the premium people will pay*.

Company Z started out valued at $1,000 and is worth $8,400 now because its earnings have gone up faster than those of the other companies; buyers are willing to pay a greater premium. This is the theory behind creating value in the vast majority of businesses.

Housing, office and retail income producing real estate is a particularly good investment because:

1. It involves a non-discretionary product.
2. You can reasonably project rental increases and expenses accurately if you control the management of the real estate.
3. If your building is financed wisely, is in good physical condition, and is located in a growing area, it will create value for you.

PURCHASE PRICE: BEHIND THE SCENES SLEIGHT-OF-HAND

There's a lot more to the purchase price than you might imagine. First, let's define purchase price as the down payment plus all debt, such as mortgages. The relationship between the debt you incur and the total purchase price lies at the heart of all real estate transactions. Professionals refer to it as leverage. And what is leverage? Webster's dictionary defines it as "the increased means of accomplishing some purpose." In real estate it refers to the use of someone else's money in a reasonable manner. The bank is willing to lend you money and you take advantage of this loan to buy more real estate. The degree of leverage in a transaction depends upon how much of that bank's money you use. Real estate professionals also use the term "structure," which refers to the degree of leverage you put into the purchase price.

In the real world, the way you structure a deal depends upon your goals. What results do you want—income, capital appreciation, or tax shelter? Your down payment could be 100 percent cash or as little as 10 percent cash, depending upon your goals—and your results will be dramatically different.

Before discussing these results, be aware that there are basically three objectives in any investment:

Generate income.

Capital appreciation (increasing net worth).

Tax shelter.

At the present time, tax-oriented investing is legislatively out of favor. But this may not be the case forever. You can take the same real estate purchase at the same price and, by changing the relationship of debt, create entirely different risk-reward programs. Our examples below show three different structures that will achieve widely different risk-reward relationships.

Let's assume that the profit and loss statement for a building indicates an annual income of $1,000 and expenses of $400. The net operating income (NOI) is $600. The purchase price for this property, without the mortgage, is $7,000. There are three ways it can be bought: all cash, moderate leverage, or extreme leverage. First, we'll look at the relationship between down payment and yield.

FIGURE 2–2
Leverage: Down Payment vs. Yield

No Leverage	Moderate Leverage	High Leverage
All cash purchase	40% down payment	14% down payment
NOI = $600	NOI = $600	NOI = $600
Down payment: $7,000	Down payment: $2,800	Down payment: $1,000
Mortgage: 0	Mortgage: $4,200	Mortgage: $6,000
Annual mortgage payment: 0	Annual mortgage payment: $420	Annual mortgage payment: $600
Annual Cash Flow: $600	Annual Cash Flow: $180	Annual Cash Flow: 0
Percent return: 8.6	Percent return: 6.4	Percent return: 0

Mortgage = Purchase price minus down payment
Cash Flow = NOI minus debt service
Percent return on investment = Cash flow divided by down payment × 100

Then we'll see how the down payment affects profits at the time of sale. In this example, we'll assume a mortgage rate of 10 percent (interest only).

At this point, it looks as though the all-cash buyer has the best deal. His yield is highest (8.6 percent) as opposed to a 6.4 percent yield for the person who bought with moderate leverage. The high-leverage buyer is saddled with a high mortgage payment that is equal to his NOI, leaving him with a zero cash flow. But let's see what happens when the property is sold. We'll assume that the real estate doubles in value five years later, and the property sells for $14,000.

We have had a chance to examine three real estate transactions. Which is the best deal? It depends upon what you're looking for. Remember, we didn't factor cash flow into the profit. If we did, and assuming no increases (which is not realistic since we sold the property at a higher price), our figures would look like this:

1. The no-leverage buyer would have received $3,000 of cash flow during the five-year holding period.
2. The moderate-leverage buyer would have received $900 of cash flow during that period.
3. The high-leverage buyer would have received no cash flow.

If you're seeking current return, then the all-cash purchase gives you the highest yield. But yield is only part of the picture. Since real estate is a cyclical business with alternating periods of

FIGURE 2–3
Leverage: Its Power Shows at Selling Time

	No Leverage	Moderate Leverage	High Leverage
Sales Price	$14,000	$14,000	$14,000
Mortgage	0	4,200	6,000
Total Money Received	14,000	9,800	8,000
Original Investment	7,000	2,800	1,000
Profit	7,000	7,000	7,000
Percent Increase	100%	250%	700%

Profit = (Selling Price divided by Down Payment) × 100

high and low vacancy over a period of time, income-oriented investors might be better off buying bonds or high-yielding stocks. If you need income to live on, real estate isn't a steady, reliable source. But if you're looking for capital appreciation over a long period of time, real estate has proven itself. In the next chapter, we'll examine your goals in more detail.

High-leverage profits in the extremely high-leverage example shown above look spectacular, but they are characteristic of a tax deal—the type of investment that is currently out of favor because of changes in tax laws. These deals are also a high-risk situation. You *must* buy at the bottom of a real estate cycle. If you don't, the chances of success are very limited; there is no room for error. Without a crystal ball, the odds of buying at the exact low point of a cycle are 7 to 1 against you. We'll discuss this more fully later in the book under our section on cycles. Too much leverage leaves you with no extra money coming in to use in case of an emergency. If you misjudge expenses, you have no room for error.

Let's go back to some basic premises about real estate. It is a long-term investment—often five to seven years or more. During that period the economy will experience good times and bad times. If you leverage too much, the operating losses you'll suffer during the bad times may not allow you to hold on to the property long enough for it to appreciate.

Important Point.   It isn't necessary to take big chances to make good money in real estate.

Investors using high leverage in real estate are taking as much risk as investors in the commodity market. When you're right, the return is wonderful; but most commodities traders lose money in the long run. So do real estate investors who buy on the basis of phantom tax advantages rather than fundamental values. Recall our example in Figure 1–7 of the difficulties in "getting back to square one" after incurring losses. You need increasingly higher geometric returns. Avoid this problem by minimizing the risk of a loss. Stay away from highly speculative investments.

In our example, we see that the moderate-down-payment investor has the best of both worlds. He receives an income and still makes a handsome profit when the property is sold.

LONG-TERM VERSUS SHORT-TERM INVESTING

People who buy stocks as short-term traders often find their profits disappointing over a long period of time. They look at the price every day and ask themselves, "Should I sell now?" A better way, in real estate and in the stock market, is to invest over the long term. This orientation removes the need to make daily buy-sell-hold decisions. When people look at the stock market every day and ask themselves, "Should I sell? Should I buy?", what are they looking at? They're looking at the price, not at the profit and loss statement or the balance sheet of the company. Yet the price doesn't tell them whether the value of the company will go higher or lower. They're basing their decision on the trend of the stock price, not on the company's value. Remember that when you buy and sell stocks or real estate, there is a cost, known as the commission. You incur that cost every time you buy or sell. Add this burden to the geometry of return that is necessary if you incur losses (when you don't study P&L statements) and you have added one more dimension against the possibility of success.

One of the reasons people have done well by owning their homes is that they distance themselves from daily decision-making. If newspapers published listings of the value of homes, you would check them out frequently—and be tempted to take action if prices shifted. But when you buy wisely and hold good property for the long term, paying more attention to fundamentals, you have a better chance of achieving success.

By its nature, real estate is a long-term investment, as you'll see in the section on cycles. Even if you buy at the bottom of the market, it still takes an average of five to six years to get to the next top point, because you're dealing with supply and demand created by the marketplace. Occasionally, wheeler-dealers buy something on a Monday and sell it on a Friday, but that's the exception. It's wiser to stay with the rules and not the exception, investing on a long-term basis, for five years or more. People who take a long-term approach to their investing are more comfortable about it. Your real estate investments should therefore be made with extra money you won't need in the immediate future. These are funds over and beyond emergency funds set aside.

CYMROT'S LAW NUMBER 5:

Buy and sell decisions should be based on fundamental changes in profit and loss statements and the balance sheet, not on price changes in the marketplace.

ACTIVE VERSUS PASSIVE INVESTING

Do you want to be involved in the dynamics of buying and selling real estate? Or would you rather sit back and hopefully collect checks? How about managing? Active investors can become involved in the day-to-day affairs, or hire someone to take care of these chores. The beauty of real estate investing is that you have a range of choices. After we discuss some of the factors involved in the role you play, you'll be able to choose the approach best suited to your temperament and available time.

Active investors are involved in all the factors that make up the following areas:

Looking at property.

Dealing with brokers.

Negotiating with buyers and sellers.

Making timing decisions.

Overseeing all aspects of day-to-day management.

Above all, they *must* research all aspects of their investment before signing a contract.

If you're an active investor, you face another choice. Should you manage actively or passively? Here are just a few of the items that active owner/managers deal with:

• Hire, fire, monitor, and train personnel involved in rent collection, leasing, maintenance, gardening, and trash collection.

• Review financial records.

• Plan surprise audits.

• Prepare budgets.

- Make purchasing decisions (supplies, equipment).
- Monitor solutions for bad service.
- Deal with problem clients (tenants).
- Negotiate insurance rates.

As an active manager, you might be called at 3 A.M. if a pipe bursts. You'll also collect rents and screen prospective tenants when there's a vacancy.

Other alternatives to active managing involve hiring a resident manager (on-site manager) or a real estate management company. Since you'll be approaching real estate ownership as a business, there are certain rules of thumb for operating most efficiently.

For example, an apartment building with less than fifteen units generally will not support an on-site manager, so you should plan on taking an active role. The cutoff in some instances might be twelve units; in others, twenty units, depending upon the income generated.

If you have a ten-unit building that collects $10,000 per month rent, you can afford a manager. But it's unlikely that the average ten-unit building will support a manager. If it generates $400 to $450 per unit each month, that's inadequate income to cover the expenses of hiring an on-site manager.

Owners of commercial real estate are less involved with these matters than those of apartment houses. Office buildings and shopping centers generally provide phone numbers for clients requiring maintenance work. Larger ones have maintenance personnel on the premises.

Utilizing the services of a manager for larger property is more efficient; it's also a goal you should reach for. This helps you leverage your time and abilities. If you actively buy and manage your own real estate, you might own a duplex or a fourplex. But when you own several duplexes and fourplexes, you can start leveraging your time. Continue to be active in real estate buying and selling, but hire a company or an on-site manager to take over other duties on your behalf. If you choose this route, refer to the chapter on management for tips on how to evaluate their performance.

If you hire an on-site manager, you'll need to screen applicants and review all of the manager's activities. That means visiting the property every week to review the facilities and the bookkeeping. You'll want to make sure that the manager is purchasing supplies efficiently. Ownership and management of a shopping center or an office building is more complex but less intense than that of an apartment house; we'll discuss the reasons in Chapter 3.

Availability of Money for Active vs. Passive Investing

Does the amount of money you plan to invest affect your choice between active and passive roles? Not necessarily. It doesn't have to be an either/or situation. A person can be active and/or passive about various aspects of management if both make sense to that particular investor. If you have hundreds of thousands of dollars, or even millions, you can choose either route depending upon your temperament and inclinations. Generally, you would need a minimum of about $10,000 in order to invest actively. But if you lack that sum, you might form a partnership with friends and relatives. A $10,000 bankroll might get you started with a $50,000 duplex.

Passive investing generally requires a minimum of $5,000. Chapter 4 has a complete discussion of passive investing and the options available. You'll learn how to find the right people to buy, manage, and sell real estate. After your initial research, you sit back and let the experts take over.

RESEARCH

Most people think the three key factors in real estate investing are: location, location, location. This is wrong. Location is just one of seven key factors that we'll discuss in detail. Instead of "location, location, location," think about "research, research, research." That's crucial to your success.

Why is research so important? Since real estate has all the good news-bad news characteristics of a business, you must evaluate everything that affects the bottom line.

If you open a dry cleaning store in the wrong part of town, it's easy to close down your operation and relocate in another neighborhood. But if you've made a mistake and bought an apartment house in the wrong neighborhood, you're stuck. Your inventory of square feet is fixed. It's impossible to pick up that piece of real estate and move it. Recognizing this fact, you must make absolutely sure that you buy in the right part of town. By applying the seven keys of the Economic Valuation System (EVS) discussed in detail later in this book, you can avoid costly mistakes. You must do your homework. This involves investigating the community— its economy, vacancy rates, and all other physical and financial factors that affect your chances of success.

When we say, "research, research, research," there are seven key areas that this research *must* be performed in. These encompass approximately 100 factors that you should evaluate when looking at any piece of real estate. They cover every aspect of the real estate business. If you investigate them thoroughly, there is a very high probability that your real estate investing will be successful. Many of these apply to your private home or a condo, as well as to larger real estate purchases. We've broken these 100 factors down into seven categories for the Economic Valuation System. Four are physical (area, location, structural integrity, and amenities), while three are financial (capitalization ratio, financing, and leverage). These seven categories are of the utmost importance because if just one of them doesn't seem right, you shouldn't buy.

CYMROT'S LAW NUMBER 6:
Think Business! Your Entire Attitude, Demeanor, and
Approach Should Be That of Perceiving Real Estate as a
Business

Chapter 1 should have motivated you to look at yourself as a business, using the basic tools of profit and loss statements and balance sheets. Now we want to build on those skills and apply them to real estate.

People whose real estate investments have been disastrous usually failed to do enough homework first. If your brother-in-law proposes that you buy a pharmacy with him, you would ask dozens of business-related questions. Does the store have a good reputation? Is it in a growing area? Who will work there? Who are the target customers? Has the store made money in the past? Why is it being sold? How many similar stores are in the same area? Can the store make money in the future?

Many people investing in real estate neglect such fundamentals. They focus on tax advantages, replacement costs, gross rent multipliers, and overlook the bottom line shown on P&L statements. And they lose money by not thinking of real estate as a business. Even when you purchase a house for yourself, it won't have a P&L statement, but by paying attention to physical location, selecting a good school district, and choosing a home with attractive features, you could be paving the way for profits later on, either on a resale basis or by renting it out.

TIPS TO REMEMBER

- Real estate investments can increase your net worth.
- Always approach real estate as a business.
- Invest in housing, shopping centers, and office buildings. These satisfy non-discretionary needs.
- In order to sell at a profit, increase the value of your property by concentrating on the P&L statement.
- Use moderate leverage for the best risk/reward returns.
- Evaluate your preference for active versus passive investing.
- Invest for the long term.
- Research all aspects of the Economic Valuation System carefully.

CHAPTER 3

EXPLORING YOUR OPTIONS

By now, you've moved off square one. You understand how real estate investing can increase your net worth, and you're aware of the differences between investing actively or passively. Now we can explore your options further.

Is income or capital appreciation more important to you? This chapter will help you decide. In our discussion, we'll expose the fallacy that owning property in order to generate income is a conservative approach.

By the time you finish this chapter, you'll be ready to contact real estate brokers. But you won't be ready to buy yet. First, you'll need to master the Economic Valuation System (EVS), the heart of this book. This system helps you distinguish top value real estate from high-risk property.

YOUR GOALS AS A REAL ESTATE INVESTOR

What will real estate accomplish for you? Traditionally, the answers have been:

- Tax write-offs.
- Income stream.
- Capital appreciation (increasing net worth).

Investing for tax write-offs is currently an obsolete approach. For many years, people thought more about tax benefits than the ultimate value of the real estate they invested in. They stalked tax shelters, with enticing thoughts of depreciation, four-to-one write-offs, and other "paper" benefits in mind. But they overlooked one basic truth: real estate is a business, and you invest in business to make a profit. Tax deductions won't increase your net worth; they just increase your paper losses. You can make good money in real estate without relying on tax breaks created by Congress. For historical perspective, consider that the first income tax laws weren't enacted until 1913, yet real estate investors made money long before that time, without tax incentives.

The Tax Reform Act of 1986 eliminated virtually all the tax-shelter benefits of real estate investments. While the House of Representatives debated the pros and cons of this bill, the media inundated us with articles about the proposed legislation. They conveyed the impression that this was the first major change in tax laws in decades. That's not true. To put it in perspective, this bill was the 19th major change in our tax code in a 23-year period.

What's the significance of these constant changes? They're a warning sign. Investing in real estate solely on the basis of tax benefits is highly risky. During some periods, real estate tax shelters are hot items, with investors jumping on the bandwagon; but there's the inevitable bust when Congress changes the benefits of such shelters. Since real estate investments are illiquid, it's foolhardy to invest today on the basis of what you think the tax laws will be years later when you're ready to sell.

As an example, let's look at changes in the depreciation schedule during recent years.

By extending the time it takes to depreciate a building, Congress has reduced the value of depreciation as a tax-saving technique.

We know from experience that the more value you have through increased profits, the greater your chance for increasing net worth, as long as we have a capitalistic society. The conclusion is: Forget about tax shelters. Seek quality instead. Investors who bought into

FIGURE 3–1
Changes in Depreciation Schedules

Year	Depreciation Period
1981	15 years
1985	19 years
1987	28 years

high-flying tax shelters ended up with poorly chosen, marginal property that couldn't generate what they needed most: profits. In any
real estate investment, reduce your vulnerability by seeking value,
not phantom tax benefits.

The Fallacy of Investing for Income

You can seek income only, capital appreciation only, or a combination of the two. Real estate transactions can be put together to
provide various percentages of both.

   At first glance, investing in real estate for income seems like
a sensible, conservative approach. But it's actually a high-risk situation. Are you skeptical? An examination of numbers will drive
home the point.

   Let's assume that you purchase real estate for a cash price of
$62,500. You receive an annual income of $10,000 from it and pay
out $5,000 in expenses per year. (Refer to Chapter 1 for definitions
of the terms used below.)

   Your basic profit and loss statement looks like this:

Income	$10,000
Expenses	− 5,000
Net Operating Income	$ 5,000

   Thus your net operating income (NOI) $5,000 per year. From
these figures, we can calculate the yield:

$$\frac{\text{Net Operating Income}}{\text{Purchase Price}} \quad \frac{\$5,000}{\$62,500} \times 100 = \text{Yield} = 8\%$$

   Now we'll introduce a new term: capitalization ratio. This is
defined as the net operating income divided by the purchase price.
Chapter 10 covers this in detail. A simple calculation provides this
figure:

$$\frac{\text{Net Operating Income}}{\text{Purchase Price}} = \text{Capitalization Ratio} \quad \text{(Formula 3–1)}$$

   The purchase price includes a cash payment plus the debt (e.g.,
mortgage). Assuming that the purchase price is identical to the
value of the property when you buy it, we can re-write the formula:

$$\frac{\text{Net Operating Income}}{\text{Value of Property}} = \text{Capitalization Ratio}$$

To simplify our calculations, assume that you made an all-cash purchase. Thus the number representing the capitalization ratio is the same as your yield. If you had a mortgage, the capitalization ratio would be then based on the net operating income before mortgage payments.

As a real estate entrepreneur, you own a business providing an 8 percent return each year. Everything will be fine if there are no changes. But real estate is a living, breathing business that's cyclical. Here's what can happen.

Suppose you increase rents next year and generate an income of $10,200. That's a jump of 2 percent. But your expenses also increase during that period. They might go up to $5,500, an increase of 10 percent. If the economy is slow and there's a high vacancy rate, you may not be able to raise rents enough to cover these increased expenses. In this scenario, let's see how your profit and loss statement changes:

Income	$10,200
Expenses	− 5,500
Net Operating Income	$ 4,700

Refer back to the formula for capitalization ratio. If your yield stays the same—at the 8 percent level—something has to suffer. In this case, it's the value of your real estate.

After completing the calculation, you'll make the nasty discovery that the value of your real estate dropped to $58,750:

$$\frac{\$4,700}{\text{Value of your real estate}} = 8\%$$

If you tried to sell your property to a buyer who also sought an 8 percent return, the most you could receive would be $58,750. In other words, you would have a loss of $3,750.

The effects snowball. If your property is now worth only $58,750, and you're taking in less income, the yield drops to 7.52 percent. What are the implications? Investing for income only involves high risk. Since you have no control over the economy, if an area becomes overbuilt, or if there's a recession, your expenses could increase—but you might not be able to cover them with increased rents.

Let's face facts: real estate is an illiquid, long-term, cyclical industry. There are only two ways you come out ahead as an income-oriented investor: (1) if you're fortunate enough to buy at the bottom of a cycle and then have prices start a long, consistent upward move. (2) it is the total overall yield during the entire holding period that you are interested in. This type of investor might be a more targeted type such as a pension fund or *Keogh* plan investor. But even professionals aren't infallible at recognizing the tops and bottoms of a cycle. If you get locked in at the wrong part of a cycle, you could face financial disaster.

With commercial real estate you can sidestep the risk of investing for income by writing triple net (NNN) leases. The tenants assume the responsibility for maintenance and utility expenses. This is typically a credit arrangement and the success of the transaction depends on the strength of the lessee.

Another problem with investing for income is the negative impact on the bottom line caused by vacancies. If a unit in your duplex is vacant for two months, you lose 1/12 of your annual income. If you started out small, purchasing a house, and it's vacant for just one month, you lose 100 percent of your income for that period.

When you invest in real estate for income, it's difficult to increase your net worth. Because you receive the money in small amounts, you're less protective of it. People tend to take cash flow and treat the money as earnings. They spend it piecemeal to maintain their lifestyle, take vacations, and purchase the latest electronic gadgets. Even though the money might add up to a significant amount over a period of years, it never increases your net worth. It just vanishes.

But if you invest for capital appreciation, when you sell the property you receive an impressive lump sum that you're not likely to squander. When people receive a large check, they protect it and invest it. You can pyramid the money you receive by purchasing another piece of real estate. By following street-smart business practices each time you buy and sell, you stand a good chance of increasing net worth. Of course, there are no guarantees when you invest for capital appreciation, but there are ways to minimize the risk.

Make Probability Work For You

Suppose you have $10,000 to invest and want capital appreciation plus some income. Can you achieve both? There are no sure-fire investments, either in real estate or in the stock and bond market, but you *can* increase your chances of achieving your goal. The system outlined below makes probability work for you, not against you.

In real estate transactions, compromise hinders rather than helps. If you aim for growth and income from a single investment, its a tug-of-war situation. People who invest in the stock market generally have a better grasp of the income versus growth concept than those starting out in real estate. For example, when a stock pays dividends, the company is diverting funds that it could use to promote growth. The probability is that you won't get much growth. Similarly, with real estate transactions, if you put all your money into a single pot, any income you receive will be detracting from possible capital appreciation.

In the stock market, a better strategy would be to put a portion of your money into an income-generating stock with a modest growth potential and invest the remainder in a rapidly growing company that pays no dividends. Each individual investment has a greater probability of achieving its goal.

If you want to invest in real estate but still want income, too, take a similar two-pronged approach. You could put part of your money in a bond fund, CDs, or a money market fund, and invest the rest in real estate that is leveraged. What is leveraging all about? It's a technique that allows you to buy more property per dollar invested. Instead of paying cash, you might make a down payment of 25 percent to 35 percent and sign a mortgage for the remainder of the purchase price. By having a mortgage, you put other people's money to work for you. When people buy real estate without leverage, the dynamics of capital appreciation versus income work against them, limiting both the income and the potential for capital appreciation. Chapter 12 discusses leverage in detail.

By taking the two-pronged approach mentioned above, the total bottom line *might* be comparable to the amount derived from a single investment in a growth-plus-income real estate investment. But the probability of achieving your goal is greater with specialized investments.

Returns from a $10,000 Investment

	Investment A	Investment B	
	Real Estate All Cash Purchase at 8% Capitalization Rate	Real Estate 40% Down Payment at 8% Capitalization Rate	9% Government Bond	Totals for Investment B
Investment	$10,000	$ 5,000	$ 5,000	$10,000
Total Value of Real Estate	10,000	12,500		
Net Operating Income	800	1,000		
Debt (Mortgage)	0	7,500		
Annual Mortgage Payment at 10 Percent	0	750		
		(interest)		
Cash Flow	800	250	450	700
			(income)	
Yield on Total Investment	8%			7%

By splitting your money between real estate and a government bond, you can afford to be more aggressive in your real estate investment. The government bond represents the conservative portion of your investment.

An Infallible Tool for Real Estate Investors

For centuries, smart real estate investors have based their purchases on certain key fundamentals, but nobody has spelled these guidelines out for the general public. Now that tax-oriented investing is out of favor, real estate gurus offer glittering generalities such as, "Buy value." But what is value? How do you determine whether a building has value or not? The Economic Valuation System (EVS), discussed in detail later on, will become your infallible tool for determining value. It's a detailed screening method applicable to the purchase of a home, condominium, shopping center, office building, or limited partnership. By following it, you'll be applying sound business practices to the purchase of any type of real estate.

The EVS evaluates seven key points:

- Area.
- Specific location within an area.
- Structural integrity.
- Amenities.
- Capitalization ratio.
- Mortgage structure.
- Leverage.

The EVS encompasses approximately 100 factors that you'll learn to use in evaluating property. If, after negotiating with the seller, you find that just one of the above key points doesn't pass muster, the deal should be declared dead. Using the organized methodology of the EVS, you'll be able to buy quality real estate that can increase your net worth. In good times or bad, the owner of good real estate has the edge over the owner of junk.

ACTIVE INVESTING: GET READY, GET SET, GO

If the dynamics of active investing appeal to you, its not necessary to go through an "apprenticeship" as a passive investor first. You can start out in the fast lane by thoroughly researching investment opportunities—choosing between apartments, office buildings, and shopping centers.

Apartments: The Best Choice for New Investors

If you haven't had any experience investing in real estate, apartments are the safest choice, offering you the greatest chance of appreciation.

Why apartments? They're generally easier to acquire since you'll find more apartments on the market than shopping centers or office buildings. You have more choices in managing them, by opting for an active or a passive role. If you choose a passive managerial role, it's relatively easy to find experienced apartment managers. When you sell apartments, you're likely to find more prospective buyers.

And there's another important plus: When novice investors make a mistake, apartment ownership offers the best chance for correcting the error in a short time frame. You can also adjust more readily to changes in supply and demand. What sort of mistakes are you likely to make? Typically, you might not charge enough rent. As you saw in our discussion of Formula 3–1, if your rents don't cover expenses, the value of your investment decreases.

Since apartment leases are generally shorter than those for offices and shopping centers, you have the opportunity to increase rents more frequently and compensate for your error sooner. Apartment leases generally run for one year. Suppose you rented an apartment for that length of time, asking $50 less than it was worth. You have lessened the value of your investment temporarily; but a year later, when the lease is up, you can raise the rent.

Commercial leases run three years or longer. This makes it more difficult to adjust to changes in supply and demand. Since your lease determines the value of the real estate, undercharging commercial property tenants is more costly for you. It could take years before you have an opportunity to correct the mistake.

The short-term leases common in apartment renting have a good news-bad news aspect. The good news is that you can increase rents more frequently. The bad news is that they adjust more suddenly when the economy slows down. Your commercial tenants might be locked into a three-year lease that cushions the blow for you; but if competition in the apartment marketplace heats up, you may have to decrease the rents sooner.

Apartment management is more intensive than that required for commercial property. Someone must be available seven days a week, 24 hours a day. Like a doctor on call in the middle of the night, that person should expect occasional emergency phone calls if a pipe bursts at 3 A.M. Commercial property management generally involves a five- or six-day week, with shorter hours.

The "someone" who must always be available needn't be you. Although you're an active investor, you can be a passive manager, hiring someone to oversee day-to-day operations. At what point is it economically feasible to do so? Here are some guidelines.

If you own an apartment house with more than 15 units, it's more efficient to hire an on-site manager. This allows you to keep leveraging your position—taking an active role in purchasing other property while someone else handles the everyday necessities. Similarly, if you own several duplexes or fourplexes, it pays to hire a manager.

Although many small investors buy individual houses, this can be risky. Your vacancy rate can skyrocket from zero to l00 percent the day a tenant moves out. If you don't have the money or the inclination to go it alone, consider pooling your money with a few other investors and purchasing a duplex or fourplex together.

Rental agreements for apartments are relatively straightforward—about two pages long—making it easier for novice investors to handle the negotiations. Commercial leases are complex documents, often 20 pages long. They involve agreements about common areas, sales participation, incremental increases based on the Consumer Price Index, tenant improvements, and other subtleties. Thus novice investors find it easier to start out with apartments.

Laying the Groundwork for Your First Investment

How do you feel about making your first real estate investment? Excited? Scared? Intimidated? Enthusiastic? It may be a combination of all these—and more. The stakes are high, with your hard-earned income on the line. How much do you really know about the business end of real estate investing? Start out by assessing your level of knowledge about the subject.

Let's assume your know-how is limited. Before visiting a broker, check out real estate classes given at local community colleges and adult education centers. You could also attend classes at private schools that specialize in real estate courses.

You'll find three trade organizations particularly helpful at this stage, and later on, too:

- Real Estate Securities and Syndications Institute (430 N. Michigan Avenue, Chicago, IL 60611). This organization has chapters in every state. Speak to someone at the local chapter to find out about currently available courses.

- National Institute of Real Estate Management (same address as above) publishes a series of guidelines, particularly for apartment owners, that reveal current management costs in all sections of the country. You'll find out the going rates in your area for such expenses as personnel, gardening, and utilities.

- National Association of Realtors (777 14th St. NW, Washington, DC 20005), possibly the largest national real estate organization, can provide you with a wide range of information. Ask them about upcoming trade shows.

In the appendix of this book, you'll find a list with names and addresses of 19 real estate-related organizations. They're a bountiful source of information.

Trade shows offer you a golden opportunity to learn about real estate from the experts. At seminars, you'll become aware of the latest management techniques and insights. Visit the booths and chat with professionals who are well-versed in the business end of real estate investing. These conversations pay rich dividends.

Subscribe to as many real estate trade publications as possible to keep up-to-date on regional and nationwide trends. The appendix contains names and addresses of major magazines and newsletters.

Narrowing Down Your Options

Read the classified ads in your local newspaper, particularly the Real Estate Investment Income section. These listings are longest on Sundays. The ads for apartments, industrial, and commercial properties can be as educational as a magazine article—and they're more up-to-date. By studying them regularly, you'll develop a "feel" for trends, purchase prices (cash plus mortgage), per square feet costs, and the marketplace in general. Do this research to gain perspective before approaching a broker. Then you can compare and evaluate his offerings with what you've observed on your own.

After this initial research, you'll feel more confident about approaching a broker. But don't stop with just one. Visit several brokerage firms. Since you're going to commit your money for a long period of time, it's essential to shop around. When you buy a car, you visit several dealers for the best deal. Here, too, you won't want to buy in haste.

You can deal with a well-known large national firm, or with a regional firm. At the regional companies, talk to the owner or manager. Explain that you've set aside X dollars to invest and discuss your goals. During this frank conversation, identify your own risk tolerance, the type of purchasing terms you want, your financial level, and objectives. When the broker knows the return you're expecting from an investment and the degree of involvement you anticipate, he can suggest appropriate transactions. If you have the time and skill to tackle repairs on a turnaround project, say so. If you want minimal involvement, make that clear. After your conversation, the manager will assign you to a broker who can accommodate your needs. You'll want to make sure that the chemistry is right, and this preliminary conversation helps.

While you're still in this data-gathering mode, you'll be taken out to see property. Compare the brokers, the types of real estate they're offering, prices, and the quality of their advice.

The seven-point Economic Valuation System will show you how to separate potentially lucrative property from the "dogs" that owners are trying to get rid of. Take your time looking. A discerning real estate investor could look at a hundred buildings before buying a single one. Street-smart individual investors do the same.

At this point, you've laid the groundwork. There's more research to be done evaluating the financial and physical factors that can make or break your investment. Armed with the data you've gathered, you'll have the courage to walk away from a deal if it isn't 100 percent right for you.

TIPS TO REMEMBER

- Invest in real estate that satisfies basic needs.
- Housing, office buildings, and shopping centers offer the best potential for increasing your net worth.
- Investing in real estate for income could have surprise risks.
- To increase your net worth, aim for capital appreciation.
- Apartments offer the best opportunities to novice investors.
- Contact trade organizations for information.
- Attend classes for real estate investors.
- Read trade publications.
- Visit trade shows.
- Study the local market by reading classified ads.
- After doing basic research, contact two or more brokerage firms.
- Work with the broker who provides the best level of service and know-how.

CHAPTER 4

ACTIVE BEGINNINGS FOR PASSIVE INVESTORS

If you've decided to become a passive investor, you can start with a bankroll that ranges from a few hundred dollars to millions of dollars. As we've seen in earlier chapters, the money you earmark for real estate investing isn't the limiting factor. Your temperament and time available enter into the picture.

While someone else does the legwork, buying and managing a diversified portfolio, you can sit back and wait for checks to arrive in the mail. *But you can't afford to be passive about choosing the investment.* Your money must go into a thriving real estate business, not a pie-in-the-sky promotion.

How can you distinguish between a solid economic venture and a shaky investment? A professional real estate investor can look at the numbers on a profit and loss statement and make a quick decision. This chapter will sharpen those skills, enabling you to uncover the clues buried in balance sheets and prospectuses. Although the Economic Valuation System (EVS) discussed later in the book is designed for active investors, you'll need to understand this system and verify that the managers of your passive investment follow its principles.

THE ABCs OF PASSIVE INVESTING

As you explore potential investments, you'll discover a wide range of offerings that have an alphabet-soup look—REITs, RELPs, MLPs, and more. These refer to Real Estate Investment Trusts, Real Estate Limited Partnerships, and Master Limited Partnerships. As a reaction to changes in tax laws, you will frequently see new real estate packages (often referred to in the trade as products).

Since Congress frequently changes its mind, encouraging tax shelters one year and throttling them the next, investing for tax benefits is risky. People with a "newspaper mentality" base their investments on the immediate, current environment, overlooking the fact that there will be a new set of rules tomorrow. Remember that you'll be selling to a buyer who will be living under new, as yet unknown rules.

As investors discovered to their dismay in 1986, anticipated tax benefits withered when President Reagan signed the new tax bill. Their tax shelter investments, weighted down with the dregs of real estate, couldn't be sold without losses. Had they purchased investment packages containing quality real estate and aimed at capital appreciation, they would have a better chance to own solid real estate holdings.

Five years from now, the list of investment offerings will undoubtedly be different than today. But the underlying principles guiding your choice will be the same. Whenever you buy, your investment must make business sense, as outlined in this chapter and in our discussion of the EVS.

As we discuss current offerings, keep in mind that it's even more important to learn how to evaluate *all* potential investments based on fundamentals. Don't dwell on the characteristics of REITs versus RELPs versus MLPs. Those are externals—merely the legal entity—the cloak that covers the investment product.

As an analogy, consider the situation if you and your relatives invest in a fourplex. It doesn't matter whether you form a partnership, a corporation, or some other legal entity. The fourplex itself doesn't change. The legal form of your active investment isn't as important as your ability to buy and operate the real estate smartly. Similarly, if the people managing your passive investment have the proper skills, the investment will do well regardless of the legal package that it's wrapped in. The bottom line is: Will this investment increase my net worth?

As a passive investor, you'll look for an investment package that matches your goals, sponsored by an organization driven by a skilled management team. Figure 4–1 shows the structure of an organization that might promote real estate investment.

FIGURE 4-1
Sponsor—Investor Relationship for a Limited Partnership

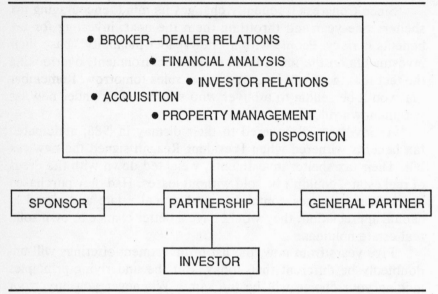

Each type of passive investment we're discussing has idiosyncracies that can be considered advantages or disadvantages. Ask your broker or financial planner about the structure, benefits, and shortcomings of newer offerings. Here's a brief rundown of investment possibilities in place as this book is written:

Real Estate Investment Trusts (REITs) are trusts that invest in diversified real estate or mortgage portfolios, or both. Their stock is usually publicly traded on exchanges and over the counter. They offer dividend income with competitive yields plus potential price appreciation. If you're reluctant to commit your money for the long term, REITs offer one major advantage—liquidity. When you decide to sell, it's as easy as a phone call to your broker. But this liquidity has a bad-news aspect, too.

Even though the real estate within your REIT may be performing well, the value of your shares will probably sink if the stock market nosedives for any reason. If the president has a heart attack, if war clouds hover, if there's an oil shortage, or if there's a political scandal in Washington, your stock will sell at a discount to its true value. Thus the money you might withdraw from your investment could decline rapidly just at the time you need cash. Even if the stock market is healthy, a REIT traditionally is priced at a discount to its net asset value. This is because buyers perceive that it's not worth its book value until the real estate owned by the REIT is liquidated.

If you're thinking of buying a REIT, don't purchase a new one just being underwritten and issued. Wait awhile. Chances are the price will subsequently drop. Or look for an older REIT selling at a discount.

When you invest in a REIT, you're not really investing as an owner; your role is closer to that of a shareholder. A REIT must pay out 90 percent of its earnings. This predetermines its working capital position. If the REIT has problem real estate, its working capital is limited.

Real Estate Limited Partnerships (RELPs) offer you a more direct route to the benefits of real estate investing. They're considered more illiquid than REITs. You invest money as a limited partner and the general partners use those funds to buy and manage real estate. By pooling the funds of many investors, the partnership can purchase more and/or larger properties, often on more favorable terms than an individual investor. This also spreads operating costs and offers a greater opportunity for diversification. The general partner makes arrangements for acquisition, management, and bookkeeping.

The minimum investment for a public offering (SEC Registered) is generally $5,000 for an individual investor, or $2,000 for an Individual Retirement Account. Private offerings are exempt from registration with the Securities and Exchange Commission (SEC), a federally regulatory commission. They require much higher initial investments, often a $25,000 minimum.

RELPs generally liquidate in five to fifteen years, at which time you should be able to measure your overall return. Some RELPs are also structured to provide you with income.

You'll frequently hear that RELPs are illiquid—but that doesn't mean it's impossible to withdraw your money. Most sponsors or syndicators can direct you to possible buyers. The biggest problem revolves around timing. If your partnership is doing well, it will be easier to recoup all or most of your money. Otherwise, you'll have to sell at a discount to your purchase price. Public programs are generally easier to sell than private ones. Chapter 14 shows how to sell active and passive investments.

Master Limited Partnerships (MLPs) are pools of limited partnerships, legally similar to RELPs, except that they generally trade in a secondary market such as the over-the-counter market. The sponsor can give you information on current bid and ask prices.

If you own a RELP that is later combined with others into a master limited partnership, your share of the new pie is determined by how successful your investment was initially. If it's performing solidly, you'll receive a larger share of the master limited partnership. Owners of good RELPs must make sure that the new MLP isn't a dumping ground for bad RELPs. For owners of badly performing RELPs, inclusion in a master limited partnership gives a broader base of real estate and a chance for better returns. But, as of this writing, Congress is investigating master limited partnerships and these legal entities may not be around in the future.

Because of the changing nature of legal entities, look at current offerings from a business point of view, not just as a particular alphabet-soup combination of letters.

Mutual Funds. Real estate-oriented mutual funds became the "new kid on the block" in the mid-1980s. They buy the stock of REITs, companies with real estate assets, and firms involved in property management or other real estate-related activities. Essentially, you're two steps away from being a real estate investor. You're relying on the ability of the fund's manager to make good stock picks, not necessarily on his real estate expertise. You're also subject to the varying performance of individual stocks which may not have anything to do with their underlying value. Like REIT investors, you share the disadvantage of seeing your investment drop in value when the stock market declines.

Active Research for Passive Investors

As you gather information about types of passive investments, you'll scrutinize them with one big question in mind: Will this investment increase my net worth?

Start by reading business and trade publications that carry advertisements for real estate investment programs. Also, look up general investment magazines that feature articles on real estate. These include the following (see the appendix for addresses):

Financial Planning Magazine

Registered Rep Magazine

The Wall Street Journal

Barron's

Fortune

Forbes

Real Estate Review

Money

Changing Times

Many local newspapers feature a special real estate section on Sundays, with syndicated articles and overviews by industry experts. Read this section for insights into current trends.

Send away for information on all passive investments that look interesting to you.

While waiting for the mail, contact a stockbroker, financial planner, or investment counselor. It's best to deal with a large brokerage firm that scrutinizes investment offerings carefully; the research process they use to verify that an investment has a reasonable chance of achieving its objectives is called due diligence. If your broker recommends one investment over another, try to find out whether the commission he receives varies from product to product. This could influence his recommendation. Also ask for a projection as to the expectations of the investment.

Talk with other people in the financial field—your attorney or accountant, for example. Ask for their recommendations, but avoid making commitments at this early stage.

Look for ads in the newspaper touting investment opportunities. Attend seminars for prospective investors. This is one situation where you *can* sometimes get a free lunch. More important, though, you'll have an opportunity to ask questions.

Soon you'll be inundated with brochures, advice, and tips. The prospectus packages you collect will be intimidating, but there's no need for you to plow through hundreds of pages of small print. This chapter shows how to zero in on the four most significant sections. The prospectus itself is a statement outlining the main features of a business enterprise. It generally comes in a package with an attractive, easy-to-read color brochure. At this point, most people follow the wrong path.

Your natural inclination is to pick up the glossy brochure and browse through it. Attractive photos emphasize the beauty of the real estate while the text is public relations hype, emphasizing the fabulous opportunites for investors. By contrast, the prospectus follows a format which is required by the Securities and Exchange Commission. But behind the mass of dull-looking print is information that can make or break your investment.

Why do syndicators send prospective investors a prospectus? What function does it serve? The answers to those questions boil down to one word: disclosure. The SEC operates on the premise that the company issuing a prospectus can do whatever it wants, but there must be full disclosure within a specified format.

As an example, suppose you want to sell a stamp collection to investors for one million dollars, and you prepare a prospectus. You would be required to include statements such as: "No collection like this has ever sold for a million dollars. It is highly unlikely that this collection will sell for a million dollars. This is a very speculative investment."

If the company making an offering is charging an outrageous sales fee, the SEC can't force them to reduce it. It *can* require the syndicator to state, "This is an extraordinarily high fee; no fee this high has ever been charged."

While the SEC operates under the principle of full disclosure, individual states operate under a "fair and equitable" principle. Before a state allows a security to be sold, a state-established commission will decide whether the investor has a fair and equitable chance to realize the objective stated in the prospectus. There's no guarantee that things will work out as envisioned—but if a state feels that the fees are excessive, it will not allow the promoter to sell this particular investment product within its borders. Most states follow federal guidelines; a few are even more stringent.

Under certain conditions, private placements are exempt from registering with the SEC, but they still need a prospectus to solicit business within the states. Although it isn't mandatory, most of these prospectuses follow the SEC format. Ask your broker for the prospectus of any public offering and double- check to see if they have similar formats. If they don't, be wary.

As a passive investor, you'll find one small degree of protection in prospectuses of real estate limited partnerships (RELPs). Almost all states insist that the investment be suitable for you. They won't let you invest in a particular RELP unless you fulfill the suitability requirement. The restrictions might read like this: $30,000 per year gross income and $30,000 in assets; or perhaps assets of $75,000. As a rule of thumb, the higher the income and asset requirements, the riskier the investment.

HOW TO READ A PROSPECTUS

Careful reading of a prospectus tells you whether the real estate package is a sound, businesslike investment, or a risky venture wrapped in showy packaging.

Instead of reading the solid mass of material cover to cover, you can focus on just four sections. You'll learn the answers to these key questions:

- Do my objectives match those of the investment product?
- Are the management fees reasonable?
- How skilled are the managers?
- What is their track record?

The prospectus we'll discuss in this chapter relates to a real estate limited partnership, but the principles apply to any real estate prospectus.

Objectives

In this short section, you might find a statement such as: "The objectives of the partnership are long-term capital appreciation . . . and equity build-up through reduction of mortgage indebtedness." Make sure the objectives are consistent with your investment expectations. If you want to increase your net worth and don't need current income, avoid investing in a partnership that stresses income. By holding down income distributions in the early years, a partnership may return 20 percent more cash in the long run.

This section may also indicate that a specific type of real estate, such as garden apartments, will be purchased. If you're convinced that office buildings offer better prospects, toss this prospectus onto the discard pile.

After finding a partnership with the same objectives that you have, you're ready to verify whether or not the management team has the experience to achieve these objectives.

The Management Team

Instead of dwelling on the organization itself, concentrate on descriptions of the management team. You aren't hiring the organization; you *are* hiring the personnel within it. The SEC requires that all key personnel involved in the company's activities discuss their experience. As you read this material, ask yourself, "Do I want these people to handle my money?" You'll want to examine the management team's experience and depth.

Is there a marriage between what these people have accomplished and the objectives of the offering? If the management proposes to buy a 22-story office complex but the people involved have handled apartments only, or if they've handled only a single office building, beware. Their experience is disproportionate to the task ahead, and success is unlikely.

What about the depth of management? How many people are listed? If only one or two people are mentioned, what happens if one dies?

Watch for subtleties in the management section. For example, how long has each person been with the company? If the firm has a phenomenal track record that goes back 15 years, make sure that the management people you're reading about were on board during the period of accomplishment. If almost everyone who achieved the impressive results subsequently left the firm, you could be left with unseasoned people who joined the company only a few months ago.

Are you comfortable with older people, middle-aged people, or younger people? Do you prefer people just starting out or someone with experience? The management team should list their ages. It can make a difference if a person is 35 years old or 75 years old.

If each person gives you a two-liner, be careful. This isn't false modesty; it might reflect a lack of expertise. The more space he or she devotes to past experience, the better you can judge the person's potential for achieving the stated goals.

The above suggestions are guidelines, but nothing is etched in concrete. You might come across a new partnership with no track record, but with a dynamite combination of people. Perhaps every principal in the company has purchased and handled one billion dollars worth of real estate and made good money for investors. If you can verify their track record in prior partnerships, it becomes safer when considering buying into their new venture.

How will the management team run the organization? Are they in control? This section should describe the roles of all the people involved, covering acquisition, management, and servicing functions. It should also spell out the methods they use to acquire property, the types of reports they provide, and how you will be kept up-to-date. This information enables you to make a common-sense judgment about their qualifications for the job ahead.

Take the position that you are mentally interviewing these people. Would you hire them based on what you're reading about their backgrounds? You're in a position to determine whether they're the kind of people you would hire to manage your money. If you have any questions, don't hesitate to contact the partnership office.

Management Compensation and Fees: Fair or Foul?

Potential investors may become glassy-eyed when they approach this section, but here's where the meat is. Using the simple guidelines in this chapter, you should be able to determine whether you'll pay reasonable fees or be ripped off. The following examples are more applicable to a public offering.

We'd all like something for nothing, but, in all fairness, the real world doesn't offer freebies. The money you invest must cover legitimate management expenses.

The prospectus should contain a complete description of all fees the general partner, his agent, or any affiliated entities will receive. These will be broken down into three time frames:

- Fees received initially.
- Fees received during the holding period.
- Fees received upon liquidation.

Fees Received Initially (Up Front)

The percentages taken out of your investment might look like this:

- Start-up (organizational)   5 percent (range 2–7
  expenses: percent)
- Sales force or broker
  commissions: 8 percent
- Acquisition costs: 10 percent
- Legal fees, title insurance: 1 percent
- Cash reserves (working capital):   4 percent (range 3–5
                                                    percent)

These numbers total 28 percent—leaving only 72 percent of your money available to purchase property. You've "lost" a big chunk of your money right off the top.

Here are a few guidelines to use when evaluating the fees in any prospectus:

- The start-up (organizational) fees should not exceed 5 percent.
- The broker/dealer fee should not exceed 8 percent.
- There should be no acquisition fee in the initial stage. If one is imposed, it should not exceed 8 percent.
- Total up-front fees should not exceed 25 percent.

What difference will a few percentage points make? Plenty. Let's make an important change in the fee structure we just examined. If you purchase shares in a limited partnership that doesn't impose an acquisition fee, your total fees will be 18 percent, leaving 82 percent of your original investment available for purchasing property.

What happens with these numbers in the real world? If you're interested in appreciation—increasing your net worth—you must get two dollars worth of real estate for every dollar invested. That's the bottom line.

If, in the first case, the partnership makes a down payment of 40 percent on real estate, you have 72 cents of your original dollar left to work for you; $1.80 worth of real estate can be bought (.72/ .40 = 1.80). That's a bit short of our goal. In the second case, without an acquisition fee, you have 82 cents of your dollar left, and this buys $2.05 worth of real estate. You have almost 14 percent more real estate working for you with the same investment! Thus a conservative down payment of 40 percent, *with no acquisition fee up front*, allows us to meet our goal of acquiring at least two dollars worth of real estate for every dollar invested. In this case, management will get an acquisition fee eventually, but it will come from cash flow or other sources later on.

A few more changes in our numbers will change the scenario dramatically. This can be done by omitting acquisition costs and reducing the other fees slightly:

	Example A	Example B
Total up-front fees	28 percent	13 percent
Percent of investment left	72	87

In Example B, you have an additional 15 percent of your money working for you (87 − 72 = 15). If the general partner purchases property with a one-third down payment, an extra 15 cents of every dollar you invested can be used to purchase more property—and the one-third down payment means it is three times more effective. Thus that extra 15 cents purchases 45 cents more real estate.

Pros and Cons About Up-Front Fees

Up-front sales fees generate heated controversy. They range from 6 percent to 18 percent. Some companies justify them by calling attention to the work they do promoting the offering, finding property to buy, and closing escrow. Others say, "We don't deserve a fee of that magnitude until the real estate starts to perform. We're using your money to buy the real estate; in addition, we'll receive fees for managing the property and selling it later on."

You're better off with a company that takes the latter approach. Management should prove themselves by creating value through cash flow. The value created in real estate—as demonstrated by the profit and loss statement—is the key to increasing your net worth.

When less money goes into up-front fees, more of your money is put to work buying more property. There's an inverse ratio between fees taken out up front and money the general partners receive upon liquidation. The more money they pocket initially, the less their motivation is to work in your best interest.

It may seem that the general partners have your best interests at heart if they defer taking acquisition fees at the outset, but there's one more point to look for in the fine print. The acquisition fee should be stated as an exact amount, without the term "present value," and without any reference to interest payments.

Fees Received During the Holding Period

During the life of your partnership, someone has to watch the store. That's the job of the general partners or the sponsors. Some partners charge a property management fee; others charge an asset management fee. Just be sure the partners you invest with don't "double dip" by taking a full acquisition fee (6 percent or more) up front and, in addition to that, charging an asset management fee every year. They are entitled to either one, or some offsetting amount, but not the maximum of both. As an analogy, consider the following: If a real estate broker sells you a house and you pay a commission (acquisition fee), you wouldn't also pay him a percentage of the value of the house as it appreciates year after year.

Property management involves collecting rents, paying bills, maintaining satisfactory occupancy levels, developing acceptable budgets, maintaining or increasing the property's value, and hiring on-site management personnel. Traditionally, the management organization receives a percentage of the gross income. In apartments, property management fees usually amount to 5 percent. In commercial property, it's usually 3 percent of gross revenues. These numbers will change over time. You must know what the current market is. If the fees are higher, find out why.

An asset management fee is based on the value of the real estate at a given time. At the time of purchase, it would be a percentage of the full purchase price. An asset management fee of just one percent per month sounds miniscule, but it amounts to a huge sum over a period of years—much larger than an acquisition fee, which happens once. Let's look at some numbers.

If we raise a dollar, an 8 percent acquisition fee would come to eight cents. If we buy $2 worth of real estate, a one percent asset management fee would be two cents. But—that asset management fee would be charged year after year, and as the asset appreciates, the dollar amount goes up.

Fees Received Upon Liquidation

The disposition fee is usually paid to the general partner, or his sponsor or broker, upon liquidation. What does it signify? Simply stated, the partner is saying, "When we sell this real estate, we're going to be paid X percent of the sales price."

That sounds reasonable—but what constitutes a fair return? This is one of those tricky situations where it pays to read the fine print. The general partner should receive no money unless the investors receive all their money back first. In other words, the disposition fee should be a subordinated fee.

If the general partner uses an outside broker for the selling transactions, watch out for excessive fees. Suppose the prospectus says that the general partner can receive a 3 percent disposition fee. The general partner may not do anything more than go to a broker and say, "Sell this property for us." The broker sells the property, charges his 6 percent fee, and suddenly you've been stuck for a total of 9 percent upon liquidation of the asset.

To avoid this situation, make sure the prospectus is clear about the disposition procedure and fees. Does it include the amount paid to an outside broker? The maximum disposition fee should not exceed a total of 4 percent, even if an outside broker is used. Make sure the prospectus states that the disposition percentage includes the fees paid to an outside broker. Watch out for situations where the partnership or one of its affiliates also serves as the outside broker. This would be a conflict of interest.

When it's time to divvy up the money, what percentage of the sales price should investors receive? In addition to the return of your original capital, a cumulative return with a preferred rate of 4 to 8 percent per year is a reasonable expectation when current interest rates are low. But stay current; these numbers only apply to 1987. *Check to see when the preferred rate starts.* Some partnerships don't start that rate until several years after investors are admitted.

What would your actual return be if you received a preferred rate of 5 percent a year and the partnership lasted eight years? A quick calculation shows the following:

100 percent of your initial investment
$$+ \text{ (5 percent per year times 8 years)} = 140 \text{ percent.}$$

With a successful limited partnership, your total return will be even greater. Under the type of arrangement just outlined, the general partner doesn't share in the proceeds until the limited partner receives 140 percent of his money back. There are various ways that the remainder of the proceeds is distributed. Guidelines for equitable distribution are as follows:

- If the partnership purchased two dollars worth of real estate for every dollar the investor put in, the limited partner should receive 85 percent and the general partner 15 percent of the remaining funds.

- If the partnership had a higher performance, purchasing three dollars of real estate for every dollar you invested, the general partner should be entitled to a larger percentage of the proceeds. The reasoning is this: Since the partnership purchased more real estate by making lower down payments (using leverage), there was responsibility for more real estate. In this case, 75 percent for the investors and 25 percent for the general partner would be fair.

THE BOTTOM LINE

Before studying track records of actual investments, you need some standard to judge the rate of return. This return is affected by the tax liability that generally surfaces upon the sale of your investment. This liability comes from the following sources of money or benefits you've received:

- Cash received from the sale.
- Notes taken back, such as a second mortgage. The value of such a note is estimated on a discounted basis—the cash you might receive by selling the note immediately at a discount.
- Tax benefits during the holding period.
- Cash received during the holding period.

How can you determine whether an investment is a disaster or a huge success? You assess the rate of return by considering how the tax liability affects your bottom line. Consider the following five categories:

1. Non-Passable Rate of Return. On sale, the cash generated from the four sources outlined above is insufficient to cover the tax liability. Thus you would receive less money than you originally invested. If you received a note and held it to maturity, even then the money generated would be insufficient to pay the taxes due.

2. Barely Passable Rate of Return. The money generated from the four sources above is just enough to pay the tax liability. While many people consider this a "break-even" situation, they would actually be losers. After paying the taxes, they would end up with less money than they originally invested due to inflation.

3. Acceptable Rate of Return. A combination of one or more of the sources above takes care of the tax liability and additionally takes care of the rate of inflation during the holding period.

4. Good Rate of Return. Sufficient cash is generated from one or more of the sources mentioned above to take care of your tax liability on sale, and to compensate for the rate of inflation during the holding period. In addition, there is some cash left over.

5. Excellent Rate of Return. Besides meeting the conditions under "Good Rate of Return," the amount of cash left over is greater than the money you would have earned with an alternative investment during the holding period. In other words, this investment outperforms the competition, after taking into account tax liability and inflation. Let's look at some numbers that demonstrate this point. See Figure 4–2.

In this example, the investor's annual tax benefits were $50 per year, for a cumulative total of $250. Inflation reduced the value of the investment by 5% per year, for a total of $250 by the end of five years.

What's a reasonable way to evaluate alternative investments? It's unfair to be a Monday morning quarterback by comparing the results to the Dow Jones or Standard and Poor's averages during a bull market, since you're not likely to have invested in the averages. In this example, we're assuming an investment in municipal

FIGURE 4–2
The Bottom Line After Five Years

Investment of $1,000. Holding Period: Five Years

Year	1	2	3	4	5	Cumulative Total
Cash tax benefits (5 percent)	$50	$50	$50	$50	$50	$250
Cash distributions	20	20	30	40	50	160
Cash on sale	NA	NA	NA	NA	1,250	1,250
Tax liability on sale	NA	NA	NA	NA	(100)	(100)
Inflation rate	5%	5%	5%	5%	5%	(25%) ($250)
Alternative investments	60	60	60	60	60	300

bonds maturing at the end of five years, paying tax-free six percent ($60) per year for a total of $300. Thus, by purchasing municipal bonds, you would receive a total of $1,300. But for your real estate investment and your municipal bond investment, you must account for the inflation factor and other plus factors, such as cash tax benefits, and cash distributions in the case of the real estate investment.

Municipal Bonds		Real Estate Investment	
Amount received:	$1,300	Amount received:	$1,250
Loss due to inflation:	(250)	Cash tax benefits:	250
Actual return:	1,050	Cash distributions:	160
		Tax liability on sale	(100)
		Loss due to inflation:	(250)
		Actual return:	1,310

This return of $1,310 is excellent. The $1,000 investment out-performed the rate of inflation as well as alternative investments. This is a realistic goal to seek. Obviously, if there are changes in inflation rates and tax laws, you must consider these changes. But, in any case, you can use these principles to define your investment goals.

Discovering Loopholes in a Track Record

The slick brochure accompanying a prospectus may claim that investors in previous partnerships enjoyed fantastic returns, but the numbers in a prospectus might tell a different story. Sometimes the omissions are as important as what is included.

Ideally, charts demonstrating the track record should have the following headings:

- Date of purchase (indicating when you actually invested money, not the date that the partnership bought property).
- Date of final liquidation (after all the notes have been taken back).
- Total money raised.
- Tax benefits (actual deductions that people in various brackets took).
- Cash distributions (the amount of distributions that were tax sheltered and the amount that were subject to taxation).
- Cash proceeds from sale.
- Tax liability from sales proceeds.
- Notes taken back (including information about amount, interest rate, and maturity).
- Profits (including a breakdown of sources).

Somewhere in the prospectus, there should be information on how long it took to raise the money. If the time frame is too long, the management lacks marketing skills and your investment might languish for months or years before the company raises enough money to buy real estate.

Let's examine some numbers. The chart we'll study contains figures from an actual track record. For purposes of anonymity, we'll call this organization the XYZ Company.

Figure 4–3 gives figures for a number of partnerships of the XYZ Company, showing what happened to each $1,000 invested.

FIGURE 4–3
Track Record for XYZ Company

1 Partnership Name	2 Year of Sale	3 Holding Period	4 Cumulative Tax Deductions (Income) From Operations Through (Date)	5 Cumulative Cash Distributions To Investors	6 Distributions Of Sales Proceeds + Net Interest Income	7 Sales Proceeds Deferred	8 Anticipated Net Interest Income
Prime	1984	6	2,000	400	960	920	340
Willows	1984	6	1,750	400	305	1700	3300
Abbot	1980	4	1,200	480	1200	∅	∅
Marvel	1976	3	3,000	275	1025	∅	∅

You'll notice immediately that some of the column headings we're looking for aren't shown in this track record. Is this a cover-up? We'll let you decide.

Let's examine the entries for their Prime partnership. Looking at Column 4, we see that the cumulative tax deductions total $2,000. Since we're looking at past history (an advantage that no longer exists), before the Tax Reform Act of 1986, investors had varying tax brackets. Someone in the 30 percent bracket had tax savings of $600 (.30 × $2,000). An investor in the 40 percent bracket had tax savings of $800. So the $2,000 shown is not your actual cash savings. Sometimes a partnership will make the numbers look impressive by giving a figure for investors in the 50 percent tax bracket; but if you're in the 30 percent bracket, the figure is inflated. Your savings would be considerably less. In this instance, when looking at Column 4, you would have to consider your own tax bracket.

During the holding period of six years, each investor received $400 of distributions. When the project was sold, the investors each received $960. In Column 7, you see that $920 has been held back. What does this mean? It's bad news.

When the property was sold, for your $1,000 investment, you received $960 in cash and a second note (mortgage) of $920 (principle) was taken by the partnership. During the period that the second note is held, you'll receive interest amounting to $340, in addition to the principle.

Superficially, the numbers look good. You put in $1,000 and it appears as though you received much more back. But beware. This is a case of what the SEC calls "selective disclosure."

Let's see what's missing. You want answers to these questions:

- When did the partnership first receive the investor's money?
- When was the real estate purchased?
- What is the actual holding period?
- What is the exact amount of the second note?
- What is the interest rate?
- What is the maturity date of the note?

The answers to these questions play a major role in helping you decide whether the track record is good . . . or a sham.

Why weren't those questions answered? A real estate professional would immediately suspect that this masks a poor track record. And he or she might be 100 percent right.

First of all, you want to know when the partnership received investor money. Some organizations hold on to your money more than a year before investing it. Suppose you turn your money over to the partnership in January and they purchase property in June. Their records will show the June date as the beginning of the holding period. What happens to your money during the six-month period? They'll pay you interest, but not on the full amount. If you pay a 10 percent commission, you'll receive interest on only 90 cents of every dollar invested. If they charge an organizational fee on top of the sales fee, that's another three percent you don't earn interest on.

In this track record, the partnership doesn't disclose two important dates—when they purchased the property, and when they sold it. All they provide is a "holding period" which, as we have seen above, may be longer than the period that they actually have possession of your money. The shorter the apparent holding period, the more leeway they have to make your returns *seem* greater.

For the Prime partnership, let's say that the property was purchased on January 1, 1980, and sold on December 31, 1985. From the amount of interest due ($340) on the second mortgage, it's reasonable to assume that it could run through 1992. At that time, investors will receive the balance of their money. The big question is this: Did they have a 5-year holding period as claimed, or a 12-year holding period? By using the 5-year period in their calculations, the general partners make the investor's return look like 27 percent. But the investors in this case must wait 12 years. When you take that into account, the return is less than half that amount. Not as an impressive a track record!

Important Point. You can't evaluate any investment unless the holding period is stated accurately.

Another questionable item in charts like this is the figure indicating your initial investment. If you put in $1,200 and paid up-front fees of $200, that left only $1,000 of your money working for you. Some partnerships will show your initial investment as $1,000 and build their track record around the return on that sum, ignoring the fact that you actually invested $1,200. It's important to ask whether the figure listed is your *total* investment or the sum left after the partnership took their up-front fees.

The Cumulative Cash Distributions figure in column 5 raises more questions. Were those distributions tax sheltered, or were tax liabilities paid? It may be wonderful to show that you received $400 in cash distributions—but, if during the holding period, you had to pay Uncle Sam taxes, your actual return shrinks. There should be some qualification as to tax liabilities related to the distributions. If that information is missing, ask questions.

A street-smart investor doesn't take anything for granted. If the real estate was sold on December 31, 1985, the proceeds might have been tied up in escrow for several months. Did investors receive the money shown in Column 6 immediately? If not, how long did they wait? You'll want to know the date when escrow closed. Some of the missing information may be in footnotes. Check them out.

In our example of an actual track record, the single most important column has been omitted. This is a classic case of selective disclosure. The sponsors haven't revealed anything about tax liabilities.

An investor in the Prime partnership put in $1,000 or more, depending upon whether the up-front fees were subtracted from the original investment as indicated on the chart. At the time of sale, according to Column 6, he received less than his investment—only $960. And there's more bad news coming. Our investor will have to pay taxes on that $960 and also on the $920 (Column 7) that he hasn't received yet, depending upon what tax law he might be under.

Someone who invested in the Willows partnership is in worse shape. When the property was sold, that person received only $305 in cash and is holding a note for $1,700 which will take many years to pay off. Meanwhile he or she will have a huge tax bill—possibly around $1,000—based on proceeds of $305 plus the $1,700 not yet received. And there's still more bad news.

Column 8 shows that the net anticipated interest income is $3,300. That's a tidy sum, which means that this is a long-term note. Assuming that the interest rate is 10 percent, we're looking at a period of almost 20 years before it will be paid off. If you add

20 years to the 6-year holding period shown on the chart, that's a total holding time of 26 years! The annual rate of return will be a disaster.

A street-smart investor would recognize immediately that the Willows partnership was a tax promotion deal involving real estate with unattractive economic features. When the property was disposed of, the partnership had to operate from a weak position. It was forced to accept a smaller amount of cash and a greater amount of second notes.

The slick brochure accompanying a prospectus may claim that investors in previous partnerships enjoyed fantastic returns, but the numbers in a prospectus might tell a different story. Sometimes the omissions are as important as what is included.

Ideally, charts demonstrating the track record should have the following headings:

Important Point.   Upon liquidation, at the right time during a real estate cycle, quality real estate will net considerably more cash. The seller won't have to sweeten the deal with long-term notes.

Now for another example. Investors in the Abbot partnership enjoyed big tax writeoffs during the four-year holding period (Column 4: $1,200 cumulative tax deductions amounted to about $360 for someone in the 30 percent bracket). After total liquidation, they received a check of $1,200. But Uncle Sam caught up with them in the end. The investors in the 30 percent tax bracket paid taxes of approximately $300 on that check, leaving them with $700. So, when we add up the numbers, they look like this:

Column 4: Tax deduction (.30 × $1,200)	$ 360
Column 5: Cash distribution	480
Remainder of liquidation check after taxes	670
Total return	$1,510

That's not terrible—but it's not impressive either. When you consider the risk involved in any real estate transaction, plus the fact that interest rates were extremely high during the holding period, investors would have come out ahead by putting their money into CDs yielding 14 percent then available.

In the Marvel partnership, the final check was for $1,025. Because of the high cumulative tax deductions and cash distributions along the way, the investor's cost basis would have been drastically reduced from the original $1,000. Someone in the 40 percent tax bracket paid around $700 in taxes after the final distribution. In other words, at the end of his investment, the amount of money he pocketed was less than his original investment. As an attempt to boost net worth, this invesmtent was a total failure.

Important Point.   Unless you receive a substantial check upon liquidation (not subject to a big tax bite) you won't increase your net worth.

Phantom Profits

In some prospectuses, the sponsors will include a column that gives a figure for profits. They might claim that a person who invested $1,000 made $3,000 in profits. In our example of the Prime partnership, when you add up the figures in Columns 4 through 8, during the claimed holding period, the numbers look large and impressive. But Columns 7 and 8 refer to second notes that haven't come due yet. When you see a chart listing profits, break that figure down. How much has the investor actually received? How long did it take? What kind of return did this amount to? Then you must take one additional step. Ask yourself what kind of return you could have gotten from alternate investments during the same period.

Questions to Ask About a Track Record

1. When the real estate was sold, did it provide enough cash to pay all of the tax liabilities for the transaction? If the investor had to dig into his pocket and write a check, the investment was a dud.

2. Did the investor get back more than his original investment after liquidation? That's a minimal requirement.

3. Did the holding period include the length of time that the second notes will be held?

4. Were the purchases and sales of property made through unaffiliated parties? In some firms, you'll find real estate sold from affiliated Company A to affiliated Company B—and that opens the door to all sorts of conflicts of interest. It's all right to have affiliated parties for managing, for providing goods and services and, for insurance—but not for buying and selling the asset itself. Look for such disclosures.

5. In a private placement, if the investor made staged payments over a period of time, when did the clock start running in terms of the holding period?

Although a chart showing the general partner's track record seems dull to the uninitiated, studying it is time well spent. Read the footnotes, too. They'll make the numbers come alive. Remember that you're committing your hard-earned money for an extended period of time. The company's track record must stand up to close scrutiny. The time you spend reading a prospectus can mean the difference between a bountiful return, or a staggering loss.

If the management checks out, if they're charging a fair price, and if they have a good track record, that's a green light for you. Here's a quick review of the features that distinguish a value-oriented economic deal from a slick promotion.

Economic Deal	*Slick Promotion*
Assets to be sold in seven years or less with acceptable returns.	Holding period more than ten years to achieve acceptable returns.
Good return regardless of inflation conditions.	High return dependent upon high inflation.
Tax deductions less than $1 for each dollar invested.	Tax deductions greater than $1 for each dollar invested.
Acquisition fees less than 10 percent of equity (preferably zero).	Acquisition fees greater than 10 percent of equity.
Positive cash flow from the outset.	Early operating losses.

TIPS FOR INVESTORS

- Read business and trade publications to get a feel for the current real estate environment and to learn about offerings available.
- Gather information from all sources: brokers, financial planners, accountants.
- Study the fundamentals of an investment package, not its legal form.
- Make sure your objectives match those of the company.
- Satisfy yourself that the management team is competent.
- Acquisition fees should be 10 percent of equity or less; preferably close to zero.
- Total up-front fees should be less than 25 percent.
- Upon liquidation, investors should receive a sum that is equal to their original investment, or more.
- To rate as an excellent investment, the return should outperform an alternate investment during the same period of time, after factoring in tax liability and inflation.
- Investors should get their money back before the general partners share in the final distribution.
- The track record should give specific information about the following:
    1. Holding periods (including duration of notes)
    2. Amount, interest, and maturity of notes
    3. Tax liabilities
    4. Breakdown of profits
    5. When figures are given per $1,000 investment, does this include the amount of your investment before or after up-front fees are imposed?
    6. When does the preferred rate start?
- Look at trends revealed in the track record. In recent years have the returns improved or deteriorated?
- Call the company if you have any questions.

CHAPTER 5

YOUR INFALLIBLE TOOL: THE ECONOMIC VALUATION SYSTEM

If you were a gambler at heart, you wouldn't be reading this book now; you would be standing in front of the slot machines in Las Vegas or Atlantic City. Since you're obviously interested in working with probabilities that are more favorable than long shots, and therefore willing to use larger amounts of money, we can move into the heart of this book: the Economic Valuation System (EVS). Its systematic methodology lays the groundwork for success.

The EVS is an orderly approach to real estate buying that maximizes your investment results. It provides you with meaningful criteria in a logical sequence, enabling you to judge all the important physical and financial aspects of any real estate purchase. The EVS incorporates every facet that will affect either your P&L statement or your balance sheet in a real estate transaction. These are:

- Area.
- Location.
- Structural Integrity.
- Amenities.
- Capitalization Ratio.
- Financing.
- Leverage.

Each criterion or sequence is part of a cumulative total. Within them, we'll provide tools you need to analyze the approximately

100 items. These items are organized into the seven categories mentioned above. You'll learn which questions are important, and the sequence in which you should ask them. If one of the seven key factors fails the test, it's a signal to walk away from the deal, or to readjust to accommodate the specific failures.

The EVS is universal. It works for all real estate purchases: single family homes, condos, duplexes, apartment houses, shopping centers, and office buildings, and most other types.

Will changes in tax laws affect the way you purchase real estate? Not at all, if you follow a fundamental approach. The EVS is timeless. It focuses on fundamentals unaffected by changes in tax legislation. It helps you make the right decisions in all cycles, consistently coming up with probabilities that are in your favor. The EVS applies today; it will apply twenty years from now; it will apply into future centuries. It works in all societies that use money as a medium of exchange and don't have unusually restrictive laws.

The Economic Valuation System works wherever you live, and regardless of the size of your investment. You can use this approach for a $50,000 private house or a $50 million apartment building. It can be used in Fairbanks, Tokyo, Paris, New York City, or a small town in Texas. As long as you live in a capitalistic society, you'll be involved in real estate; you'll live in it, own it or lease it, work or shop in it. The EVS gives you the capability of looking at real estate intelligently to judge its value.

WHY USE THE ECONOMIC VALUATION SYSTEM?

Real estate is a business, and the EVS encompasses the techniques for analyzing your prospective purchase as a business. If the property passes all seven major criteria, you've chosen a business with a much higher probability for success.

Mistakes can be costly, and you don't want to throw away your hard-earned money. The average home is priced at more than $100,000, making your potential outlay for a down payment at least $10,000. If you're an active investor, you might be purchasing property worth hundreds of thousands, or millions, of dollars. Even as a passive investor, a rock-bottom investment is in the $5,000 range.

FIGURE 5–1
The Great Juggling Act: The EVS Simplifies Decision-Making

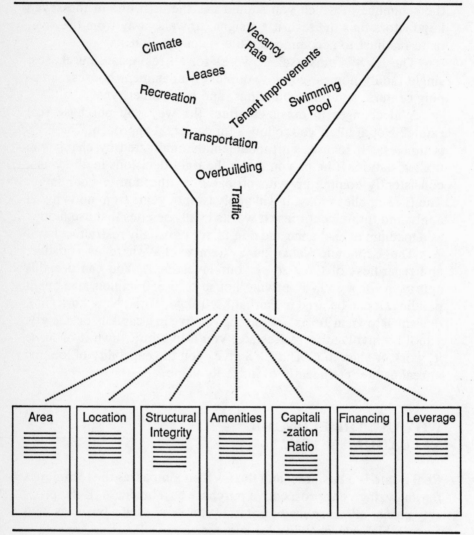

If you were buying a car or a stereo system, you'd research the purchase carefully. In real estate investing, research is even more essential. The EVS will serve as your tool, your game plan. It increases the probability of your success.

Whether you are active or passive, the EVS enables you to be in control. A broker might rave about a building he's trying to sell. If you are active, you will want to decide for yourself whether or not to buy. Before you sign any contract, the EVS helps you gather information independently. Then you can make the right decision. If you are passive, the EVS gives you a track to determine the acquisition capabilities of the people you are hiring.

The benefits of using the Economic Valuation System can be summarized as follows:

- The EVS is systematic.
- It's comprehensive.
- It puts you in control.
- It will help you avoid costly mistakes.
- The EVS boosts your probability of success.

HOW DOES THE ECONOMIC VALUATION SYSTEM WORK?

The EVS deals with more than 100 issues in 2 different categories (physical and financial). You've seen some of them in the illustration above. For purposes of clarity and meaningfulness the more than 100 issues used by EVS are very heavily weighted toward apartment purchasing. This is being done to increase the success ratios of newer investors. But the seven keys of EVS apply to all income producing real estate. We've taken these items that prevail in all real estate transactions and organized them into seven key categories. Each of these categories is considered in sequence, as shown in Figure 5–2.

Subsequent chapters contain in-depth discussions of each of the key categories, along with point ratings and the weighing system. If just one of the seven categories fails to pass muster, it's a danger signal—a "deal killer." In real estate, you'll come across

FIGURE 5–2
The EVS Helps Lay the Groundwork for Decision-Making

Selection of an optimum
area is at the core of EVS.

Once the best area is
selected, you choose the
optimum location within it.

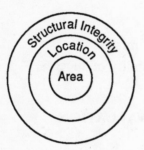

Now you are ready
to evaluate the
structural integrity
of a potential purchase.

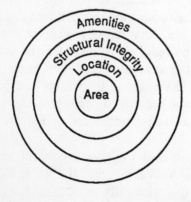

The fourth step
involves evaluation
of amenities.

FIGURE 5–2
(*Concluded*)

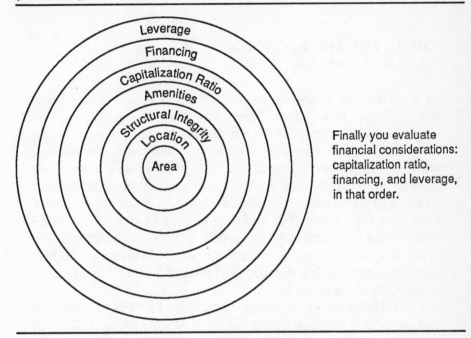

Finally you evaluate
financial considerations:
capitalization ratio,
financing, and leverage,
in that order.

this term occasionally. What's the significance? If you can't adjust or change a problem, don't complete the transaction. Kill it. Here are a few examples of deal killers:

- When you study the capitalization ratio, if the return on income is too low, negotiate a reduction in price, or kill the deal.
- If you discover structural problems, what are your alternatives? The seller might fix them before you buy; he might leave money in escrow for you to fix them, or he might reduce the price enough to cover your expenses needed to fix the problem. If none of these adjustments take place, don't buy.
- If you are not sure of the area, you cannot change it; but you might ask the seller to guarantee a certain return over

a period of time until the area develops. Take a chance with *his* money if he claims the area is good.

HOW TO USE THE ECONOMIC VALUATION SYSTEM

Let's review our definition of real estate: a business that buys, sells, or leases square feet. The prospective purchase must pass certain physical criteria for the key factors of area, location, structural integrity, and amenities. You always start with the physical elements; the greatest financial terms are of no value if the building is falling apart. If the area is good, then you can consider specific streets; and go further in deciding which side of the street is best. If the area isn't right, then the deal should be dead. You won't want to take your analysis any further. For example, what difference will superior construction make if you're in an area with high unemployment and few prospective tenants? None. You shouldn't consider purchasing the building.

You'll learn how to evaluate the building itself. Is the structure solid, or will it collapse during the next storm? Does it have the facilities and amenities to attract the type of clients you want?

As a businessperson, you will also need a methodology to evaluate the financial side of your real estate. In an orderly fashion, you'll analyze income and expenses. Is there enough money before debt service? What type of debt should you incur? The EVS enables you to answer these important questions in a meaningful sequence, and on a cumulative basis.

For each piece of real estate under consideration keep your data in an orderly fashion, using a file folder or loose-leaf notebook. Identify each property with the name (if applicable), address, seller, number of units, square feet, purchase price, down payment, and mortgage description. Each of the following seven chapters concentrates on one key factor and provides sample forms so you can follow the most convenient format.

Build a file with a written analysis of everything in sequence, moving from one key factor to another in a forward progression. The EVS arranges your questions into a logical sequence. We give extra weight to particularly important factors.

CONTRACT NEGOTIATIONS

If you've always thought of contracts as the point of no return, think again. They're more of a starting point. Street-smart real estate investors do some initial research, satisfy themselves that a certain piece of property looks promising, sign a contract, and then complete their research using the EVS. This procedure makes sense because there are certain costly investigations that require professional review. You don't want to commit your money to these investigations until you have the property tied up on a "subject-to" basis.

A good contract allows you to back out if you discover a deal-killer. Initially, when you express an interest in the property, the seller is sending you the following message: "My real estate is worth X dollars." After negotiating, when you sign the contract, in essence you're replying, "I agree to X price, but subject to my now conducting, during the next 30 days, a thorough inspection of the area plus the structural and financial status of the real estate itself. I want to look at the leases, and, to do this, I will give you a deposit as an indication of my good faith. I am signing the contract because you are telling me that this buiding is well-constructed and in a growing area; I need to check that out."

You need the protection of a contract before investigating certain aspects of the real estate in depth. One of the most important expressions in a real estate contract is "subject to. . . ." When you purchase any type of business, you are going to agree on a price subject to verification of many things that make that property valuable. For a private home, this might include a termite report, checking the plumbing and electrical lines, and much more.

As a potential purchaser of any type of business, you would examine the physical facilities and the client relationships; you would substantiate financial allegations and do whatever else that particular type of real estate would require in the form of investigation. Remember, you can never over-investigate; you can never examine too much.

Inserting a clause to the effect that you will buy "subject to a satisfactory inspection" provides you with a unilateral, non-binding contract. If you pay inspectors to check out the structural integrity before signing a contract, the seller might change his mind and decide not to sell to you after you've paid for the inspections. The seller will probably want something a little more specific than just a general "subject to a satisfactory inspection." You probably will be asked to identify the problem. For example, you might state, "subject to verification of the rent law" or "subject to verification of the roof condition, or the HVAC system (heating, ventilation, and air-conditioning)."

Thirty days is a reasonable, acceptable time for an inspection, but if you need more time to complete your examination, get more. You might have to increase your deposit since you're asking the owner to take his property off the market for a longer time; but that is a worthwhile use of money to make sure you complete your investigation thoroughly.

For your protection, the contract may be worded so that you don't have to spend more than a specific figure (for example, $2,000 or $4,000) for repairs. If the inspector finds something amiss, the seller may agree to a stipulation such as, "Based on the termite inspection, the seller will pay the first $2,000 for repairs"; or, "The seller will pay the first $5,000 of roof repairs required by an acceptable roofing inspector; otherwise the contract will be null and void."

Research After Signing a Contract

If you're purchasing an apartment building, shopping center, or office building, you want to make sure that it will attract clients (tenants). If the economy in an area is weak, your real estate won't generate the anticipated profits; hence a market study is essential. Since these studies are expensive, you want to have a contract in hand before initiating work on them. You might study retail sales per capita, bank deposits, and solvency of banks. The next chapter shows you how to gather this information.

When you buy a piece of real estate, you're making a major committment in an area. You can't move your building; thus you must be *very* careful to make sure this is the right area for your investment. Real estate investors planning a major purchase might pay as much as $25,000 to a consultant for a detailed study of an area.

When purchasing an apartment building, specify that you want to look at the leases, the credit applications and their payment records, and other pertinent information. If you are considering the purchase of a shopping center or office building, review all leases or spreadsheets necessary. If the seller claims that his office building or shopping center is in a growing area with a healthy economy, research the validity of his claims after signing the contract. If they are not substantiated, you would then have grounds for killing the deal.

Naturally, you'll tackle some research on all seven key categories of the EVS before signing a contract—but you won't commit extensive funds to the bulk of this research until after you're sure that the seller is serious with you and signs a contract. Use the chart in Figure 5–3 as a guide.

Your research on the area and location will involve a market study. To evaluate the structural integrity, you'll hire experts in the construction field. On the finance side, your research of the capitalization ratio will involve a study of profit and loss statements. The mortgage and leverage investigations always take place after signing a contract.

You must undertake all these studies *fast*. An orderly approach is mandatory. That's where the Economic Valuation System proves its worth. Without it, you run the risk of overlooking some of the 100 items that should be considered. Any item you overlook reduces the probability of success. First you must make sure the area

FIGURE 5–3
When to Do the Major Part of Your In-Depth Research

Key Factor	Before Signing Contract	After Signing Contract
Area	x	x
Location	x	x
Structural Integrity		x
Amenities		x
Capitalization Ratio		x
Financing		x
Leverage		x

is right. Then hire engineers, inspectors, and other specialists. Finally, check out the financing.

Real estate investing is a prime example of caveat emptor—let the buyer beware. You're buying a business predicated on an intensive investigation. This investigation involves hundreds of facets covering a wide variety of subjects. The EVS helps you conduct an orderly investigation. Use a form similar to Figure 5–4 to evaluate the results of your investigation.

CYMROT'S LAW NUMBER 7:
If You Can't Remedy Any Problems Uncovered by the Economic Valuation System, Kill the Deal

If you've decided to become a passive investor, you still need an orderly system to evaluate the property in your investment, whether it's a real estate investment trust, a limited partnership, or some other legal entity. Your research won't be as extensive as that of active investors, but you still need to use the Economic Valuation System to judge certain important aspects of the real estate being purchased. You won't have access to information on structural integrity, but you can ask the right kinds of questions and make sure your sponsor is doing the right kind of research. You can also do some homework to verify that the real estate is in a growing area.

When you invest in real estate using the EVS, you've put probability on your side. You'll be investing in a business that's destined for success; one that will out-perform the vast majority of other types of investments.

TIPS TO REMEMBER

- Use the Economic Valuation System to conduct an orderly investigation of all physical and economic factors affecting a prospective real estate purchase.

FIGURE 5–4
Economic Valuation System Issues Summary and Comments

PROPERTY NAME

TYPE OF PROPERTY

ADDRESS

SELLER

NUMBER OF UNITS

TOTAL NUMBER OF SQUARE FEET

PURCHASE PRICE

CASH DOWN PAYMENT

MORTGAGE DESCRIPTION

Critical Issues Summary

		Rating			
	Actual	Passing	Bad	Average	Good
Physical					
Area		(14)	(29.5)	2	33.5
Location		(11)	(21.5)	0	17.5
Structural integrity		10	(10.5)	21	55.0
Amenities		(10)	(30.0)	10	41.25
Financing					
Capitalization Rate		(4)	(19.0)	9.5	39.35
Financing		2.25	(5.5)	10	21.0
Leverage		6	6	15	24.0
Total		(21.75)	(110.0)	67.5	231.6

RECOMMENDATIONS & COMMENTS

DATE: _____   SIGNATURE _____

- The EVS covers over 100 items in seven key categories—area, location, structural integrity, amenities, capitalization ratio, financing, and leverage.

- The logical sequence of questions in the EVS speeds up your research and increases your probability of success.

- Sign a contract subject to satisfactory conclusions resulting from market studies, financial evaluations, and structural inspections.

- If just one of the seven key factors fails to pass muster, and correction of the problem is impossible, kill the deal.

CHAPTER 6

THE AREA: YOUR POINT OF NO RETURN

In the previous chapter, we introduced the Economic Valuation System and explained that its 100 items consolidate into seven key physical and financial points. The first key point—and the most crucial one of all—is area. If you make a mistake here, you're doomed from the outset. The building you purchase might be constructed like the Rock of Gibraltar, but if the area is wrong, your mistake is fatal. There's absolutely no way to compensate.

For our purposes, we'll define area as a piece of geography that includes living, employment, shopping, and entertainment within 20 minutes travel time, as shown in Figure 6–1. Thus, in addition to housing, there will be support activities within a reasonable traveling distance.

We've restricted our definition of area so we can focus on increasing the odds in your favor. Your first question should be, "Is this a good area?" You can come up with a commonsense answer by asking yourself, "Would I want to own a business here?" You could be thinking of businesses as diverse as a restaurant, a shoe store, or a pharmacy. If your answer is "no" then you wouldn't want to own real estate in that area. Once again, all the principles that apply to the success of other businesses also apply to the success of real estate.

Employment is the anchor in any area. As long as employment is high, the area has potential, even though its economy might be in a temporary decline. There must be a sound economic base and a reason for people to work in an area. Diversity of employment is also a very important factor. The base needs to be broad. Look

FIGURE 6–1
Typical Activities within an Area

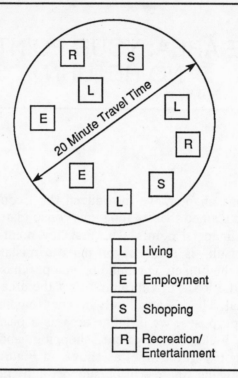

L	Living
E	Employment
S	Shopping
R	Recreation/ Entertainment

at the situation from a business point of view. Profit and loss statements are the key to future value; but without clients who can create income for your real estate, the income side of a profit and loss statement collapses. Employment becomes the nucleus that binds together living, shopping, and entertainment. Employment generates the need for housing. Gainfully employed people also shop for more goods and services. As people shop, additional employees are needed to staff the stores, generating a positive momentum. The more employed people you have in an area, the greater the need develops for entertainment and cultural activities.

Research, Research, Research—But Where?

When using the Economic Valuation System, you'll need facts and figures relating to population growth, employment, retail sales, bank deposits, and community trends. Finding the answers you seek might seem like a formidable task, but a wealth of information is at your fingertips, wherever you live. You'll uncover valuable data—most of it free—in U.S. census reports, studies by local Federal Reserve Banks, Chambers of Commerce, local real estate associations, and trade associations, that have prepared economic analyses. Libraries, business colleges, and business associations can also provide statistics relating to the local economy. Incidentally, there are 12 Federal Reserve Banks in major cities throughout the country, so there's bound to be one in your region. (See Appendix.) Additional information is available from national groups such as the National Multi Housing Council, the National Association of Realtors, and the National Realty Committee. (Addresses of these organizations are in the appendix, along with a list of on-line information sources.)

Put Yourself in Control

There are two ways to buy real estate—sit back and let commission-seeking salesmen submit proposals, or make your own decisions about areas to investigate. The latter approach is critical to success. A seller generally wants to get rid of property he feels has outlived its potential. Smart buyers take an aggressive stance, seeking opportunities on their own.

Using the Economic Valuation System, you'll make educated choices, not guesses. First, you'll select an area or city. Real estate people generally divide a metropolitan area into four area quadrants—northeast, northwest, southwest, and southeast. You'll want to orient your thinking the same way. Sometimes quadrants are divided by a river, major highway, railroad or some other physical obstruction. At other times, the boundaries are set arbitrarily. In the next chapter, you'll learn how to fine-tune your choice down in a particular quadrant and neighborhood that represents the best investment.

Using the Area Valuation Worksheet

If you're planning to buy a home for your family, you'll find many of the items on the Area Valuation Worksheet helpful (See Figure 6–2). Investors who are planning a major outlay *must* investigate all 22 criteria listed. We'll discuss each one in turn.

FIGURE 6–2
Area Valuation Worksheet

PROPERTY NAME _____

TYPE OF PROPERTY _____

ADDRESS _____

_____

SELLER _____

NUMBER OF UNITS _____

TOTAL NUMBER OF SQUARE FEET _____

PURCHASE PRICE _____

CASH DOWN PAYMENT _____

MORTGAGE DESCRIPTION _____

AREA-PROPERTY STATISTICS

STATE _____

CITY _____

QUADRANT _____

AREA-PROPERTY VALUATION

Condition	Subject	Bad	Avg	Good	TOTAL SCORE
(5%), National Avg, +5% (5 Year Average)	1. Migration	(2)	0	2	
(5%), National Avg, +5% (5 Year Average)	2. Earnings Per Capita	(2)	0	2	
(5%), National Avg, +5% (5 Year Average)	3. Retail Sales Per Capita	(1.5)	0	1.5	
(5%), National Avg, +5%	4. Bank Deposits Per Capita	(1.5)	0	1.5	
75 Average Sun Days 125 Average Sun Days 175 Average Sun Days	5. Climate	(1)	0	1	
125%, 175%, 225% of Rent Costs	6. Average Annual Carrying Costs Paid, Owner vs Renter	1	1.5	2	
(5%), National Avg, +5% (5 Year Average)	7. Unemployment	(2)	0	2	
(5%), National Avg, +5% (5 Year Average)	8. Job Creation	(1)	0	1	
Yes, Proposed, No	9. Rent Control	(3)	1.5	0	

FIGURE 6–2
(Continued)

AREA-PROPERTY VALUATION

| | | Rating | | | TOTAL |
		Bad	Avg	Good	SCORE
Condition	Subject				
Number of Bills Passed Effecting Real Estate (Subjective)	10. Legislative Environment	(2)	(1)	0	
10%, 20%, 30% of Total	11. Permits Issued Number Units	(2)	0	2	
10%, 20%, 30% of Total	12. # Units Construction Started	(3)	0	3	
	13. Condition of School System	(1.5)	0	1.5	
	14. Condition of Museums	(2)	0	2	
Subjective	15. Condition of Airport	(2)	0	2	
Decisions	16. Condition of Roadway System	(2.5)	0	2.5	
	17. Condition of Railway System	(1)	0	1	
	18. Condition of Shopping Facilities	(2)	0	2	
	19. Condition of Recreation Facilities	1.5	0	1.75	
(5%), National Avg, +5%	20. Revenue Tax	(1.75)	0	1.75	
(5%), National Avg, +5%	21. Sales Tax	(.5)	0	.5	
(5%), National Avg, +5%	22. State and Local Taxes	(.75)	0	.75	
	TOTAL	(29.5)	2	33.5	

Use a separate worksheet for each area you're considering. You'll observe that you need some hard facts and figures before filling out this sheet. It's not enough to obtain local data; you need a frame of reference. Thus you'll compare local figures with national figures over a five-year period of time. That time span gives you the necessary perspective; otherwise, your data might be distorted by the current business cycle.

You'll use the national figures as a benchmark for the first four items on the list: migration, earnings per capita (per working person), retail sales per capita, and bank deposits per capita. If you invest in areas where the local figures are better than the national average, your probabilities of success improve.

Look for trends with each of these items. Generally, you'll find that local trends move in the same direction as those nationally, but the rates may vary. If the national trend is on an upswing and the trend in your area is going down, instead of using the Economic Valuation System for that particular item, you'll need to ask questions such as: What is causing the local figures to decline? How long is this trend projected to continue before this area moves in the direction of the national average again?

If national figures move down while local figures move up, again you'll want to find out why they diverge. You might be approaching the peak of a particular market.

Now let's consider each item on the Area Valuation Worksheet.

1. Migration. The population of an area increases in two ways: by an increase in the birthrate, or by people moving into the region. Look for an area into which grown adults (working people) are moving. It's estimated that one working person can support six others (baker, butcher, candlestick maker, etc.)

If census reports reveal that the national average is increasing at a certain rate, is the rate in your city or area the same? Is it faster? Slower?

Here's how to handle the scoring: If the area is growing at a rate of 105 percent or more of the average, mark down a score of two. If it's growing at the rate of 95 percent or less of the national average, score a minus two. If the growth rate is roughly the same, score a zero.

2. Earnings Per Capita (Per Working Person). When compared to the national averages, figures for earnings per capita tell you the extent to which people will have additional discretionary income. This ties in with the standard of living. The greater the earnings per capita, the more money people will have to spend on food, housing, and entertainment. Existing businesses expand and new ones are attracted to the area. This financial activity leads to greater community development. Score this factor the same as Migration.

3. Retail Sales Per Capita. Figures on retail sales per capita tell you how much money people are spending in that area. Note that this item is slightly less significant than migration and earnings per capita, so the good and bad ratings scores are worth 1.5 points.

4. Bank Deposits Per Capita. Obtain this information from the Federal Reserve Bank in your area. If national figures are high and those in your area are low, this thin margin of reserves indicates that the area is weaker than average. There's less discretionary income. High bank deposits per capita offer a cushion to the economy by providing extra reserves for people to draw on; thus more resilience. Businesses and people will have additional money for emergencies. Spending won't dry up as soon as the economy falters.

5. Climate. Most of us take climate for granted, but it has an important effect on the degree of activity in an area. Moderate, pleasant climates add to the vibrancy of an area. People go out frequently and do more; they shop longer hours and seek entertainment at night as well as during the day. And they spend more money. Thus 175 sunny days will earn an EVS score of 1, while 75 sunny days will score a minus one.

6. Average Annual Carrying Costs Paid Versus Rent. If you want to invest in housing, this item tells you which has an edge in the current marketplace—a house or an apartment. All people— except those who want to permanently rough it in the woods— need a roof over their heads. At this point, you want to find out if they're prospective tenants for your apartment, or if they're more likely to buy a house.

These people will be asking themselves: "Should I live in a private house? A condo? An apartment house?" Although almost everyone would prefer to live in a private house, affordability and stability are the strong driving forces. Finances often force a compromise between what people want and what they can afford.

Before filling in the blanks on this item, you'll need to find out what monthly carrying costs are for an average house and for an apartment unit. Suppose a person could rent an apartment for $100 per month. If he or she bought a house, what would the carrying costs be compared to that rent? The direct carrying costs might include: mortgage payments, insurance, taxes, and average fix-up costs to maintain the property. In addition, the indirect carrying costs might be the loss of interest or dividends that would have been earned on the down payment.

The more it costs to carry a house, the better it is for the owner of an apartment house; apartment living would look more attractive to budget-conscious people. Obviously, the bigger the spread between house payments and apartment rent, the more people will want to rent one of your apartment units. If carrying costs are $225 per month on a house, your apartment unit would be more attractive than it would if carrying costs for a private house were $125 per month. Thus, if carrying costs are 125 percent of apartment rent, score one on the evaluation sheet. If carrying costs are 225 percent, score a two.

7. Unemployment. Unemployment figures tell an important story; it's revealing to look at trends. Obviously, the lower the unemployment rate in your area compared to the national average, the better the overall economic picture will be. When unemployment is low, bank deposits go up, retail sales increase, and earnings per capita rise. The area attracts more people because there's more work. The economy becomes robust and your prospects for profits increase.

8. Job Creation. The more an area grows in terms of creating new jobs, the healthier it is for your real estate investment. New jobs and a high rate of employment lead to less crime and welfare, and a host of important plusses. The improved quality of life attracts people who want to live in a pleasant atmosphere. Their satisfaction generates more support for community's cultural activities. One positive aspect feeds another. New businesses start up in the area or move into it. Old businesses are successful and expand their operations, hiring more people and creating even more employment. A "wheel of fortune" is created, as illustrated in Figure 6–3.

9. Rent Control. The high point rating for this factor on our Area Valuation Worksheet underscores its importance. Rent control spells trouble. Since the value of your real estate is based on a profit and loss statement, any law that restricts your income damages your profit margin. Rent control usually portends the beginning of more legislation affecting real estate unfavorably.

FIGURE 6–3
The Wheel of Fortune

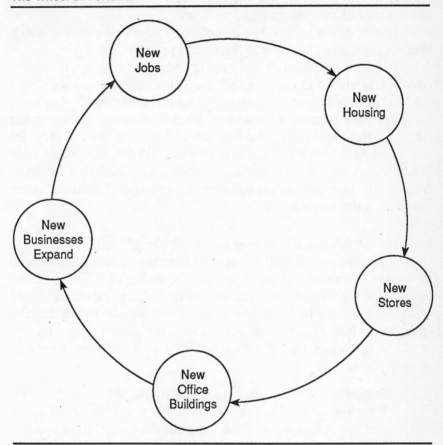

If a law decrees that your income can only be a certain amount while vendors who sell you goods and services can charge anything they please without restriction, your expenses will increase. This will happen for two reasons:

- Your real estate is getting older and more expensive to maintain.
- Even with inflation under control, prices will still increase two to three percent per annum.

You're caught in the classic "profit margin squeeze." Expenses mount while your income is fixed. Thus your profit margin as a percentage of sales is going to decline.

In this environment, the incentive to own real estate withers. People look elsewhere for investment opportunities.

In some communities, colleges are a boon; in others, they have worked against real estate interests. The University of California in Berkeley is an outstanding college with numerous Nobel Prize winners; but because of students' liberal leanings, Berkeley has some of the most restrictive rent control laws in the country. On the other hand, Stanford University has a less liberal student body and this has kept rent control out of Palo Alto, California. Because real estate laws are less restrictive, many major businesses have located in the community.

10. Legislative Environment. If you're planning to invest in a community—whether the amount of money is several thousand dollars or a million dollars—you must be aware of the laws on the books and legislation being considered that affect real estate. Some laws and bills may be favorable; others might not. An overwhelming number of bills might foreshadow too much government interference. A few examples of laws that might make landlords uncomfortable are:

• Deposits must be earning interest on behalf of tenants. Whether that's good or bad is not a point that merits discussion in this book. Be aware that such legislation adds an additional amount of responsibility to the owner of real estate.

• Families with children cannot be turned away. This can be very unfavorable to landlords.

What type of environment have the laws mandated? If too many are unfavorable, you can reach a point where it isn't worth the hassle to be a landlord.

11. Permits Issued: Number of Units. Information on the number of permits issued for new construction indicate the competition you'll face as a real estate owner. Learn how many builders have permission to construct new apartments, homes, office buildings, or shopping centers. To obtain percentage figures, divide the number of permits issued by the total supply of units in existence. With commercial real estate, you'll be evaluating this data in terms of square feet rather than units. Obtain this information from your local real estate trade association or from a large real estate brokerage firm in the community.

If there are permits to build office space that would result in a 20 percent increase, you might anticipate that there will be 20 percent more companies leasing office space. If permits for apartment units are up by 10 percent, you might expect that 10 percent more people will move into the community. In either case, there's another question to ask: Does the community have the ability to handle all this excess? If it can't absorb this level of expansion, there will be a surplus of units over what is necessary; and this additional square footage is bad news. As with any other excess, whether it's building units or unsold stereo sets on a retailer's shelf, prices decline when there is too much merchandise. When that happens, profits decrease.

12. Number of Units Under Construction.   In combination with permits issued, you need to know the number of apartment units under construction, and the number of square feet of commercial real estate under construction. This takes numbers out of the theoretical realm and into the real world; you find out what's happening right now. Permits give someone the right to build, but that person might change his mind later on.

When a building is under construction, you know it's going to be on the market within a finite time—perhaps in the next month or two, or in six months. If you look at numbers of permits only, you don't have any idea when the building will come to the market. It could be 12 to 18 months, or never. Obtain this data from the same sources as the number of permits issued.

In some U.S. cities, the percentage of unoccupied office buildings at this writing is as high as 28 percent because of poor absorption. Such grim figures make it essential that you know what is being built in your area. Would you invest in the restaurant business if you learned that four more restaurants were under construction nearby? It's exactly the same for apartments, shopping centers, and office buildings.

National averages have no bearing on the next seven items on our EVS chart. You'll evaluate each of them as bad, average, and good based on more subjective criteria. Finding answers requires some form of informal investigation—studying the subject in question, asking questions, and obtaining a consensus opinion.

13. Condition of School System. There are several ways to evaluate the condition of a school system, but they're time-consuming. If you wanted to spend a great deal of time, you could check out data provided by the U.S. Department of Education. But you can take a short cut. If you talk to a cross-section of people within a community you'll find some overall agreement about the school system. For example, how does a high school rate? You might ask the administration about the percentage of graduates who go on to college.

Families tend to move into communities with good school systems; thus good school systems will help promote communities. This is one of the key reasons why the city of Palo Alto has grown and become the heart of Silicon Valley.

14. Condition of Museums. Successful museums attract a great deal of money for displays, and they attract people who appreciate the cultural benefits of living in that area.

15. Condition of Airport. This is very important. Airports generate a great deal of employment by serving as arrival and departure points for people attending business conventions. You can track the success of some of the cities in this country based on their airports. To cite a few examples: Dallas, Chicago, New York, Newark, San Francisco, and Tampa. By contrast, Kansas City and Houston put their airports in the wrong location and have suffered as a result.

16. Condition of Roadway System. People want to avoid congestion and long, slow commutes. Many communites don't have the ability to expand roadway systems because of geographical limitations. People stay closer to home and rarely shop. The inability to get to businesses restricts growth. Keep in mind the rule for growth: Growth can go in only two directions—up or down—not sideways. The most dramatic example is that of Juneau, the capital of Alaska. The only way to reach that city is by boat or plane. It sits right at the edge of the base of the mountain, with no access roads and no room for expansion. Legislation has been proposed to move the capital to another city; if it passes, Juneau will be killed economically.

By contrast, Sacramento, California has been growing because, of its location as the hub of several interstate and intrastate highway systems.

17. Condition of Railway System. Railroads are important for shipping supplies and people and providing a link to other parts of the country. The economic health of an area hinges on commerce—by air, rail, water, and highway.

18. Condition of Shopping Facilities. Referring to Figure 6–1, Typical Activities within an Area, you can see how the condition of shopping centers fits into the overall picture. Are the shopping centers in your area attractive enough to encourage more people to shop and spend money? If the answer is yes, stores will expand and grow and so will the community. Here are two examples of shopping centers that won't grow.

- If a 25-year-old shopping center in Minnesota doesn't have covered walkways, it's not conducive to shopping. People in cold climates prefer protection from the elements.

- Similarly, a big shopping center in Houston that lacks air conditioning would be considered outdated.

19. Condition of Recreational Facilities. People who pursue recreational activities are healthier; they get out more, spend money, and have a positive attitude. Active individuals look for hotels and office buildings with gyms. They're interested in jogging areas and health and exercise facilities. Does your area have adequate recreational facilities that promote increased activity?

20. Revenue Tax.

21. Sales Tax.

22. *State and Local Taxes.* When a community is unable to support itself through normal taxes, such as business, real estate, and sales, it must seek additional forms of revenue or increase the basic taxes to unreasonable levels. The more a local government burdens people with taxes, the less money its citizens have to spend. This vicious circle reduces the growth potential of an area. Unemployment increases; spending decreases. A recession might result. It's important to compare these taxes to national averages.

Totalling the Results

If your total score for an area is 33.5, that's excellent. A score of 2 is good. The minimum you should settle for is 14.

This Area Valuation Worksheet allows you to look at the overall results and weight them. If certain factors are undesirable, they may be overshadowed by others that are extremely positive. Let's look at the state of California as an example.

California has one of the highest rates of state taxation; but when you put everything together, the state still gets a passing grade. It has an excellent university system, a diverse economy, high employment, good climate, cultural advantages, and other overwhelming features that are able to overcome the negative aspects of a high tax rate. If California didn't score well on other features, then the state wouldn't be as attractive for investors.

TIPS TO REMEMBER

- Selecting the right area is your first and most crucial decision. Making a mistake is fatal. Research all factors carefully.
- Look for growth in an area as measured by migration plus per capita earnings, retail sales, and bank deposits.
- Evaluate the competitiveness of your proposed real estate purchase by studying figures for permits and buildings under construction.
- Job creation is the anchor to an area.
- High employment spurs growth—and real estate profits.

- If taxes and adverse legislation are oppressive, it's harder to make money in real estate.
- A good climate attracts people and businesses.
- Well-located and maintained roads, airports, shopping centers, and recreational facilities enhance an area.

CHAPTER 7

McDONALD'S SECRET: CHOOSING THE BEST LOCATION

Now that you've selected a good area for your real estate investment, it's time for fine-tuning. You need to choose the best location within that area. According to a conventional dictionary definition, location is "a position or site occupied or available for occupancy." Since we're looking at location from a business point of view, we'll define it in a way that helps you achieve your business goals. Location is an exact place for a piece of real estate that is most convenient to achieve the objective for that particular real estate.

When we say exact place, we'll be talking about certain specifics. Is the location on the left or right side of the street? Is it on a corner, adjacent to a main thoroughfare, on a dead-end street?

The key point in our definition is that the location must be the most convenient for achieving the objectives of the real estate. Different types of real estate have different objectives. In your search for the right location, always regard your real estate as a business. That business has clients—the people who will utilize its square feet. Those people are commonly known as tenants, but calling them clients helps you keep a business perspective in mind. Your clients are customers, and your aim is to please them.

First, define the type of real estate you want to buy—residential units, shopping centers, or office buildings. Then, when you look at prospective locations, keep in mind the objectives you must satisfy for the clients who will be buying or leasing your square feet.

FIGURE 7–1
Pinpointing an Exact Location within an Area

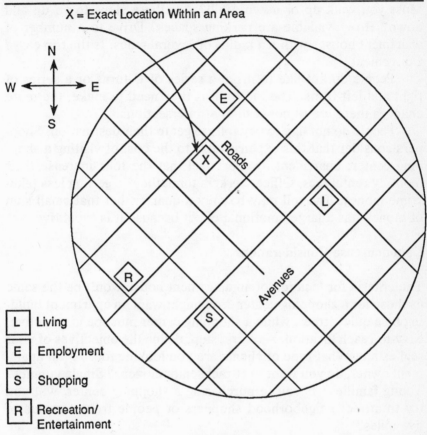

X = Exact Location Within an Area

L	Living
E	Employment
S	Shopping
R	Recreation/ Entertainment

Research from Behind the Wheel

When you look at specific location, put yourself into the shoes of a client of that building. If it's an apartment house, drive to those facilities where your tenants might work, shop, or go to the movies. If you're considering the purchase of an office building, walk out of the lobby and see how comfortable you would feel going to nearby restaurants or shops on your lunch hour. Also, drive to the neighborhood where employees might live. Evaluate the ease and convenience of your trip.

If you're purchasing a shopping center, see how comfortable it is to walk from shop to shop. How easy is it to get to your car? Must you walk up or down a hill? Are there steps to go up and down? How available are parking spaces? Drive to a number of apartment houses within a radius of several miles. Is the trip easy? Convenient?

People do not like to make a series of U-turns or a series of right and left turns. The more turns they need to make, the more chances there are of congestion at intersections.

People do not like to pay tolls to get to their destination. Shoppers consider that this expense adds to the cost of visiting a shopping center; apartment dwellers feel that the tolls increase their monthly rental fees. Office workers think they're getting less take-home money. The toll may be only a quarter, but that small sum of money has a large emotional effect because it is repetitive.

Commonsense Considerations

The criteria for location of an apartment house won't be the same as those for a shopping center. You might want an apartment building on a quiet street, while a shopping center must be in an active, easy-to-reach location. As a first step, define the objectives of your real estate. What type of clients are you looking for? As an apartment owner, do you want to attract senior citizens? Single yuppies? Young families? If you're purchasing a shopping center, will you try to attract neighborhood shoppers or people from a radius of five miles?

People think of McDonald's in terms of hamburgers and french fries, overlooking the fact that this company is one of the most successful real estate firms in the country. They're experts in site selection. Each store location is chosen to maximize the number of customers. Have you ever had to make a U-turn to go to McDonald's? No. They're generally on the "correct" side of the street. Why are they more successful than other hamburger franchises? Do they have a better hamburger? No. They have better locations.

Although common wisdom makes it seem that "location, location, location" is critical in real estate investing, keep in mind that the three most critical words for your purposes are "research, research, research." This process applies to all seven EVS criteria, but you have more room for error in some of the categories. Of the seven keys in our Economic Valuation System, five can be changed. Area and location are fixed. That's why you must put such heavy emphasis on these factors, researching them extensively. Any mistake you make is totally uncorrectable. Mortgage terms can be altered. If an apartment building needs extra amenities, you can usually add a swimming pool or a tennis court. If the income estimate from a shopping center is inaccurate, you can take steps to offset it by increasing rents. But a poor location will haunt you forever.

The location you select depends upon the clients you seek to attract. Let's relate this statement to your personal needs. If you're buying a home and your family includes school-age children, you would want to be within walking distance of the school, or within walking distance of a bus stop that services the school. But, if your children are grown, you wouldn't want to live adjacent to a high school.

As the owner of an apartment house, you're aware that tenants won't want to be next to a major six-lane highway, particularly if they have children. On the other hand, if you own a shopping center, your clients (the owners of the shops) might want to be adjacent to that same six-lane highway.

Location and area work together, hand in hand. How would your real estate investment do if you had a good area and a bad location? You might expect average results; even though the location isn't optimum, the good area might pull up the value of your investment. How would a good location do in a bad area? Probably not very well. The area would pull down the good location. Area is the most critical; then comes location.

What Do Your Clients Want?

Before we apply the Economic Valuation System to site selection, let's examine the differing needs of your clients. Once you decide whether to invest in residential units, an office building or a shopping center, be aware of the needs of your prospective clients.

Apartments and Other Residential Units

Most people prefer relative quiet. They don't want an apartment on a main thoroughfare or adjacent to one. People would rather listen to their TVs or stereo sets, not to traffic whizzing by. People like balconies—but not facing a busy, brightly lit area, particularly a commercial street with flashing lights.

More and more, you see apartments taking on the look of homes. They are landscaped with more trees and spacious natural settings. Although the buildings are further back from the street, it's not necessary to drive far to reach them. Apartment dwellers generally don't want to travel more than 15 or 20 minutes to shops or to work. By contrast, people who own their own homes may be willing to drive an hour to work to protect their investments and lifestyle.

If you have a choice as to the side of the street, be aware that people prefer to make a right turn from their parking lot into the traffic pattern that takes them directly toward work. They don't want to go out of their way for several blocks before making a U-turn.

Shopping Centers

Your shopping center clients want to be near activity; they want to create the feeling that customers are actively engaged in looking at merchandise, spending money, and interacting with others. Your shopkeeper clients want to be near major thoroughfares.

To survive, a shopping center needs thousands of people going through the facility; by contrast, the road to a 100 unit apartment house would service only about 200 people. The center needs wide roads that lead into it, allowing large numbers of cars to come and go easily. A regional center should be near major thoroughfares, and interstate highways with cloverleaf exits.

Office Buildings

Unlike shopping centers, where foot traffic is minimal because of the proximity to major highways, it's desirable for office buildings to provide facilities for pedestrians. People who work in office buildings want sidewalks nearby so they can walk to local stores or restaurants during lunch breaks. The office building would not necessarily be adjacent to a residential area, or to a configuration of main highways.

Which direction will most employees be commuting from? Keep their traffic flow in mind. If possible, purchase a building on the side of the street most people come from. Otherwise, they'll be approaching it from the "wrong" direction, faced with the prospect of driving past the building and making a U-turn later.

Detective Work—Using Your Imagination

Before buying, most novice real estate investors look at a piece of property a few times, perhaps on sunny springtime days. Under those conditions, everything looks great. But you're getting an incomplete view. For example, in California it very rarely rains during the summer, so you must project what will happen during an extended rainy season. In cold climates, you'll need to visualize what happens when it snows.

Look at all the physical features of that location and imagine what will happen during other times of the year. Is the property near an earthquake fault or flood plain? During severe rainstorms, an adjacent stream might overflow. A building in a picturesque valley might end up half submerged in an instantly created lake when it rains. Or the hill that the apartment rests on may erode, washing away the landscaping. That hillside location might also be uncomfortably windy during the winter. Your clients will then want to turn up the heat, increasing your heating costs. To avoid surprises, you would need to project the wintertime heating costs. In other words, you *must* look at that real estate and its surrounding land as it will be 365 days a year. What are the worst weather conditions you can expect? Could you cope with them?

The Difference Between Day and Night, Weekdays and Weekends

Most people look at real estate in the daytime, but that isn't enough. It's important to go back at night and find out what happens to that property after dark. For example, an apartment house could have a serene atmosphere in the daytime; at night, you might find the parking lot full of motorcycles, with lots of beer drinking, noise, and a host of problems that result from this activity. If a large number of friends and their children visit your clients on weekends, this has a direct impact on the expense side of your P&L Statement.

At a shopping center, you may discover that the lighting is inadequate. The eerie nighttime atmosphere might drive prospective shoppers away. During weekends, you'll have a chance to observe the type of customers and the direction they come from. Whatever the real estate, go back to the location at night and on weekends to see what's going on. You want to make sure that the conditions at those times don't contradict the objectives of that real estate.

EVALUATING THE LOCATION

For each location under consideration, you'll prepare a Location Valuation Sheet. The one in Figure 7–2 focuses on items common to all income-producing real estate.

Start filling out your form with a description of the property. Indicate the quadrant and define the location further by noting the nearest intersection and major road.

Now we'll go through the evaluation section by section. A passing grade for location would minimally be (11).

1. Ingress to Property

2. Egress from Property

Ingress and egress refer to the ability to get into a property and get out of it conveniently. Factors that effect ingress and egress include the following:

Is the location in a valley?

Is the location on the side or top of a hill?

Is the property on an earthquake fault?

How far is the property from a stream or river?

Let's look at specifics for apartments, shopping center and office buildings to evaluate features your specific clients would want.

FIGURE 7–2
Location Valuation Worksheet

PROPERTY NAME _____

TYPE OF PROPERTY _____

ADDRESS _____

SELLER _____

NUMBER OF UNITS _____

TOTAL NUMBER OF SQUARE FEET _____

PURCHASE PRICE _____

CASH DOWN PAYMENT _____

MORTGAGE DESCRIPTION _____

LOCATION-PROPERTY STATISTICS

Quadrant _____

Intersection _____

Name of Near Major Road _____

LOCATION-PROPERTY VALUATION

Condition	Subject	Bad	Avg	Good	TOTAL SCORE
		Rating			
	1. Ingress to Property	(2)	0	2	
	2. Egress from Property	(2)	0	2	
	3. Property on Main Highways	(2)	0	2	
	4. Property on Commercial Thoroughfares	(2)	0	2	
	5. Property on Dead End Street	(2)	0	2	
	6. Access to Freeways	(2)	0	2	
	7. Access to Neighborhood Shopping (Residential)	(.5)	0	.5	
	8. Access to Regional Shopping (Residential)	(.5)	0	.5	
Subjective Decisions	9. Access to Employment (Residential)	(.5)	0	.5	
	10. Access to Recreational Facilities (Residential)	(.5)	0	.5	
	11. Access to Airport (Commercial R.E.)	(.5)	0	.5	
	12. Access to Public Transportation	(.5)	0	.5	
	13. Access to School systems	(.5)	0	.5	
	14. Zoning	(2)	0	2	
	15. Toxic Waste Disposal	(4)	0	0	
	TOTAL	(21.5)	0	17.5	

Shopping Centers. Regional malls, which generally have 250,000 square feet or more, need to have a well-lit major highway with an exit that leads almost directly into the mall. You can't have a regional mall that would require customers to drive through residential areas. You also cannot have regional malls that would require shoppers to drive through high employment areas; those potential shoppers would get caught up in rush-hour traffic. After shopping, people want to get onto a main highway immediately outside that will take them to the local streets they live on. But they don't want to drive on local streets to a shopping center.

The convenience factor is more important for people going to a shopping center than for those leaving it. Thus, if a major highway disgorges people on the right side of the road, make sure you buy a shopping center on that side of the road.

Neighborhood (strip) shopping centers, which have approximately 100,000 square feet, are generally on commercial thoroughfares. Traffic lights simplify ingress and egress. A divider in the road forces people to drive past and make a U-turn, a major inconvenience. Seven-Eleven stores found in neighborhood shopping centers are single-purpose convenience stores. Like McDonald's, their success depends upon location.

Office Buildings.   Whether the office building is on an avenue or road, people should be able to drive into the parking lot easily. If they're coming from the opposite side of the street, a divider on the road in front of the building prevents them from making a right or left turn directly into the parking lot. In some instances, they might have to drive half a mile or more and then wait for traffic to pass before making a U-turn to drive back toward the building. Employees dislike that inconvenience.

Apartment Houses.   People want to drive in on a level road and find a parking spot easily. Like office workers, they're easily annoyed by having a divider in the road opposite the building. If the building is on a quiet street, ingress and egress are easier. When people leave for work or shopping, there's no need to wait several minutes for a break in the traffic before driving out of the parking lot.

3. Property on Main Highways

Is traffic so heavy that it's difficult to drive out of the parking lot? On some busy streets, it may take five minutes of sitting in the car before getting onto a main thoroughfare.

Shopping centers on a major street require a traffic light. The constant flow of cars going in and out should be able to move without long delays. Stop signs are ineffective since they allow cars to move out slowly and only one at a time.

Office complexes don't necessarily need to be on a main highway. However, if they're on a commercial thoroughfare, employees can shop and eat nearby.

4. Property on Commercial Thoroughfares

For a neighborhood (strip) shopping center, a commercial thoroughfare is ideal. People can drive there easily from home to do their convenience shopping. Before purchasing a strip center, take an auto traffic count. McDonald's and other fast-food restaurants consider traffic information an important part of their research. They count the number of cars moving in both directions past a particular location they're interested in. Then they buy on the side with the most traffic.

Make sure your shopping center is on the side of the street with the heaviest traffic. If the traffic is evenly divided, choose the side of street that has homeward bound drivers. People tend to shop more on their way home from work—but they're in no mood to make U-turns. That's why the odds favor businesses on the "correct" side of the street.

While traffic lights are a necessity near shopping centers, too many of them can be a nuisance near office buildings or apartments. Must your clients go through a series of red and green lights to reach their office building or apartment house? Are these lights electrically timed? If so, are they timed so that traffic moves in a fluid manner?

5. Property on Dead-End Streets

Dead-end streets are unsuitable for shopping centers or for office buildings. They can't accommodate the huge numbers of cars that would be driven in and out. People want to access these buildings from different directions. With a single entry and no exit point, it's just not convenient. A dead-end street is attractive only for residential units; traffic is generated only by people who live there.

The following evaluations (6–10) relate to residential property. Judge them by the convenience of their access.

6. Access to Freeways

7. Access to Neighborhood Shopping

8. Access to Regional Shopping

9. Access to Employment

10. Access to Recreational Facilities

11. Access to Airport
This is important for commercial real estate—both office buildings and shopping centers. Successful airports breed success in two ways: they become significant employers; and, in addition, they generate inflows of people that need support services, such as hotels, restaurants, and other businesses.

12. Access to Public Transportation
This factor is significant for all three types of real estate investments.

13. Access to School Systems
This would apply to certain types of residential property. Evaluate this factor only if you're renting to people with schoolchildren of various ages. It would make no difference to senior citizens or yuppies.

14. Zoning
Since you're not buying real estate in the middle of the wilderness, you must learn about nearby zoning for three reasons:

1. You'll find out about competing buildings.

2. If property nearby is slated for a use that's incompatible

with your prospective purchase, you'll be forewarned—and able to look elsewhere.

3. The majority type of real estate will establish the look and style of a particular area or part of an area.

Be sure to look at zoning in the immediate neighborhood and also in the quadrant. You want the big picture. Zoning maps that you purchase from the local zoning board will show what the urban plan is and what dedications have been made in certain areas. If there is any vacant land nearby, you *must* find out about its zoning and intended use. Is there enough of a buffer between your building and the new project? How much traffic and noise would that type of development generate? You wouldn't want a gas station or a night club built on land adjacent to your apartments.

Be very careful in areas that have no zoning restrictions.

If you're considering the purchase of an apartment house and there is a vacant lot nearby zoned for apartments, that's bad news. You'll face increased competition. If you're contemplating the purchase of a shopping center or an office building, apartment zoning nearby is welcome news. Additional people would be coming into the area as potential shoppers and employees. Therefore, the real estate you're buying would become more attractive.

Zoning for upscale office buildings or expensive apartments near an apartment building is good; but a mobile home park generally detracts from an upscale neighborhood. If you're thinking of purchasing a shopping center surrounded by land zoned for large apartment buildings, shoppers would have difficulty getting in and out of the center. Be aware of all potentially disruptive zoning nearby.

15. Toxic Waste Disposal

Recognizing that toxic wastes can move through soil, you should check to see if manufacturing plants or other businesses dispose of toxic waste in the area where you are purchasing real estate. What effect, if any, will that toxic waste have on your real estate? Contact environmental officers in the city government, and local environmental groups.

Title Report

Finally, you should obtain a title report, which is an examination of the land and improvements, to see if there are any prior liens on them. This report will also indicate whether there are any easements (giving someone else rights to the land below or air above it). Easements may affect your ability to do what you want with the real estate and also impact future resale value.

Hilltop Locations: The Aesthetics Are Nice, but the Problems Aren't

Most office buildings and shopping centers are not located on the tops or bottoms of hills; that type of site adds an extra inconvenience to egress and ingress. Look for flat locations in order to avoid potential problems of drainage and flooding. Apartments can do well on top of a hill because people enjoy the view. Employees on the ground floor of an office building appreciate landscaping, but a view isn't necessary for those on upper floors. And, in shopping centers, people are interested in bargains, not scenic vistas.

Although hilltop locations are fine for apartment houses from an aesthetic viewpoint, these sites pose structural problems which we'll discuss in the next chapter.

TIPS TO REMEMBER

- The more convenience you give people, the more they will want to rent or lease your square feet. They're paying the rent for a location that's easy to reach.
- Research carefully. If you make a mistake on location, you'll be locked into it forever—or until you can find a buyer who makes the same mistake.
- Retrace the footsteps of your clients, traveling from residential areas to shopping centers and office complexes.
- Visualize the effect of changing seasons and weather conditions on the property.

- Make daytime, nighttime, weekday, and weekend visits to the property.
- Be aware of local zoning and its impact.

CHAPTER 8

STRUCTURAL INTEGRITY: BRICKS AND MORTAR DON'T TELL LIES

Once you purchase real estate, you're locked into the area and location. Now we'll talk about the physical structure of a building, the third factor on the Economic Valuation System, and the first one you can alter. We'll define structural integrity as the approval or qualification of all mechanical and structural improvements, as well as the supporting land. Since you can change the physical structure, why is this pre-purchase evaluation so crucial? Real estate is a capital-intensive business. If you buy property that needs repairs, you face massive expenses. Durability holds the key to greater profits for you.

Just one expenditure for fixing your real estate could easily wipe out two years of anticipated earnings or cash flow.

Let's assume that you planned to invest $50,000 as a one-third down payment on residential units. The full purchase price of your real estate is $150,000. That might buy a triplex or an apartment building with up to six units. For this example, we'll talk about a five-plex. Initially, you might expect yields of 2 to 4 percent based on the amount of money you invested, not on the purchase price. We'll assume a 3 percent yield; that would work out to a $1,500 annual cash flow. [$50,000 down payment × 3 percent yield = $1,500 cash flow]

Now for the horror stories. If you had to replace three carpets more than you planned, you would spend more than $1,500—a full year's cash flow. If you had to replace any part of the roof, or if you discovered foundation problems that you hadn't anticipated, those repairs could cost $5,000 each. Any minimal investment in your landscaping would come to several thousand dollars. It just takes a couple of mistakes in judgment and your yield vanishes. You then have a negative cash flow. That's why you must be extremely careful when you check out the structural integrity of a building. Never forget the importance of research, research, research. The worksheet/checklist in this chapter (Figure 8–2) offers guidelines to follow.

If you invest a substantial sum of money and buy a large building complex, painting costs alone could come to $50,000. Redoing the blacktop parking area would set you back $100,000. Upgrading the landscaping could cost $50,000. That's also what you would pay for a swimming pool. Putting in a tennis court might cost $25,000. Roof replacement would come to $75,000. These are very costly. In order to avoid unpleasant surprises after you buy, take precautions before you sign on the dotted line.

If your research uncovers defects in structural integrity, you have several alternatives:

1. Walk away from the deal.
2. Ask the seller to make necessary repairs.
3. Ask the seller to lower his asking price accordingly.
4. Have the seller set aside money you can use for designated repairs.

THE GOOD NEWS AND BAD NEWS ABOUT REPAIRS

Let's start with the bad news first. Two factors drive up your expenses: age and inflation.

When you buy a building, it's inevitable that you'll have to replace things from time to time. In an apartment house, this includes carpeting, drapes, appliances, and anything else that goes with the unit. The cost of replacements increases each year; you must factor that in. These increases come about for two reasons:

1. The building is getting older and each year more things need replacing.

2. Even though inflation is not rampant at this writing, it always looms as a factor. Historically, under the capitalistic system, deflationary times exist for only several years during each 100–year period. That means we're in an inflationary period most of the time.

Even an apparently low inflation rate of 2 or 3 percent can have an adverse affect. Factor in that percentage, plus the age of your building, and it's easy to see that you'll constantly be facing increases in your expenses.

Now for the good news: If you buy in a good area with a good location you should be able to more than offset the increased expenses by rental increases. *If you buy a structurally sound building, you can control expenses and operate more successfully.*

If you doubt that there's magic in numbers, you're in for a pleasant surprise when you examine Figure 8–1. As a real estate investor, you'll find that expenses generally run less than 50 percent of income. So for every 50 cents that expenses go up, you need to raise the income by only 25 cents to break even. Thus, over a period of time, the cash flow (money available after debt services) increases dramatically.

FIGURE 8–1
There's Magic in Numbers

Income:	$1.00	
Expenses:		
Operating	.50	
Expenses:		
Mortgage:	.47	
Total expenses:	.97	
Cash flow	.03	(1.00 minus .97)

If you raised the income by 5 percent, the total income would be $1.05.

If your expenses increase by 5 percent, the figures would look like this:

Operating Expenses:	.525	
Mortgage:	.470	
Total Expenses:	.975	
Cash flow:	.075	($1.05 minus .975)

Even though your expenses and income increase by the same percentage, your cash flow in this case more than doubles.

If your income and expenses both increase by 5 percent, you would see some surprising results. Figure 8–1 shows some numbers for a typical piece of real estate:

To express this another way, if the percentage of the increase in income and expenses is the same, your profit margin goes up. This is one of the big profit features of real estate.

In commercial real estate, the tenant pays all expenses and the income is fixed to some type of consumer price index. You can expect rent increases on lease renewal and also on the basis of the contractural agreement in the lease. For example, a three-year lease could be written to include an increase each year during the life of the lease, in addition to the increase that follows a boost in the consumer price index.

Owners of a shopping center can anticipate even greater increases in income. According to common practice, they receive a percentage from the sales income of businesses in the center. The more successful the leasees are, the more income they will generate for the landlord. This money is additional return to the landlord, thereby increasing the value of his shopping center.

THE PERILS OF IGNORING "MINOR" REPAIRS

You'll rarely come across a perfect building. You may notice cracks in the pavement, worn carpets, dirty walls, potholes in the parking lot, and other seemingly minor defects. The temptation is to say, "Well, I can ignore some of these minor repairs for a while." But is it safe to do so? The answer is *no!*

Once you own a building, some repairs will be done in emergency situations; with others, you have a choice of taking care of them quickly, or stalling. For example, leaky pipes fall into the emergency repair category, while you might choose to ignore dingy walls and potholes in the parking lot. Stalling might buy you time, but it comes at the expense of profits. Here's the scenario.

Dingy walls and crumbling pavement in a parking lot detract from the appearance of your building. Thus your real estate business might not be as competitive as others in the neighborhood. Potential clients will lease elsewhere. Since your negligence poses the risk of leasing less square feet, you can expect vacancies. You certainly can't hope to raise the rents because your square feet are now unattractive and less useable.

Thus, if you don't take action, you face two unpleasant situations:

- *By ignoring necessary repairs, you lessen the value of your investment.*
- *When something is not fixed quickly, it will cost much more money to fix ultimately.*

Taking these warnings out of the theoretical realm and into the real world, let's look at three scenarios:

1. Suppose you own a building on a hill and each time it rains, part of the landscape erodes. You might temporarily fill it in with more dirt, but that isn't tackling the problem head-on. Two months later, you may find that the erosion has become so severe it cuts under the foundation. That involves major expenditures.

2. If you have a few potholes in the parking lot, you could fill them in immediately at fairly minimal expense. But you choose to ignore them. Months later, you might find that instead of patching, you have to dig up the entire parking lot and re-pave it.

3. A small part of the roof needs to be patched. You ignore it. By the end of the rainy season, you might need to replace the entire roof, in addition to repairing interior water damage.

The cause of your problems won't go away. Deterioration continues. Months later, instead of being able to fix the damage with a patch job, you may need an expensive replacement. Your costs then escalate.

In the process of getting worse, a minor problem becomes major, impacting the overall structure. That's the case in our first example above. So when you look at cracked steps or sidewalks, potholes, erosion, and other seemingly minor problems in a building, you *must* have money set aside for repairs before making an investment.

By examining a building's structural integrity carefully, you can anticipate necessary capital improvements. If you think you

---

CYMROT'S LAW NUMBER 8:

Capital improvements should not come as a surprise. They have to be anticipated and the money available for them needs to be there.

---

can handle them, that's fine. If the outlay seems overwhelming and the present owner won't make repairs, walk away from the deal. You don't want to buy something that will lose its value almost immediately. If you're forced to charge lower rents because the property is deteriorating, it's extemely costly. Suppose a freshly painted apartment with good carpeting rents for $500 per month. Since you want to wait a while before fixing up the unit, you reduce the rent by $50 per month. Over the period of one year, you'll lose $600 in rent. But your loss doesn't stop there. Your building will lose $7,500 in value. In the chapter on capitalization ratios, we'll explain why, for every dollar of rent you lose, the building could lose $12.50 in value. That sounds scary—and it is.

With these horror stories in mind, let's examine the process you'll follow to verify structural integrity.

FIRST STEPS IN VERIFYING STRUCTURAL INTEGRITY

All structural examinations should be done by a professional. But before you hire someone, you need to lay the groundwork. Your preliminary research on structural integrity will help you save money when you hire a professional inspector or engineer. In addition to enabling you to give adequate direction to the professional you hire, research will help you save money by avoiding wasted time spent on areas not requiring further investigation. As an example, assume the roof is new, rains have recently fallen, and there is not a single complaint of a leak; there is no staining or standing water, and visual inspection confirms all walls are at right angles. Based on these factors, you would not direct the inspector to spend much time on the roof. If any of these conditions were not met, you would request the inspector to investigate further.

Visual Inspection

If you were purchasing a manufacturing plant or a retail store, you would inspect the inventory. In the case of real estate, the square feet are your inventory. This is your business! Make a visual inspection of the entire building. Verify that the walls are at right angles to one another. Look for cracks in the walls. Try out the mechanical equipment to make sure it works. Turn on the air-conditioning system. Turn on faucets. Is the water pressure adequate? Is the water dirty-looking? Flush the toilets. Look for water stains on the ceilings or walls. They'll lead you to leaks.

Suppose you're buying an apartment building with 100 units. It would cost a fortune if the professional inspector you hire goes through each unit. By visually inspecting the apartments yourself, you ferret out the ones that seem to have problems and can ask the professional to zero in on those specifically. You might ask him to check out 20 units that have stained ceilings or walls, sinks with low water pressure, or electrical sockets that don't work.

Look at Recent Work Orders

In any well-run building, the current management will have a set of work orders. These are forms used for authorizing repairs. When tenants complain that something isn't working, the owner will write up a work order before repairs are done. These can be a valuable reference for you.

Ask to see work orders for the past three years. When you review them, look for patterns. If nine out of ten work orders involved leaks, find out where those apartments are located. If they're on the top floor, you would authorize the structural engineer you hire to check the roof carefully.

Talk to Clients/Tenants

Interview a cross-section of tenants and you'll discover a wealth of information about the building. Ask questions such as, "What things would you like to see fixed. What don't you like about this building?" You may learn that mud gathers in a particular area during rainstorms, one of the sewers backs up occasionally, water pours over a section of the flat roof, or one side of the building is very cold on windy days. For an accurate cross-section, make sure the people you interview are from various parts of the building.

If you're purchasing a shopping center, you would talk to some of the retailers who rent space, and also to shoppers strolling through the mall. Similarly, if you're purchasing an office building, talk to the tenants and their employees.

Interview the Staff

Speak to the leasing agent, maintenance person, and the on-site manager. What things would they like to have fixed if enough money was available? Which are high-priority items in their opinion?

Interview the Potential Seller

You'll be having many conversations with the potential seller about terms later on. Right now, you want to zero in on possible structural defects and weaknesses. Ask for an update of all capital improvements done in the last three years. From this, you can extrapolate certain information. If you know the building is 25 years old and the heating system was replaced two years ago, there's some assurance you won't face major repairs of that system. But if the original roof is still on the building, chances are it will need capital improvements in a few years. This approach is similar to that you would take in buying a home for your family. You would talk to prospective neighbors, and ask what sort of repairs people nearby have completed in recent years. For example, have many people replaced their heating systems? If so, and the home you're buying still has the original furnace, you could assume that it's likely to develop problems soon.

Now that you've done this research—walked through the building, and spoken to clients, staff people, and the present owner—you're in a better position to hire the right type of professional engineer. Depending upon the weaknesses you've uncovered, you can determine which type of expert to hire. Also, by pointing out clues to possible structural defects, you'll be in a better position to direct his inspection and insist that he carry out your instructions explicitly.

HIRING THE RIGHT PROFESSIONAL

What type of professional inspector should you hire? You may need more than one, depending upon the type of building and its site. You could end up paying a termite inspector, soil engineer, mechanical engineer, and more. Find out whether, within the expert's specific industry, it is necessary to have a license. If so, make sure you utilize the services of a person who has that license.

If you're purchasing an all-brick building, you might not need a termite inspector. By contrast, with a wood-frame building, you would want to know about the condition of the wood, making a termite inspection mandatory. If the building is on a hill, hire a soil engineer to check the soil. Before purchasing a building that sits on a waterfront, check with the U.S. Army Corps of Engineers to find out about the condition of the bulkheads.

Inspectors in each of the specialties we've mentioned might charge from $1,000 to $50,000. What determines the charge? The instructions you give this professional determine the extent of the inspection. If you're unsure about instructions, your broker should be able to offer some guidance.

Before hiring a professional, ask for references, and *always* check them out. You want to find an individual with a good reputation, who has done similar work in your area. How long has this person been in business? How large is his business? Any representation is only as good as the person or company backing it. It's important to ask this professional for a breakdown of repair costs you might incur, including both parts and labor.

THE STRUCTURAL INTEGRITY WORKSHEET

After filling in a basic description of the property at the top of the form, you're ready to indicate the four key characteristics: terrain, foundation, siding, and roof. The terrain might be described in terms of the site itself. Is it flat or hilly? Is the building on fill? Are there creeks or streams on the site? The other three characteristics are self-explanatory.

Before we move to individual items on the worksheet, let's examine the philosophy behind our grading system. The point score may appear arbitrary, but, in most cases, it's determined by bottom-line considerations. The more durable your driveway, roof, exterior, and so forth, the less money you'll need to spend on maintenance over the long haul. In other words, you'll enjoy greater profits. That's why this grading system can help you make money and create value over a period of years. The minimum acceptable grade is 10.

1. Driveway

Apartment Houses.   Since driveways cover a large area, they have a strong impact on people approaching the building. Some apartment houses may have an entry with mosaic brick, but the overall driveway will be either asphalt (blacktop) or concrete. A driveway in good condition can give an older building a new look; by contrast, one that is full of potholes and cracks can make a new building seem like a tenement.

You'll note that a good concrete driveway is worth three points on our worksheet, while a good asphalt driveway is only worth two points. What's the difference? A concrete driveway lasts longer, is stronger, and is a better investment. It expands and contracts less, is less prone to cracking, develops fewer potholes, and offers better drainage. If you buy a building with a good concrete driveway, that's a distinct advantage. But if the concrete needs repairs, that's bad news, since it costs more money to fix concrete than a blacktop pavement. Incidentally, in most cities, you'll notice that heavily trafficked roads are made of concrete for durability, while side streets generally have asphalt paving.

Shopping Centers.   Large shopping centers generally have asphalt paving. Because of the large parking areas required by shopping centers, its cheaper to patch asphalt if problems arise.

Office Buildings.   More and more of the office buildings constructed these days—particularly upscale buildings—have concrete driveways. For an analogy, you might consider which is preferable—a wood-framed building or a brick one? Of course, a brick building is the first choice, for looks and durability.

FIGURE 8–2
Structural Integrity Worksheet

PROPERTY NAME _____
TYPE OF PROPERTY _____
ADDRESS _____
SELLER _____
NUMBER OF UNITS _____
TOTAL NUMBER OF SQUARE FEET _____
PURCHASE PRICE _____
CASH DOWN PAYMENT _____
MORTGAGE DESCRIPTION _____

STRUCTURAL INTEGRITY-PROPERTY STATISTICS
TERRAIN _____
FOUNDATION _____
SIDING _____
ROOF _____

STRUCTURAL INTEGRITY-PROPERTY VALUATION

Condition	Subject	Bad	Avg	Good	TOTAL SCORE
	1. DRIVEWAY				
	Concrete	(1)	1	3	
	Asphalt	(2)	0	2	
	2. PARKING AREAS				
	Covered #_____				
	Per Unit #_____	0	2.5	3.5	
	Open #_____	1	2		
	Per Unit #_____				
	3. PARKING AREAS				
	Concrete	1.5	2.5	3.5	
	Asphalt	1	2	3	
	4. Bumpers	(.5)	0	.5	
	5. Roofs				
	Flat	.5	1	2	
	Mansard	1	1.5	3	
	Pitched	1.5	2.5	4	
	6. Siding	1.5	2.5	5	
	7. Foundation	(1.5)	3	5	
	8. Balconies	(1.5)	1	2	
	9. Stairways	(1.5)	1	2	
	10. Paint Condition	(1.5)	1	2	
	11. Insulation				
	(a) Exterior Walls	(2)	0	2	
	(b) Interior Walls	(2)	0	2	
	12. Crawl Space	(.5)	0	.5	
	13. Ducts	(.5)	0	.5	
	14. HVAC (Heating, Ventilation & Air Conditioning System)	(1)	0	1	
	15. Trim	(.5)	0	.5	
	16. Windows	(.5)	0	.5	
	17. Drainage	(1.5)	0	1.5	
	18. Site	(1.5)	0	1.5	
	19. Landscaping	(1)	0	1	
	TOTAL	(12.5)	23.5	54.5	

2. Parking

People want convenience, and if the weather is particularly hot, rainy, or cold, they prefer covered parking areas. In addition to the convenience, this "extra" helps protect their cars from the elements. Under "Condition" on our worksheet, scoring for covered parking is as follows:

"None" would be scored zero.

.75 means that there is covered parking for three-quarters of the units, and this would be worth 2.5 points.

1.5 means that there are 1.5 covered spaces for each apartment unit. This is worth 3.5 points.

The more covered units an apartment building has, the more attractive it is for potential tenants—and for you as an owner. You can charge extra money for covered units, or increase the overall rent.

In an office building, people like the convenience of covered parking; they can walk directly from their cars into the building. For shopping centers, covered parking is unrealistic, except, perhaps, in cold northern areas. Elsewhere, it's important to offer covered malls with parking facilities conveniently close to the building.

3. Pavement in Parking Areas

The discussion for subject number one—driveways—applies in this instance also.

4. Bumpers

There are two types of bumpers in parking lots of apartments, shopping centers, and office buildings:

- One type is placed in the roadway to discourage speeding. It consists of a hump that makes drivers slow down.

- The second type of bumper is a piece of concrete located at the edge of grassy areas to keep cars from damaging the landscaping when people park. Bumpers are used in this case rather than curbs because curbs can break apart, leading to repair expenses. The "bad" in our evaluation sheet refers to the number and condition of the bumpers.

5. Roof
There are two basic types of roofs: flat and pitched. The mansard roof listed on our worksheet is flat for the most part, but has an overhang that goes around the roof, giving it a French Provincial look. Pitched roofs merit the highest ratings. A good one earns twice as many points on our rating chart as a good flat roof. Pitched roofs look attractive and they last longer because drainage is no problem. By contrast, flat roofs have built-in complications. Water gathers in puddles, putting extra weight on certain parts of the roof. This weighs down the building and weakens it. In cold climates, a pitched roof is definitely advisable since it avoids a huge buildup of snow. Some investors won't buy an apartment building anywhere without a pitched roof because of its long life.

A good flat roof lasts 10 to 15 years while a good pitched roof lasts 15 to 25 years.

You'll notice very few pitched roofs in shopping centers and office buildings. Why? A pitched roof takes up valuable space that can otherwise be leased. For example, an office building with a pitched roof might lose the equivalent of two stories. Since leasees will pay for the cost of roof maintenance, owners would rather lease that space and increase the value of their building. In urban centers, tall apartment buildings have flat roofs, but since garden apartments are zoned for only two or three stories, pitched or mansard roofs make economic sense for them.

6. Siding
Brick siding is best. It looks better for a longer period of time, and there's no need to paint it periodically. Wood siding requires painting every five to seven years. Pressed board, which is made from paper that is pressed together and treated chemically, requires painting every three years.

7. Foundation
A concrete slab can be above grade or below grade. Below grade is preferable because it provides dramatically increased stability. A solidly-constructed, below-level slab of concrete should be "locked" into the soil. It won't slide or shift and is less susceptible to the effects of mud movement. The deeper a foundation is set

into the ground, the stronger it's going to be. Some foundations literally sit on top of the soil. They're susceptible to wind movement and any shift in the ground. Most importantly, mud can soften the foundation.

8. Balconies

Wood balconies require painting. The paint tends to chip, leading to rot. In that case, you would be saddled with replacement costs. A stucco/concrete balcony is better, while metal balconies are the best. Again, as in roofing materials and siding, we're seeking the advantages of structural materials that last a long time.

9. Stairways

Metal stairways have the same advantages as metal balconies. They last longer than wood stairways and are more economical in the long run.

10. Paint Condition

Make a commonsense judgement on this item. On an all-wood building, paint in bad condition is a serious matter, whereas the paint trim on a brick building isn't as crucial.

11. Insulation

R-11 and R-19 are energy-rated amounts of insulation. The difference between them might amount to three to four inches of insulation. In some areas of the country, this is unimportant; in other areas, it greatly impacts heating costs. Judge this factor objectively without assigning a point rating.

12. Crawl Space

This space underneath a building has two possible uses:

> You can use it to get from one part of the building to another part.
>
> You can use it as storage.

A crawl space is an "extra" that can be considered an attractive feature. At its worst, a crawl space might serve as a place where water gathers.

13. Ducts

Ductwork carries hot or cold air in office buildings, shopping centers, and homes. The condition of the ducts is an objective feature. Determine where the ducts are and what condition they are in.

14. Heating, Ventilation, and Air-Conditioning System

This machinery is commonly referred to as the HVAC system. You'll find it on the roof, on concrete pads set in the ground, or in sleeves (metal holders). Sleeve-type installations are often seen in apartment buildings where an air-conditioning unit is mounted on windowsills.

Find out the age of the system and ask whether the original guarantee is still in effect. You might also ask to see utility bills over a period of time to see if there's any change in the overall trend.

In shopping malls, most HVAC systems are mounted on the center of the roof, even though it's inefficient from an energy standpoint. In this case, you won't be stuck with higher utility bills since lessees pay them.

HVAC systems for office buildings can be on the roof, on a pad beside the building, or, in rare cases, inside the building. Most new office buildings are completely sealed so tenants can't open the windows; this necessitates an effective ventilation system.

Newer apartments have HVAC units on a pad adjacent to the building. Older structures have air-conditioning units in sleeves or on the roof, which is inefficient—and more costly for you.

15. Trim

Metal or wood trim enhances the appearance of a building. Check to see its condition.

16. Windows

Metal casing is preferable to wood-frame windows. Double-paned windows offer the advantage of increased insulation. They last longer and are less prone to cracking.

17. Drainage

We've put drainage near the bottom of the list, but this doesn't minimize its importance. Water can be very destructive, and poor drainage causes significant water damage. The purpose of drainage is to gather the water and direct it away from the building. When water comes down from a high area, through gutters and drainpipes, it hits splash blocks on the ground, and these direct the water away from the building. If a building lacks gutters, water floods over the edge of the roof, drips by the windows, stains the side of the building, and—most importantly—drops straight down, forming puddles beside the building and ultimately undermining the foundation. Gutters are a minor investment—yet, without them, you can undermine the foundation itself. Through erosion or settling, water breaks apart anything that is not waterproof, even concrete. It might get underneath a concrete driveway and erode the steel supports. Water carries soil away and can ruin landscaping.

Before buying a building, mentally envision what would happen during a rainstorm. Where will water run? Where will it gather?

18. Site

Very few developers know how to construct a building correctly on a hill. A hillsite requires a different type of engineering and architecture because of natural erosion. Ideally, you would want to own a building on a flat area—on sound bedrock with soil that doesn't move.

On a hilltop location, the building can be on level ground or on a site that is slightly rounded. On flat ground, the site doesn't necessarily mandate that the building be on a totally flat area. The ground can be built up with a berm to add visual interest.

Buildings constructed on fill can be dangerous. You never know if the compacting process is complete or not. If shifting continues, your building will crack in the future.

Check with the city planning commission to find out whether the building was constructed on fill. Talk to neighbors, and ask your broker about the site's past history. If you're buying in earthquake country, hire a geologist.

If you buy a one-year-old home on a hill, you're in a potentially dangerous situation. If the fill is five years old and nothing has happened in the past three years, that's more reassuring. How can you evaluate the effects of shifting? Look for right angles and cracks inside the building. The slightest shift generates cracks and off-right angles that are apparent to the eye. Look at ceilings and corners for these telltale signs. If the fill is unstable, as indicated by these hints, the building will crack like Jello if an earthquake hits.

19. Landscaping

Landscaping is one of the best investments you can have on a piece of land, but it's expensive. A mature tree can cost between $50 and $100. When treated correctly, trees get larger and become attractive amenities. By "correctly" we mean that they're well located, with no danger of crashing into buildings, and also that they're free of infestation.

Today, people are interested in the outdoors and in natural settings. If your site lacks landscaping, it will cost you a great deal of money to plant trees and shrubs. In addition, if you don't have the mechanical system (such as sprinklers) to preserve the landscaping, installation is another expense you face.

If you're interested in an apartment house with sparse landscaping, either pass it up or protect yourself by learning about the cost of fixing it up. Before buying, contact at least one landscape architect and ask for plans that you could follow to add shrubs and trees. The cost is likely to be substantial. Armed with an estimate, you can renegotiate the seller's offering price, or at least set aside money for the work on your own. You *must* upgrade the landscaping to make your building competitive with others in the neighborhood.

Every item you invest in should have a guarantee, as a sort of insurance policy for your pocketbook. For example, the person who sells you trees should guarantee that they're healthy. If the trees die from lack of water, that's your fault; but if they had some undetected sickness in the beginning, they should be replaced free of charge.

TIPS TO REMEMBER

- A durable building generates greater profits.
- If you discover defects, walk away from the deal, ask the seller to repair them, renegotiate the price, or have the seller set aside money for repairs.

- When neglected, minor repairs become major repairs.
- A preventive maintenance program will help you avoid capital improvements that come as a surprise.
- Back up your own visual research by asking hard questions of the owner, manager, and tenants.
- Hire professionals to evaluate the building and site.
- If your building isn't attractive and in good shape, it won't be competitive, and you'll lose money.
- Landscaping is an excellent long-term investment that will enhance the real estate much more than your investment.

CHAPTER 9

AMENITIES: FRILLS VERSUS NECESSITIES

Frosting on a cake. That's how the general public looks at real estate amenities. They think of swimming pools, community rooms, and covered parking as frills. But as a business-oriented real estate investor, you think of such items differently. Amenities are support facilities that attract and keep the type of client you seek. A swimming pool could be a frill or a necessity, depending upon your clientele. You evaluate amenities by asking, "How will this item impact my profit and loss statement?"

When you buy real estate, think about today *and* tomorrow. The more an apartment's features and amenities resemble those of a private home, the easier it will be for you to sell at a profit later on. The more functional amenities office buildings and shopping centers have, the larger the potential profit on sale. Such amenities in commercial buildings might include escalators, elevators, covered parking, and employee recreation.

Before evaluating specific amenities, let's return to basics. Real estate is a business that buys and sells square feet. When you purchase a building, you're acquiring a floor, walls, and a ceiling on a parcel of land. By themselves, square feet mean nothing. What makes that building able to accommodate apartment units, a shopping center, or offices? The answer is simple—the features that go into a building, allowing it to get the job function completed make it stand out from the competition.

How do you distinguish between necessary amenities and frills? Evaluate the needs of your clients and the function of the building. For example, if you want to attract young singles to your apartment building, a swimming pool might be a necessity. If you seek a clientele of senior citizens, the same pool could be a frill.

The Empty Box

Suppose you purchased a 36,000-square-foot building with no interior walls. What could you do with it? If you divided it into partitions, each ten feet square, and called it a shopping center, retailers wouldn't be able to keep an adequate inventory of stock and shoppers wouldn't have enough room to walk in and out of the cubicles. If you called your structure an apartment house, you wouldn't attract clients to such tiny rooms. People want space to spread out and entertain.

Suppose you decide against installing interior walls. You'd never find apartment tenants willing to live commune-style in 36,000 square feet of open space. If you decided to call the structure an office building, you would have difficulty finding a lawyer or executive who could work effectively in that open space. So what makes the difference between your 36,000-square-foot building standing as a white elephant versus performing a useful function? The interior of a building must be designed to accomplish a function for your prospective clients.

By now, you should automatically think about real estate as a business. Take this approach one step further by thinking about your customers as clients, not tenants. Once you have this mindset, you recognize that there are certain steps you should take when prospecting a client and closing a transaction. The principles that go into the owner-client relationship differ from those in an owner-tenant relationship. The latter is traditionally viewed as an adversarial relationship—one that does not build a successful business.

In order to build a successful real estate business, you must develop a support relationship between yourself and your clients. Amenities are one of the key ingredients—the catalyst or glue—which makes that support a reality. The following business analogies serve as examples.

If a person opens a restaurant and wants to attract a certain clientele, he'll incorporate specific amenities that attract and keep the clients he seeks. He might plan the restaurant with a Spanish or Mexican theme and carry it out with appropriate decorations.

This concept would be carried out further in several ways: the menu design, the way the waiters and waitresses dress, and in the food itself. Customers who come to this restaurant for a Spanish or Mexican experience will be happy. The owner has used the support facilities to attract and keep the type of client he seeks.

The basic idea is the same in specialized clothing stores. Today you can find stores for tall people, short people, and even overweight people. Tall mirrors make viewing easy for customers in a store for tall people. Salespeople are generally well-dressed tall individuals. The walls might feature photographs of tall people dressed attractively and comfortably. In a store for petite women, clothing is easy to reach and salespeople are generally the same height as their customers, to avoid a feeling of intimidation.

If you owned a brokerage firm that wanted to attract commodities investors, you would provide the facilities, research people, and communications equipment that served those clients best. Or, if you sought conservative investors, you would have a research staff well-versed in municipal bonds and knowledgable salespeople who could explain their intricacies to clients. You might also have an inventory of municipal bonds on hand.

Whatever business you are in, you need support facilities to attract and keep the type of client you seek. Real estate is no different than other business in this respect.

A Tale of Two Buildings

Following is a brief study of the amenities in two apartment complexes in a well-known U.S. city. We'll refer to them as Apartment Complex A and Apartment Complex B.

Apartment Complex A is adjacent to a research center which employs many engineers in their middle-to-late twenties. These people earn an annual income in the mid-$30,000 range. This apartment building supports their lifestyle with three swimming pools including one for playing volleyball, a large Jacuzzi, several tennis courts, and an attractive recreation room with social activities taking place much of the time. People enjoy living there; this well-run apartment complex is very successful.

Apartment Complex B is in another part of the city, adjacent to a medical center, where many of its residents work. Some are on the graveyard shift, going to work around midnight. Others return home from work around 5 A.M., while it's still dark. Their income is about the same as those who live in Apartment Complex A, but these people are in their mid-thirties. The amenities in this complex are quite different than those in Apartment Complex A.

The tiny Jacuzzi can't accommodate more than three people without becoming crowded. There's just one swimming pool and it's not much larger than a bathtub. The recreation room barely accommodates a foursome at a card table. So far, that doesn't seem particularly inviting. But let's look further. Complex B has security guards, beautifully appointed apartment units, and a well-built structure that prevents outside noise from bothering those who live there. These people don't want to party; they don't want an active social life. They want to come home to a secure, comfortable place where they can relax and unwind. Apartment Complex B fills those needs.

If we switched things around and gave these medical people the amenities of the first building, they would complain of noise and move out. And, if you traded the activities in Complex A for security guards and thick walls, the swingers would become bored and vacate.

In our "Tale of Two Buildings", we're talking about two different lifestyles. *As an owner, you must know which lifestyle is going to exist in your building. You can also dictate the type of client you will attract by the amenities you provide.*

If you don't want a noisy young crowd, don't provide big pools, large Jacuzzis, and recreation rooms. This isn't to say that older people don't enjoy these facilities; they're just not as important for most senior citizens. Be aware of different types of facilities that appeal to older, middle-aged, younger, single, and family people. Each group has different desires, and the amenities you provide must satisfy their needs.

You'll find the same situation with amenities for a private home. A family with four children wouldn't buy a two-bedroom, one-bath home, nor would they want a house with a fireplace in each room. By contrast, two people with no children wouldn't be interested in a large backyard with a swingset. The family with children would consider a spacious kitchen a necessity; the childless twosome would settle for a smaller kitchen. People look for important features that complement their lifestyle.

Style

Every building has its own style: this could be contemporary, Victorian, provincial, woodsy, or any of many other designs. Whether you're looking at a private house, a condominium, or apartments, be aware that each of these styles gives a different feeling. The exterior style should be consistent with the style that you wish to introduce inside. If your building looks provincial on the outside and has contemporary features inside, this inconsistency is aesthetically disturbing. It's disruptive.

When you think about the design of office buildings and apartments, consider comfort also. Recognize that the way the building looks on the outside affects the way it is furnished on the inside.

AMENITIES FOR TODAY AND TOMORROW

Since nobody has a crystal ball that predicts changes in the economy and in lifestyles, try to develop a sense of future changes. Be aware of contemporary trends and avoid non-proven vogues. Before you focus on specific amenities, it's necessary to determine how long you plan to hold on to the real estate. Make a financial projection, the same way you would in any business. Do you want to keep the property for two years? Five years? Are you thinking of retaining it permanently, or giving the real estate to your children some day? You must have some idea of how long your holding period will be. How does this time line affect amenities?

CERTAIN CHANGES MIGHT COME ABOUT IN THE FUTURE THAT WOULD PROMPT YOU TO INSTALL AMENITIES YOU DON'T NEED NOW. YOU MUST MAKE SURE THAT YOU HAVE THE FACILITIES FOR THESE AMENITIES.

For example, if you purchased a shopping center that continues to grow, you would need to accommodate the additional traffic and also provide extra parking space. If people can't park easily, they'll shop elsewhere. To cope with temperature extremes, you might want to convert your shopping center into a covered mall. A controlled climate is a desirable amenity in most parts of the country.

If you own a two-story office building in a growing area, there are two ways you could increase your income: increase the rent or enlarge the building to generate more income. But does the zoning allow you to make the building larger? If not, can you get that zoning changed? Plan ahead and make sure your future options can be carried out.

Suppose you purchase an apartment building without a pool or tennis court. You might not need these amenities today, but what about the future? Do you have the space for these additions? How about the zoning?

As a real estate entrepreneur, you must plan more carefully than an ordinary businessperson must. Any amenity you add is going to require more space. Make sure you have that space and the capability to get zoning approval. When you think of amenities, always think of today *and* tomorrow.

THE AMENITIES WORKSHEET

Since amenities touch people's everyday lives in many subtle and not-so-subtle ways, our amenities worksheet is the longest in the Economic Valuation System. This list can also be used as a checklist if you're buying a private home for your family. The minimim acceptable score for amenities would actually be negative 10!

1. General Appearance
There's nothing scientific about the general appearance. People gaze at a building and either feel good about its overall appearance or turn away with negative perceptions. The general appearance is affected by major and minor items. Is the parking lot full of potholes? Are the doors worn, cracked, or in need of paint? Are they painted in tasteful colors or garish reds? Is the siding or wood trim worn? Are the glass doors of the shopping center or office building substantial or flimsy? Does the appearance discourage people from going inside? Are sidewalks cracked? Does the building have a dirty, unkempt look?

Is the side of the building stained by water that dripped down from the roof? Does the trim need repainting? Is the lighting ad-

FIGURE 9–1
Amenities-Worksheet

PROPERTY NAME	
TYPE OF PROPERTY	
ADDRESS	
SELLER	
NUMBER OF UNITS	
TOTAL NUMBER OF SQUARE FEET	
PURCHASE PRICE	
CASH DOWN PAYMENT	
MORTGAGE DESCRIPTION	

AMENITIES - PROPERTY STATISTICS

NUMBER OF ACRES	
NUMBER OF UNITS	
NUMBER OF SQUARE FEET	
NUMBER OF BUILDINGS	
ARCHITECTURAL DESIGN	

LOCATION-PROPERTY VALUATION

Condition	Subject			Bad	Avg	Good	TOTAL SCORE
Subjective	1. General Appearance			(2.5)	2.5	5	
	2. Curb Appeal			(3.0)	1	3	
	3. Functional Design			(6.0)	2	6	
	4. Density			1	2	3	
	5. Community Building			(2.5)	0	2.5	
	Lounge	Yes	No				
	Kitchen	Yes	No				
	Sauna	Yes	No				
	Exercise Facilities	Yes	No				
	Fireplace	Yes	No				
	Entertainment Facilities	Yes	No				
	Restrooms	Yes	No				
	6. Swimming Pool Additional Pool			(1.75)	0	1.75	
	7. Jacuzzi			(.5)	0	5	
	8. Tennis Court - Lighted			(1.0)	0	1	
	9. Basketball Court			(.5)	0	.25	

Column header group: *Rating*

FIGURE 9–1
(*Concluded*)

Condition	Subject	Rating Bad	Avg	Good	TOTAL SCORE
	10. Childrens' Playground	(.5)	0	.5	
	11. Picnic Tables	(.25)	0	.25	
	12. Barbeque	(.25)	0	.25	
	13. Unit Mix - Compared to Market	1.5	2.5	3.5	
	14. Kitchen	(2.5)	0	2.5	
	All Electric				
	Full Appliances				
	Trash Compactor				
	15. Washer/Dryer Connections	(1.0)	0	1	
	16. Patios - Enclosed	(1.5)	0	1.5	
	17. Balconies	(1.5)	0	1.5	
	18. Laundry Facilities	(1.5)	0	1.5	
	19. Smoke Alarms	(.5)	0	.5	
	20. Individual heating	(.75)	0	.75	
	21. Individual Air-Conditioning	(.75)	0	.75	
	22. Fireplaces	(.75)	0	.75	
	23. Storage	(.75)	0	.75	
	Individual				
	Community				
	24. Cable Television Access	(.25)	0	.25	
	Resident Paid				
	Owner Paid				
	25. Controlled Access Fencing	(.5)	0	.5	
	26. Leasing Office	(1.5)	0	1.5	
	On-Site				
	Separate Building				
	TOTAL	(30.0)	10	45.75	

equate at night? Are any of the lighting fixtures broken? Weeds, cracked sidewalks, and litter in the traffic flow areas generate a negative feeling. In a shopping center, you might see old notices or signs that apply to events which took place months ago. This indicates a neglectful attitude that most likely carries over to other aspects of maintenance.

First impressions are important. If they're negative, people won't want to go into a shopping center or office building. And, they certainly wouldn't want to live in an apartment building that

2. Curb Appeal

If you're driving by and looking at the real estate from the curb, are you tempted to park and go into the building? If you're looking at an apartment house or an office building, do you want to seek out the leasing agent's office? Would you leave your car and browse in a shopping center? Getting prospective clients to visit a particular neighborhood is half the battle; once they're in a neighborhood, curb appeal will attract or repel them.

There are two types of curb appeal:

1. Bad or good curb appeal. A negative impression turns people away, a positive impression attracts people.
2. Selective curb appeal. This relates to the functional design of the building.

For example, a fast-food stand might be on the same block as a posh restaurant. Both could be well-constructed, attractive, clean-looking buildings. If you're hungry, which one would you go to? You would select the one that satisfies your present needs. If you're traveling with children and want a quick snack, the curb appeal of the fast-food place would tempt you to stop there. But, if you and your spouse are looking for a fine meal on a Saturday night, you would go to the fancy restaurant.

Suppose you owned a large accounting firm that needed more space for expansion. You might drive past an office building for lease, but never stop and get out of your car because it's obvious that the building is too small to accommodate your staff. That's selective curb appeal. If the building doesn't allow for the livable performance of what you want to happen, you wouldn't bother going any farther than the curb.

3. Functional Design

In a shopping center, can people move easily from one store to another? Case histories of several large shopping centers reveal that they failed miserably because of poor traffic flow. Customers had to go up and down several stairways to reach separate promenades, each with just a few shops. If your shopping center has stores on more than one level, escalators or elevators should be provided. Customers want to be catered to. They don't want to expend too much effort to spend their money.

Most people who work in suburban office buildings drive to their jobs and park in a designated area. If these parking facilities aren't connected to the building or located conveniently beside it, people feel frustrated. The arrangement is useable but inefficient.

In some apartment houses, parking is far from the entrance. When people must walk up a hill to reach the front door, it's even more aggravating.

Look for a functional design in your real estate business—one that allows your clients to go about their business as easily and efficiently as possible.

4. Density
This refers to apartment buildings; it indicates the number of apartment units per acre. If you purchased a 144-unit building on 12 acres, the density would be 12 units per acre. The average building constructed today has a density of more than 18 units per acre. An apartment complex with a density in the low teens takes on a park-like setting. Instead of three or four stories, it has one or two. Low density is an attractive feature, but as land becomes more expensive, developers build higher density apartment buildings.

5. Community Building
Why is a community building important in an apartment house complex? Keep in mind that apartments compete with private homes. The average private home has approximately 1,600 square feet and occupies a quarter of an acre. The average apartment unit has only 800 square feet, which basically accommodates a kitchen, bedroom, lavatory, and combination living/dining room. Since there's a tradeoff between living in an apartment or a private house, other facilities must be made available to the apartment dweller. A community building accomplishes that role.

The community building serves as a combination living room, family room, library, and entertainment center. It allows your apartment building to compete more successfully against private homes. Prospective clients feel they're gaining an important extra which eliminates the need for ownership of a private home. A community room with several thousand square feet allows them to entertain large groups and may even provide exercise space.

6. Swimming Pool

Is there a pool? What is its condition? Is the pool open enough hours to satisfy most people? Is it clean and attractive? Incidentally, the average 1,600-square-foot house we referred to above would not have a swimming pool.

7. Jacuzzi

People are increasingly concerned about health. This popular amenity is included in many new apartment complexes.

8. Tennis Court

If the apartment complex doesn't have a tennis court now, can you put one in? Do you have the space to put it in a north-south orientation so the sun doesn't get in the players' eyes? Lights installed at the court allow people to enjoy playing tennis in the evening after work. Like pools, tennis courts are an extra that people who own private homes rarely have.

9. Basketball Court

10. Children's Playground

11. Picnic Tables

12. Barbecue

The type of clients you wish to attract will dictate your interest in the amenities described in 5–12 above.

13. Unit Mix

Look for a unit mix consistent with the type of tenants you seek. For example, singles are interested in one-bedroom apartments; middle-aged people like larger rooms for the furniture they've accumulated. With commercial real estate, you might provide smaller offices for certain types of office buildings. In shopping centers, you might offer differently shaped rental units to suit various types of retail businesses.

14. Kitchen

Years ago, men weren't interested in kitchens. Today they like to cook and spend a great deal of time in the kitchen, so this room has become important for attracting male and female clients. In the past, people considered frost-free refrigerators, self-cleaning ovens, and garbage disposal units as extras. Today, these items are standard, everyday features. Only trash compactors remain in the luxury category, but more and more people are asking for them.

15. Washer/Dryer Connections

Traditionally, large apartment complexes had a community building with a washer/dryer room, or a separate facility in each building. Today, to give more of a private home feeling, expensive apartment complexes have washer/dryer hookups in each unit. Tenants can then buy or lease their own machines.

If you're thinking ahead about the possibility of a condominium conversion, most communities require that each unit have its own washer/dryer hookup, so look for this amenity in the building you buy. It's a plus for today and tomorrow.

16. Patios

17. Balconies

Patios and balconies can be an asset or a liability. Some patios consist of a slab of concrete and offer no privacy. That doesn't generate much of a homelike atmosphere.

Often, balconies hang over a main thoroughfare with round-the-clock traffic noise and carbon monoxide fumes. Some face a busy street with blinking neon lights at night. This isn't what people envision when they think of the ambience of balconies. As an owner, you would incur the extra cost of bricks and mortar, but such balconies won't generate extra income. Balconies that afford privacy and quiet are more of an asset to you and your clients. You can charge more rent when balconies face lakes, pools, ponds, or private open areas.

18. Laundry Facilities

Washing the laundry is an ongoing activity in apartment houses. Does each building have its own facility? What condition is the room in? Does it have a comfortable, secure feeling? Is the room well-lit? Can people sit there and read magazines while waiting? Some clever landlords paint the walls of their laundry rooms blue; when tenants hold up white clothes, they appear cleaner against a blue background. The person then feels that your appliances are doing an excellent job.

19. Smoke Alarms
In most cities, smoke alarms must be provided by law.

20. Individual Heating Controls

21. Individual Air-Conditioning Controls
Can your clients control their lives, or do you pull the strings? As a landlord, you want to control costs; but if you're lord and master of the air-conditioning and heating systems, clients will be miserable. People have different ambient temperature requirements. They're sure to complain when someone else manipulates the controls, dictating whether they will be too hot or too cold. They shiver in the winter when the heat isn't turned up adequately, and in the summer if the air-conditioning system shoots blasts of cold air into the rooms. Conversely, they melt in the winter from too much heat, and bathe in a pool of sweat on hot summer days when the air-conditioning unit isn't set at a comfortable level.

This issue of control also applies in office buildings and shopping centers. In an office, people's productivity nosedives when they lack the ability to control the room temperature. When the landlord doesn't allow clients to adjust the thermostat, the relationship becomes adversarial. Uncomfortable people become angry and won't cooperate when you try to raise rents in the future. They'll vacate instead. If clients are comfortable in their facility, they'll be happy; you'll enjoy a good, long-term relationship.

22. Fireplaces
Fireplaces provide a warm, cozy environment that certain types of people find attractive. Gaslit fireplaces are best. They're cleaner, easier to start, and provide more heat.

23. *Storage*

Storage can consist of individual units where each client keeps a key to space that belongs to him or her; or it can be community space, generally a large room, under the supervision of a custodian. These storage arrangements apply to apartments, shopping centers, and office buildings.

Clients generally prefer individual storage facilities. Each keeps his or her own key and can gain access to their belongings anytime. There's less chance of pilferage, and more convenience since clients don't need to hunt for the custodian each time they want to look for something in the storage area. With community storage, it's time consuming to seek the custodian and then prove to him that certain items in the community room actually belong to you. In a shopping center, shopkeepers can keep their own inventory separate from other retailers' property. In an office building, there's more privacy if records are stored in a private area.

24. *Cable Television Access*

As technology moves forward, access to cable TV has become more important. People want to have a wider choice of programs and channels available, particularly for sports and entertainment. By providing cable TV, your apartments become more competitive. Who pays for access to cable TV? Sometimes residents pay; in other situations the owner provides the service "free" but increases the rent to cover expenses.

25. *Controlled Access Fencing*

Does the office building or apartment building have security gates? What type? Do they provide *real* security or are they token preventative measures? Genuine security fencing often requires clients to use a special card in order to enter the perimeter areas and the building itself. The use of security fencing doesn't necessarily imply that the neighborhood is bad; it's an attractive feature with snob appeal. Since people like to feel elite, security fencing in upper-end office buildings and apartments is a desirable amenity.

26. *Leasing Office*

Our discussion of leasing offices applies to shopping centers, office buildings, and apartments. It is extremely advantageous to have a leasing office in the building itself.

How large should a building be before it merits its own leasing office? You would want an on-site leasing office in an apartment building of 100 units or more, an office building with 100,000 square feet or more, and a shopping center with 150,000 square feet or more. If the leasing office is at another location, potential clients must get into the car and drive to the facility. An on-site leasing office is more efficient; the person is at the facility already. It's easy for the client to come in, sit down, and talk to the agent. The fact that they're on the premises indicates that they have selected the area already; now you have the opportunity to show them your facility and sell them on the idea of leasing space in it.

If a shopping center or office building is 100 percent leased for the next few years, you don't need to reserve space for an on-site leasing agent. In an apartment building, you should provide an on-site leasing agent since apartment occupancy has more of a transitory nature. Turnover in suburban apartments generally averages 65 percent per year, requiring a continuing marketing effort on your part. By contrast, leases generally run a minimum of three years in office buildings and shopping centers.

Why did we specify a minimum of 100 units in an apartment house before you would hire an on-site leasing agent? The number is not etched in concrete; but if you have fewer units, the economics don't allow for an on-site leasing agent or manager.

If you have 100 units or less, your manager or assistant manager would handle the leasing. Should you choose to work through a property management company, expect to pay 4 to 6 percent of your gross revenues to them.

An on-site manager is more expensive. In addition to paying him a salary, you give him an apartment rent-free. Let's see how that eats into your cash flow.

Suppose you have 14 units, with annual gross revenues of $100,000. If you paid a property management company five percent, that would come to $5,000 per year in fees. If you had an on-site manager, you would be "giving away" one-fourteenth of your income—or $6,000—to the manager. In addition, you would be paying him a salary. The numbers are even more convincing if the number of units drops to ten. You would be giving away one-tenth of your income in the form of the manager's apartment; that would come to $10,000 in lost income. However, if you're considering the purchase of a luxury building with high rents, an on-site manager is more affordable.

TIPS TO REMEMBER

- Amenities are support facilities that attract and keep the type of clients you seek.
- The features and amenities that go into a building are of major importance.
- Know the type of clients you seek and provide amenities that satisfy their functional needs.
- You can select the type of clients you want by the amenities you choose to provide.
- Make sure you have the space and zoning to add extra amenities in the future.
- Certain amenities enable you to raise rents and to sell at a profit in the future.
- The more the amenities in an apartment building resemble those of a private home, the easier it is for you to attract and keep clients.
- In commercial space, a good amenities package means stronger leases, better lessees, and increased value in the real estate.

CHAPTER 10

THE CAPITALIZATION RATE: LOOKING AT THE BOTTOM LINE

Now that you know how to evaluate the physical characteristics of real estate, we'll move on to financial considerations. What is the value of a particular piece of real estate? This figure changes constantly. You'll need this information when you purchase property, while you own it, and when you're ready to sell it. Capitalization rate—the key to a successful real estate venture—is the return derived from your investment dollar, regardless of mortgage rates or tax benefits.

There's no mystique to the measurements experts use to determine value. We'll start by discussing three commonly used methods, and then expose their weaknesses.

1. Gross Rent Multiplier

The Gross rent multiplier represents the relationship of the annual collection of rent to the potential purchase price.

Gross rental income × Gross rent multiplier
= Value of the real estate

One of the accepted measurements is that the value of the real estate is valued at a multiple of the total annual collection of rent.

This type of evaluation is similar to the price/earnings ratio of stock. You'll recall that the P/E ratio is the price of the stock divided by the earnings of the company. That figure, which might be seven times, ten times, or twenty times, represents what people historically have been willing to pay.

In current practice, a typical figure for the gross rent multiplier might be seven times. If the future looks bright, as determined by the marketplace, the figure might be eight or nine times, or possibly even ten.

2. Replacement Costs

Some people measure the value of real estate by its replacement cost. For example, commercial real estate might have a replacement cost of $100 per square foot. Thus a shopping center or office building with 25,000 square feet might be priced at $2.5 million. If it costs $40,000 to replace each unit in an apartment building, then a building with 100 apartments might be valued at $4 million.

3. Income Per Square Foot

This method of establishing the value of real estate is based on comparables—the value of similar property. Thus, if a similar building sold for a certain price, you might use that as a "ballpark figure" for establishing the value of the real estate you're interested in.

All of these measurements have a certain importance as guidelines for establishing price—*but from a business standpoint, none of them has any validity when determining the true value of the business of real estate.*

As we've discussed in earlier chapters, real estate is a business that buys, sells, or leases square feet. We've shown that the value of a business is supported by the earnings of that business. As the earnings increase, so does the value of the business. Conversely, if earnings decline, the value of the business goes down. None of the measurements we've discussed has anything to do with the earnings of the business. In an indirect way, they impact earnings, but not enough to serve as a reliable measurement of value.

There is one measurement that is directly tied to the earnings of the business of real estate; and it's simple to use. You don't need to consider tax benefits or the value of the mortgage. This single measurement is the *capitalization ratio*. Assuming that you purchased the property for cash, the capitalization ratio is the percentage return calculated by dividing your net operating income by the purchase price.

$$\text{Capitalization ratio} = \frac{\text{Net operating income}}{\text{Purchase price}}$$

In Chapter 3, we defined net operating income (NOI) as the amount of money available before debt service.

Gross income − Expenses = NOI (net operating income)

In the business of real estate, you receive income from your clients who use the square feet. Then you subtract expenses for conducting this business. If you look at the NOI as a percentage of return in relation to the purchase price, you can establish the type of yield (cash return) available.

Before buying real estate, you must ask, "What kind of cash return can I expect?" The capitalization ratio answers that question. It's appropriate to analyze this ratio both quantitatively and qualitatively.

We're looking at the heart of a business—its essence— examining its earnings without considering debt or tax benefits. Based on analysis of the profits of that business, which is a quantitative measurement, we're asking, "What is this business worth?" We're not concerned with gross rent multipliers, or relationships dealing with square feet. We're zeroing in on the yield. Why? *The yield determines what the price of the real estate might be.*

A QUANTITATIVE LOOK AT CAPITALIZATION RATIOS

If the NOI equals $100, you determine the value of the real estate by considering what a fair yield would be in the marketplace. For example, that yield (capitalization ratio) might be 8 percent. Use the formula below to determine the value of the real estate.

$$\text{Purchase price (value)} = \frac{\text{NOI}}{\text{Capitalization ratio}} = \frac{\$100}{.08} = \$1{,}250$$

Small Changes in the Capitalization Rate Lead to Major Changes in the Bottom Line

Numbers can be deceptive. Changing the capitalization rate one percent from 8 percent to 7 percent, or from 8 percent to 9 percent, may seem like an infinitesimal difference, but the following example demonstrates its powerful impact on yield and the ultimate value.

Suppose you purchased real estate for $1,000, all cash (no mortgage). The annual income is $150 and expenses are $70. That leaves $80 as your net operating income. Using the formula above, you'll find that the capitalization rate (yield) is 8 percent.

Changes in the yield of the capitalization ratio will change the price of your real estate. This is similar to the action in the bond market; when prices rise, yields fall, and vice versa.

As we mentioned above, a change in yield from 8 percent to 7 percent, or from 8 percent to 9 percent, *seems* like a one percent move—*but these represent major moves in the price of the real estate* (Figure 10–1). The significance lies in the relationship of one percent to the original yield. A move from 7 percent to 8 percent represents a move of approximately 14 percent in the value of the real estate.

$$\frac{\text{Change in Yield}}{\text{Original Yield}} = \frac{1}{7} = 14.2 \text{ percent}$$

If you purchased real estate with a capitalization rate of 8 percent, it's to your advantage to sell it at a capitalization rate of 7 percent. Why? The value will increase to $1,143. As a rule of thumb, then, you want to sell real estate at a lower capitalization rate than you purchase it for.

Playing with these figures can be illuminating. If you buy at a capitalization rate of 8 percent but sell at a capitalization rate of 9 percent, you'll suffer a significant loss.

The below example deals with an all-cash purchase—but that's just the tip of the iceberg. If you use leverage—making, for ex-

FIGURE 10–1
Small Changes Have a Big Impact

Purchase Price: $1,000 Cash NOI = $80	
Capitalization Rate	*Value (Price) of Real Estate*
7 percent	$1,143
8 percent	1,000
9 percent	889

FIGURE 10–2

The Powerhouse Effect of Leverage on Capitalization Rate and Price

Purchase Price	=	$1,000
Down Payment	=	300
Mortgage	=	700
Capitalization Rate	=	8%

From Figure 10–1, we've seen that the value is $1,143 when the capitalization rate declines to 7 percent. That's an increase of 14.3 percent over the $1,000 cash price paid.

Value	=	$1,143
Mortgage	=	700
Equity	=	443
Appreciation	=	$ 143

Now, let's look at profit potential.

$$\frac{\text{Appreciation}}{\text{Down Payment}} = \frac{\$143}{\$300} = 47\% \text{ increase}$$

ample, a 30 percent down payment, you multiply the effect of changes in the capitalization rate by three. Let's see what the numbers look like in this instance by following the fortunes of an investor named Jack Smith (Figure 10–2). He bought property for $1,000 and made a down payment of $300. His mortgage is $700 and the capitalization rate is 8 percent.

In our example, the capitalization ratio declined 1 percent, from 8 percent to 7 percent. For the all-cash buyer, the value of his investment increased 14.3 percent. Since Jack Smith made a 30 percent ($300) down payment, the value of his investment increased 47 percent.

Another investor, Ed Murphy (Figure 10–3), wasn't so fortunate. He also purchased property at $1,000 with a 30 percent down payment and a capitalization rate of 8 percent. But when it came time to sell, the cap ratio went up to 9 percent. That meant bad news.

Ed Murphy invested $300 as a down payment and that equity is now valued at only $189—a loss of $111. On a percentage basis, that's a loss of 37 percent.

In both cases, we're assuming the earnings stay the same and the capitalization ratio changes.

To be realistic, figure out your resale price based on the same capitalization ratios in effect when you purchased the property.

FIGURE 10–3
A Swift Decline

Purchase Price	=	$1,000
Down Payment	=	300
Mortgage	=	700
Capitalization Rate	=	8%

From Figure 10–1, we've seen that the value declined to $889 when the capitalization rate increased to 9 percent.

Value	=	$ 889
Mortgage	=	700
Equity	=	189
Loss	=	111
% Loss	=	37%

However, your profits will be greater if the NOI or future capitalization ratios are lower than they were at the time of purchase. Increased earnings make that scenario possible.

What happens if earnings increase? In Jack's case (Figure 10–2), if the NOI increases from $80 to $100, since he bought with a 30 percent down payment, he can sell for a better multiple. Higher earnings allow him to sell for a low capitalization rate and a higher premium to the earnings.

Historically, you'll find that when real estate markets heat up people are anxious to buy. This results for a variety of reasons.

• Very low or no vacancies in an area.

• Low interest rates allow mortgage money and leverage to exist, permitting people to buy more real estate for less money.

• Perhaps there's some inflation, but the environment is positive and people enthusiastically buy real estate.

In this scenario, people tend to pay less attention to capitalization ratios and will pay higher rates of interest, attempting to justify the real estate by gross rent multipliers or replacement costs. Another instance where people tend to justify higher costs for real estate occurs when tax legislation is more favorable toward real estate investing. People then disregard intrinsic values.

Prospective buyers return to basics when the real estate market runs into difficulty. They look at capitalization ratios more carefully. When all the fluff is cut away, they seek real value and scrutinize yields. The capitalization ratio seems to rise when real estate is in a bear market. When vacancy rates are high, landlords make rent concessions, and nobody dares to raise rents.

Whether we're in a real estate bull market or bear market, *you should always pay attention to the capitalization ratio*. It is the only intelligent way to buy a business.

CYMROT'S LAW NUMBER 9:

Determine the value of the business by the rate of return your investment in that business will bring. This approach will protect your downside; it ultimately survives all the temporary situations described above.

A QUALITATIVE LOOK AT CAPITALIZATION RATIOS

Now that we understand the value and importance of capitalization ratios, it's time to explore the difference between quantitative and qualitative analysis. Merely coming up with an arbitrary number—that the yield is 8 percent or 9 percent—isn't enough. People who look at things on a quantitative basis only can be misled. For example, they might assume that real estate with a 9 percent capitalization ratio is a better buy than one with an 8 percent capitalization ratio. That could be extraordinarily misleading. Using the bond market as an analogy, you might ask: If a AAA bond yields 8 percent and a AA bond yields 9 percent, which one is a better value? You must look at the quality and strength of that yield. We're talking about qualitative analysis—analyzing the substance behind the yield.

Let's think about math again. The capitalization ratio is made up of two ingredients—income and expenses. We must understand those numbers with two things in mind:

- What are those figures today?
- What are they likely to be tomorrow?

By determining today's income and expenses, you determine today's yield, and the value of the real estate based on those numbers. But if it appears that the real estate will have a lower income and increased expenses in the future, leading to a lower yield, the price should be adjusted accordingly. The seller may anticipate that income is likely to drop while expenses rise, generating a lower yield in the future. If you're aware of this fact, you need to adjust the price accordingly. Conversely, the seller may anticipate that the income will rise and expenses may be controlled. He might adjust the expenses down, resulting in a higher net operating income, which will create a lower capitalization rate, and thus a higher price. In order to negotiate a fair price, you must determine the current value based on *today's* income and expenses.

Don't take anything for granted. The broker or seller may show you an operating statement and claim that, based on the price, the capitalization ratio is 8 percent or 9 percent. Do your own research. Analyze income and expenses now, not later. You are going to buy based on today's numbers, not on tomorrow's projections.

First, ask questions. Are the numbers you received from the seller or his representatives actual current cash-in-the-bank numbers, or some type of pro forma numbers that may be pie-in-the-sky dreams? Pro forma numbers are unacceptable for this type of analysis. In strong real estate markets, you'll find that people tend to try to sell on tomorrow's value. Don't fall for this pitch. Buy on today's value. You must look at income that is being put into the bank today—real cash in the bank.

Analyzing Income

When you scrutinize income, look at all its aspects. Is the trend up or down? Do any leases have special arrangements that you will have to incur later on, such as free months at the end of the lease, or reductions of rent income at the end of the lease?

Next, examine the type of tenants in the building. When a lease is signed for a commercial or a residential building, a credit analysis should have been done. Review all these credit analyses. Here are some of the areas you should investigate:

1. Has each tenant the capability to sustain future rent increases?

2. Examine the delinquency record of income to see whether one or more tenants (for whatever reasons) do not pay their rent on a timely basis. How many tenants pay late? Why?

3. How many checks have bounced? And, how many bounced, were redeposited based on insufficient funds, and bounced again? Find out what the problem is.

4. Are there adequate security deposits on hand?

5. On commercial leases, develop spreadsheets to analyze lease expirations as to the amount of square feet and income.

6. Read all the leases and review them for special arrangements. Before purchasing commercial property, make sure the seller gives you an estoppel; this is a legal document that protects you against any unknowns. The estoppel document assures the buyer that he is responsible for the leases in place; if there are any other unknown, previously negotiated arrangements, those are the seller's responsibility. An estoppel document is analogous to title insurance. Both provide you with protection and peace of mind.

While performing this qualitative analysis, incorporate all the analyses of area and location that you've completed with the Economic Valuation System. This helps you determine the overall strength of the location and area so you can make a determination as to what the future occupancies will be.

Remember, supply and demand create or destroy value. Capitalization ratios measure value.

At this point, you're measuring the current value, but you'll also want to determine the future value. That future value is determined by the future supply-demand ratio or availability of that particular real estate. If there will be too much of that real estate—whether it's office buildings, shopping centers, or apartments—this excess of supply over demand will dramatically impact the income side of the ledger. Review very carefully everything we've discussed in the chapters on area and location.

When you evaluate commercial leases, see if the tenants have been paying the billings for expenses. *It is particularly important to find out if they have been paying the billings for consumer price index (CPI) increases. It is equally important that they pay the percentage of sales specified in their leases.*

Going a step further, review the fairness of each of these provisions and any limitations, to make sure that your investment has upside potential. Certain large tenants may have more favorable types of leases; you need to be able to see the upside on each of these and make sure you have fair measurements. Specifically, make sure that the price index used (whether it is local or national) has moved historically in relation to the rate of inflation.

You want to have the opportunity to participate in a percentage of sales, but you must be careful to see at what level that percentage of participation starts. If the level is too high, the percentage becomes meaningless because you'll never have the opportunity to benefit from it.

Review the income side to determine its source. Is the money coming from tenants who are occupying space, or from tenants who no longer occupy the space but are subletting it. In that case, they might be paying the lease on an obligated vs. usage basis. Is the income from a third party, perhaps the prior seller, in reponse to some type of financial guarantee? These leases must be occupied by bona fide tenants in place—individuals or companies that you can anticipate will continue to occupy that space in the future. This is what creates the value of the real estate. You're buying a business, and if it doesn't have clients (tenants), the value is lessened because it will generate less income now and in the future.

In addition, one of the most underestimated costs in the real estate business is that of lease-up expense. It is always much more than anticipated. *Not only do you have vacant space, and receive no income from it, but the additional expense from the cost of attracting tenants is going to exceed your expectations.* It takes a long time to attract tenants, and to start collecting rent from them. If you buy a building that needs to be leased up, resign yourself to costly delays.

In the typical scenario for the lease-up of a commercial building, a facilities manager representing your potential client inspects the building and reports on it to his vice president. The vice president then waits until the president returns from a prolonged business trip. They hold meetings, discuss the prospective move for weeks, look at other property, and then, perhaps months later, make a decision.

If you're renting apartment units, the process is equally slow. Even if a prospective tenant likes your apartment, he or she will look at others, think about all of them, take time off for a vacation, come back for another visit with his friends, wife, or mother-in-law—and then make a decision. If you're trying to lease ten apartments, your delay is tenfold.

Finding clients for your real estate business is no different than finding them for any other business. It's a slow process.

Analyzing Expenses

The expense side of the P&L ledger is far more difficult to analyze. When you buy real estate, chances are you will install new management. Thus it's unlikely that your expenses will be identical to those of the previous owner. Your income will be the same because you anticipate having the same tenants, who contractually will pay the same rent. But the expense side of the P&L statement can differ in many ways.

Frequently, a buyer may say, "This real estate is a good buy because it hasn't been managed correctly. I can add value to the building through my superior management skills." It's wiser to anticipate managing the building as poorly as the current owner. Even though you examine the expense side carefully, assume that expenses will change, most likely for the worse. One problem many buyers have is that their ego gets in the way. They presume they will manage better than their predecessors; they're convinced they have superior management skills which will improve the bottom line immediately. That's a bad assumption. It's more reasonable to assume you're at least as inefficient as the current manager.

Don't look at the net operating income too optimistically. Presume that if the prospective seller is running the real estate at a certain cost, your expenses will be similar, not less. Verify the seller's numbers, audit them, and if they are validated, use them as your base for determining the value of the real estate, unless there are extenuating circumstances.

Let's examine some of the items that appear on the expense side of profit and loss statements. Some of them apply to apartments; others to commercial real estate, both office buildings and shopping centers. Apartment owners generally absorb the cost of all the expenses except utilities. In an office building and a shopping center, the owner generally passes operating costs on to tenants but will absorb capital expenditures, such as structural changes relating to walls and roofs, or perhaps a major change in the parking lot. Some negotiations between owners and tenants may go as far as having the lease cover certain capital expenditures; but traditionally, the triple net (NNN) lease takes care only of the operating expenses of the real estate. Even under those conditions, if commercial property is managed poorly and expenses run high, the situation may appear fine on the surface because the landlord passes through these expenses to his lessees. But if the burden continues to escalate to the point where the tenant's rent keeps going up as the result of absorbing expenses due to the landlord's mismanagement, the tenant will not renew his lease. Further, the landlord won't be able to increase the base rent on that particular space.

This same theory applies to tenant-paid utilities in apartment buildings. If the utility costs paid by the residents are excessive, you limit your ability to increase the base rent. As far as the tenant is concerned, his utility costs and his base rent add up to his total rent.

What does this signify? This situation impacts the real estate owner's real earnings. When he passes through those expenses, that's a wash; it is not an increase of income for him. All he is doing is taking expenses as a debit and receiving a credit from the tenant. *Nothing beneficial to the owner will show on the bottom line.* He can take increased base rent down to the bottom line; but as expenses increase, the bottom line suffers. Even in commercial property where the landlord doesn't pay these expenses, they impact his profit and loss statement.

To sum up, there are two major effects of increased tenant paid expenses:

- An indirect effect: The owner can't raise rents.
- A direct effect: He doesn't have an increased cash flow.

If it should be necessary to reduce rents because of some problem, the value of the property declines rapidly. Let's look at Arnold Mason's story. He's an apartment owner who based his calculations on a capitalization rate of 8 percent. When he reduced the rent on just one apartment unit from $500 monthly to $450 per month, his expenses stayed the same. Over the time span of one year, he "lost" $600 in rent. (12 months × $50 per month lower rent). *For every dollar that the net operating income is reduced* *when the capitalization ratio is 8 percent, the value of a building declines $12.50.* Thus, in this instance, the value of Mason's building dropped by $7,500 ($600 × 12.50 = $7,500). Just imagine the mushrooming effect if he had to reduce rent on 5 or 10 units!

Let's examine some of the expenses incurred with both commercial and residential property. These include several categories.

1. Grounds Maintenance
You incur expenses for landscape service, landscape supplies, equipment, sprinklers, and repairs to asphalt and concrete. In most instances, you would rely on outside services. This means that you must negotiate with the most efficient service you can find, get the best contract possible, and have the best job done. And you must supervise these activities. Any type of outside contract needs to be supervised and managed in order to assure quality performance.

2. Administrative Expenses
You must do a certain amount of advertising. In the case of shopping centers, this can be extensive. It is accomplished with posters, billboards, and entertainment activities that successful shopping centers provide to attract customers. Real estate ownership also involves accounting and legal expenses, licenses, and organizational dues.

Apartments also require extensive advertising. The turnover in garden-style apartments is approximately 65 percent on an annual basis. That means your business loses 65 percent of its clients every year. To compensate, you need a well-thought-out marketing plan; advertising is an integral part of that plan, along with other tools on the expense side of the ledger.

3. Real Estate Taxes/Insurance
Are you paying the lowest possible real estate taxes? If not, can you appeal? Would you do this yourself or hire an expert? Do you have the best insurance coverage? Is it the cheapest? Have you shopped all the agencies that provide the best type of service?

4. Capital Expenses
You will need someone—either in-house or an outside person—to oversee purchasing of carpets, drapes, furniture, and the handling of ground improvements.

On the expense side of the ledger, you can characterize management as a nickel-and-dime business, but those expenses add up to millions of dollars in many instances. So you need to look at expenses today and predict what future expenses will be as the real estate gets older.

When projecting future income and expenses, make sure you define accurately today's exact income and expenses. All future predictions are based on what is happening today. If your understanding of today's figures is incorrect, all future projections will be incorrect—even if you accurately predict the percentage changes. Your figures for net operating income and anticipated yield will be unreliable. Thus the value placed on the real estate will be erroneous. Those are severe consequences!

Use the worksheet in Figure 10–4 to determine capitalization rate and property valuation. A minimal acceptable score would be (4).

TIPS TO REMEMBER

- Use the capitalization ratio to determine the value of real estate at the following times: before buying, during the holding period, and before selling.
- Recognize the significance and impact of seemingly small changes in the capitalization ratio.
- You must have accurate figures on today's income and expenses before you can estimate future earnings and expenses.
- Don't expect to accomplish miracles at first; assume that your expenses will be the same or higher than those of the present owner.
- If owners of commercial property manage inefficiently, even though their tenants pay for certain expenses, the bottom line will be impacted adversely.
- Don't be deterred by new vogues or fashions. Yield analysis using the capitalization ratio is a proven survivor.

FIGURE 10-4
Capitalization Rate Worksheet

PROPERTY NAME _____
TYPE OF PROPERTY _____
ADDRESS _____
_____

SELLER _____
NUMBER OF UNITS _____
TOTAL NUMBER OF SQUARE FEET _____
PURCHASE PRICE _____
CASH DOWN PAYMENT _____
MORTGAGE DESCRIPTION _____

CAPITALIZATION RATE-PROPERTY STATISTICS
CURRENT INCOME ANNUALIZED _____
CURRENT EXPENSES ANNUALIZED _____
CURRENT NOI ANNUALIZED _____
PURCHASE PRICE _____
CAPITALIZATION % _____

CAPITALIZATION RATE - PROPERTY VALUATION

		Rating			
Condition	*Subject*	*Bad*	*Avg*	*Good*	*TOTAL SCORE*
	1. Tenant Profile	(3)	0	3	
20-25%, 25-35%, 35%+	Income % of Rent				
20-30, 35-40, 45+	Age				
0-33%, 33-66%, 67%+	Blue Collar				
	Professional				
(5%), Avg., 5%+	2. Rent per Square Foot	(2.5)	0	2.5	
(5%), Avg., 5%+	3. Physical Occupancy	(2.75)	0	2.75	
80/85/90	4. Economic Occupancy	(3)	0	3	
	5. Delinquency Rate	(2)	0	2	
To 65%, 65-100, 100+	6. Resident Turnover	(2)	0	2	
(5%), Avg., 5%+	7. Rent Per Unit Average	(1.5)	0	1.5	
0-5%, 5-10%, 10%+	8. Average Collections	1	2	3	
	Past Five Years				
Subjective	9. On-Site Manager	(.5)	0	.5	
Subjective	10. Leasing Agents	(.25)	0	.25	
Subjective	11. Maintenance Personnel	(.25)	0	.25	
	12. Tenant Paid Utilities				
No, Yes	All			3	
	Partial		2		
	13. Owner Pays				
	Common Area Only		1.5		
	All	(4)			
	Gas	(2)			
	Electric	(3)			
	Water	(.5)			
	Hot Water Heating	(.25)			
Subjective	14. Overall Maintenance & Repairs	(.5)	0	5	
Subjective	15. Real Estate Taxes	(2.5)	0	2.5	
Subjective	16. Insurance	(2)	0	2	
*-7.5, 7.5-8.5, 8.5+	17. Capitalization %	2	4	6	
	TOTAL	(19.0)	9.5	39.25	

*Changes in alternative investments could effect acceptable capitalization rates.

CHAPTER 11

MORTGAGES: CHARITY
BEGINS AT HOME

So far, you've learned how to evaluate the physical characteristics of real estate and to judge whether it's a good investment in terms of yield. Now you're ready to overcome the obstacle course of mortgages. The fine print in these documents is fraught with dangers; you can't afford to read them casually. Some of those sneaky provisions might leave your personal assets vulnerable to attachment; others might force you to share part of the appreciation with your mortgage lender.

Mortgage evaluation is one of the seven keys in our Economic Valuation System. As usual, let's start off with a definition. Webster's explanation is rather complicated, but it covers the main points: "A mortgage is a conveyance of property on condition that the conveyance becomes void on payment or performance, according to stipulated terms." Stating it more simply, we can define mortgage as a debt on property or land. The borrower (mortgagor) borrows money from a lender (mortgagee) and uses either land or improvements on the land, or both, as the collateral to secure such borrowing. When you pay off the mortgage, the real estate is yours, free and clear.

A well-chosen mortgage gives you a financial boost. An oppressive one can drag you down, like a massive rock hanging from your neck—even though it's just a piece of paper. In addition to considering how a mortgage affects your costs, keep in mind that a good mortgage can make your property more attractive to prospective buyers when you're ready to sell.

Why should you consider mortgaging property? A mortgage allows you to control more assets with less money. The extent with which you mortgage a property (or create additional debt by putting in less of your money) is determined by factors we'll discuss in the next chapter on leverage.

You'll recall that our formula for purchase price is as follows:

Purchase price = Down payment + Mortgage

The mortgage can represent as much as 90 percent of the purchase price, or as little as 10 percent.

What constitutes a good mortgage? What types of mortgages should you avoid? For now, we can dispense with numbers and discuss the principles behind obtaining the best mortgage possible. We'll discuss types of mortgages, the terms and conditions that determine their cost, and the length of time that you'll be in debt.

Years ago, when life was simpler, people had fewer choices. If someone wanted an ice cream cone, they chose between vanilla, chocolate, and strawberry. Now you can choose from hundreds of flavors. Similarly, at one time the choices between mortgages were few. Today you're faced with an ever-changing variety of mortgages.

Whether you're a novice investor or someone who has previously been involved in mortgaging property, you must be aware of your rights—and opportunities—to negotiate an advantageous mortgage. Your concern about interest rates doesn't end when you sign on the dotted line. Continue to be aware of changes in interest rates as long as you own the real estate. There may be opportunities to gain a financial advantage by refinancing—replacing one mortgage with another.

The Lender's Point of View

Before we discuss strategies you can use to obtain a good mortgage, let's take a broad view of mortgage lending. How is a mortgage created? As a first step, the lender obtains money from outside investors. That mortgagee might be a bank or savings and loan association, an insurance company, or other lending institution. The lending agency's ability to obtain money rests on its capability to provide investors with a good return on their money. In turn, that lender also needs to make money on the transaction. Thus the lender profits from the spread between what his organization pays investors and what his organization receives from you, the borrower.

Your Role as a Corporate Treasurer

When you prepare to negotiate a mortgage, put on the hat of a corporate treasurer. The corporate treasurer of a company is responsible for managing and creating cash. There are several ways by which a treasurer creates money. Right now, we're interested in the way that relates to real estate. The technique the corporate treasurer uses—and the one that you as a private individual will use—involves borrowing money. When the corporate treasurer borrows money by securing real estate with various loans, these are his objectives:

1. Borrow money as cheaply as possible.
2. Push out (extend) the period of time over which the mortgage has to be paid back as far into the future as possible.

The treasurer utilizes these principles for all forms of borrowing. In the case of a corporation, such borrowing may involve issuing bonds (wherein people can invest in the debt of the company); issuing commercial paper (which is simply an IOU on behalf of the corporation); or establishing bank lines of credit. Whatever method is used to borrow, the same two principles mentioned above will always prevail.

As your own corporate treasurer, you'll also try to negotiate the cheapest cost and push the debt out as far as possible, delaying the repayment time. What's the benefit of pushing the repayment as far as possible into the future? You'll be repaying with dollars that you've had the use of during the time the mortgage was in effect; and, because of inflation, you'll be paying much cheaper dollars later on. Today's dollars buy goods and services at today's prices. Even under the most modest inflationary rates (2 to 3 percent annually), you'll be paying back the debt in the future with dollars that are worth less.

HOW TO OBTAIN THE BEST
POSSIBLE MORTGAGE

There are two ways to obtain a mortgage. You don't have the luxury of an either/or situation. The *only* way to make sure you obtain the best possible mortgage is to follow both techniques.

1. Find a reputable mortgage broker.
2. Shop on your own for the best available mortgage.

A mortgage broker is a person who has connections with various money markets on a broad geographic scale. Well-known mortgage brokerage firms operate on a national scale. Retain a mortgage broker, but do not pay any money until he or she has brought you a mortgage that you have accepted and that has actually been committed and funded to you by the lender.

How can you be sure that the broker is presenting you with the best possible mortgage? There's only one way: you must also shop the market on your own. If the mortgage broker does his or her job correctly, the mortgage obtained for you should cost you less than the one you obtain on your own, even including the broker's fee.

Compare the mortgage obtained by the broker with the one you've been able to obtain on your own. Then commit yourself to the one with the lowest cost. It's too risky to let a broker do all the work while you sit back. Because of the amount of money you'll be committing and the contractural agreement you're about to take on, make sure that you have given that mortgage every chance to be the best.

Despite the strong arguments in favor of taking this two-pronged approach, many people are very reticent to shop for a mortgage. Yet these same people will drive a mile down the road to put ten gallons of gasoline in their car—if they can find a station selling gas at two cents a gallon cheaper. Or these same people may go to three different clothing stores, attempting to save $25 on a suit. Yet when we talk about a mortgage, we're talking at least five figures and probably six. In many cases, the mortgage might be a seven-figure sum. That's $50,000 or $100,000 or even $1 million of debt which will extend for years. When you look at mortgages in that light, it's not a matter of "should I or shouldn't I shop?" You have no choice. *You shop for the best transaction you can possibly get. Anything less is totally irresponsible.*

What does this type of shopping involve? You will prepare a checklist of things that make up a mortgage. (We'll discuss the details of this checklist shortly.) Then visit all the local banks, taking this checklist with you. If traveling is inconvenient, phone the banks and ask the senior loan officer whether the bank is interested in making mortgages at this time on the type of property you're interested in buying. A number of these banks may quote price and cost terms on the phone. In addition, go to the bank where you already have a relationship to see what terms they might make available to you. Now you're ready for even more research.

The Sunday newspaper of every major cosmopolitan area has a real estate section that carries articles dealing with trends in the real estate market. Many of these newspapers have special sections that present sample mortgage rates available at various lending institutions. Shouldn't you expect a large degree of uniformity in your area? Not at all.

There's a large disparity of interest rates, points, initial costs, and terms of the mortgages offered. Many of these disparities relate to motivation. If a bank has considerable deposits on hand and is interested in getting these deposits into a loan portfolio, the bank will offer competitive mortgages. Remember, money is a commodity to a bank—it's a product. If they have too much of an inventory of that product, they'll try and move it; and, in the process of moving it, they will make their mortgage offerings as competitive as possible.

On the other hand, some banks may not be in a competitive position—not as motivated—and therefore their mortgages won't be as attractive. All banks are not equally motivated since they don't have equal amounts of excess deposits on hand. Because of this disparity, it's essential that you shop around.

When you visit a bank, try to see the most senior loan officer, or even the manager. The higher the officer, the more latitude he or she has to negotiate with you. The situation is similar to other shopping scenarios. How many times does the car salesman have to go check with his manager to see if he can structure the deal that the client wishes to make? In a bank, the product they're offering is money, and the person in a high-ranking position has the latitude to offer you the most attractive rates.

Now that you know your responsibilities in obtaining a mortgage, exactly what are you going to negotiate for? First, let's see what makes up a mortgage.

SEVEN KEYS TO A GOOD MORTGAGE

The principles behind a large mortgage (for an apartment house, a shopping center, or an office building) are no different than those involved when you purchase your own home. Using the Economic Valuation System, we'll examine seven keys involved in the makeup of a mortgage. These have been weighted so that you can determine the passing grade for any mortgage you're considering. The minimum passing grade would be 2.25.

The seven keys involved in our discussion pertain to all mortgages regardless of the size of the contractural debt involved. These seven keys need to be analyzed individually—but ultimately, you'll look at them as a total. For example, one of the seven keys involves the cost of obtaining a mortgage. At some banks that cost might be very high, meaning that they attach a number of points (which we'll explain shortly) to the cost of obtaining a mortgage. But, on the other side, the interest cost on that mortgage might be very low. This could translate into more cash being required at the front end of the transaction because the amount of the mortgage plus its cost requires more of a down payment. But, over the holding period, you might be able to benefit from a lower upkeep and achieve a much larger savings along the way. Thus you need to look at the *entire* mortgage. You're interested in the bottom line—not individual figures along the way. If the mortgage receives a passing grade on our weighting system, chances are you're looking at a good mortgage—if there aren't extenuating circumstances that make it onerous. A passing grade would be a minimum score of 2.25. There are so many possible combinations that it's essential to look at all seven keys, weigh them, and then evaluate the total. Remember, your own personal capabilities need to be factored in.

FIGURE 11–1

PROPERTY NAME _____

TYPE OF PROPERTY _____

ADDRESS _____

_____

SELLER _____

NUMBER OF UNITS _____

TOTAL NUMBER OF SQUARE FEET _____

PURCHASE PRICE _____

CASH DOWN PAYMENT _____

MORTGAGE DESCRIPTION _____

ECONOMIC EVALUATION SYSTEM—MORTGAGE VALUATION

	Rating		
	Poor	Average	Good
Front End Cost			
1.5 / 2.5 / 3 Points	1	2	3
Current Terms			
Market Fixed			6
Market Variable		2.5	
Maturity			
Less Than Est. Hldg. Period	(1)		
Same " " "		1	
150% " " "		3	
200% " " "			5
Lock In			
1 Yr			1
2 Yrs		.5	
3 Yrs	0		
4 Yrs	(1)		
Prepayment			
To 1.5%			2
1.5%-2.5%		1	
2.5% +	0		
5% +	(1.5)		
Assumption			
Yes, No Cost			2
Yes, Reasonable Cost		1	
No, More 50% Mort	(1)		
No, Less 50% Mort	0		
Non-Recourse			2
Recourse	(3)		
TOTALS	(6.5)	11	21

Here are the seven keys—the seven ingredients that go into a mortgage. They all belong on the checklist you'll take to the bank.

1. What is the total front end cost?

2. What will the mortgage cost along the way?

3. What is the maturity? (When will I have to pay back the money I borrow?)

4. Is there a lock-in feature which means that I can't pay off the mortgage or reduce it for a certain period of time? This feature decreases transferability.

5. Is there a prepayment clause that will force me to pay a penalty if I pay off the mortgage ahead of schedule? Is there an assumption clause in the mortgage allowing someone to assume the debt from me?

6. Is the mortgage recourse or non-recourse? If it's recourse, the lender can look beyond the collateral and possibly reach out for my personal assets.

7. How solid is the bank's commitment? Is there a chance of a bait-and-switch situation? If the bank or lender offers me a deal that I'm committed to and I have spent money on that commitment—either through a due diligence examination, or by ceasing my search and thereby missing other opportunities—is it possible that suddenly the bank will withdraw its commitment, declaring that the mortgage is no longer available?

Now let's examine each of these keys in detail.

1. Initial Cost of Mortgage

Ask the prospective lender for a list of all costs that go into obtaining a mortgage. To determine the value of the real estate you're borrowing money against, the lender may have to obtain an appraisal. Who will pay for that appraisal—you or the lender? If the money comes out of your pocket, exactly what will the charges be? If you pay, make sure you'll receive a copy of the appraisal. Often people who pay for the appraisal never even receive a copy. Yet you might need it for borrowing in the future; thus a copy in your possession could save you money later on. Within a certain period of time, an updated appraisal could be substituted for a full-blown new appraisal—and updating costs considerably less than starting from scratch.

Some lenders charge just for giving the potential borrower the privilege of filling out their forms! Their justification? "It's our policy. If you want to do business with us, pay the fee." At this stage, you don't want to turn down the opportunity to secure a good mortgage; you'll be asking questions and weighing all seven factors. You certainly want to know if it's going to cost you money to fill out those forms. Some lending institutions insist that they must run a credit check to determine if you're creditworthy—and they'll attempt to charge you for this even though they'll make a substantial profit on the mortgage later on.

Finally, you'll have to consider points, which is another way of expressing percentages. When the lending institution tells you they are going to charge you one point, one-and-a-half points, or two points, what are they telling you? They're going to charge you 1 percent, 1-1/2 percent, or 2 percent of the amount of the loan as an up-front fee. On a $500,000 mortgage, your fee would be $5,000, $7,500, or $10,000 respectively. Some lenders will allow you to pay these points over a short period of time, such as one to three years. Others take it out of the mortgage itself. Thus, on a $500,000 mortgage with a one point (1 percent) charge, you will owe the bank $500,000 and pay interest accordingly, but you will receive only $495,000 from the bank. They automatically take out the $5,000 fee.

The above costs are the major ones that go into the front end of a mortgage; some banks may charge for other aspects of the initial processing. Find out what these other fees are. What will the total up-front costs add up to? Lending institutions may have their own jargon for these fees; you'll want to find out the total cost of the front end fees that go into obtaining the mortgage. Some lenders will charge less points but more for a credit check; others will charge more points while imposing a very modest fee for the credit check. *You must find out the total up-front cost.* You'll notice on our EVS chart that, under mortgage valuation we have 1.5; that's the total front-end cost, 1.5, 2.5, or 3 points. That ranges between good, average, and poor. If the points total cost of the front-end mortgage fees is 3 or more, that's a poor rating.

2. Mortgage Costs Along the Way

Once you obtain a mortgage, what will your costs be during the holding period? What interest rate are you paying? What are your monthly costs in dollars? Could any outside events affect those dollars and the interest rate? Basically, there are two types of interest rates—variable and fixed.

Fixed-Rate Mortgages

The fixed-rate mortgage is exactly what it implies. When you take out the mortgage, you and the lender agree to a fixed interest rate. It won't change over the life of the mortgage.

The rate of interest is not necessarily an exact percentage of the money you've borrowed because another ingredient may affect the amount of money you pay the lender. That ingredient is amortization. Amortization refers to the rate at which you pay down the principal. Through this process, each monthly payment includes the interest and a portion of the principal. Thus you're reducing the amount of principal you owe. The length of amortization (shown in the amortization schedule in Figure 11–2) will determine how much of each payment is principal being paid down. On an amortized mortgage, each payment will come to a higher amount than if you just took the interest rate and multiplied it by the outstanding principal.

A mortgage can be partially amortized or fully amortized. With a partially amortized mortgage, when the term of the mortgage is up, you would be required to pay off any remaining principal. A fully amortized mortgage schedule is planned so that there is no remaining principal balance at the end of the term. In other words, there is no balloon payment.

What's the difference between paying off the mortgage in 15 years versus a 30-year period? With a 15-year term, you are paying off the mortgage sooner, so the money dedicated toward the paydown will obviously be larger than if you were taking 30 years to pay off the mortgage. Which is better? Neither. Just be aware of all the options that exist. The correct one is that which makes you feel most comfortable.

Suppose you and your neighbor both take out $50,000 mortgages with the same interest rate. Does this mean that you'll incur

10%

MONTHLY PAYMENT
Necessary to amortize a loan

TERM AMOUNT	1 YEAR	1½ YEARS	2 YEARS	2½ YEARS	3 YEARS	4 YEARS	5 YEARS
$ 25	2.20	1.51	1.16	.95	.81	.64	.54
50	4.40	3.01	2.31	1.90	1.62	1.27	1.07
75	6.60	4.51	3.47	2.84	2.43	1.91	1.60
100	8.80	6.01	4.62	3.79	3.23	2.54	2.13
200	17.59	12.02	9.23	7.57	6.46	5.08	4.25
300	26.38	18.02	13.85	11.35	9.69	7.61	6.38
400	35.17	24.03	18.46	15.13	12.91	10.15	8.50
500	43.96	30.03	23.08	18.91	16.14	12.69	10.63
600	52.75	36.04	27.69	22.69	19.37	15.22	12.75
700	61.55	42.04	32.31	26.47	22.59	17.76	14.88
800	70.34	48.05	36.92	30.25	25.82	20.30	17.00
900	79.13	54.06	41.54	34.04	29.05	22.83	19.13
1000	87.92	60.06	46.15	37.82	32.27	25.37	21.25
2000	175.84	120.12	92.29	75.63	64.54	50.73	42.50
3000	263.75	180.18	138.44	113.44	96.81	76.09	63.75
4000	351.67	240.23	184.58	151.25	129.07	101.46	84.99
5000	439.58	300.29	230.73	189.06	161.34	126.82	106.24
6000	527.50	360.35	276.87	226.87	193.61	152.18	127.49
7000	615.42	420.40	323.02	264.68	225.88	177.54	148.73
8000	703.33	480.46	369.16	302.50	258.14	202.91	169.98
9000	791.25	540.52	415.31	340.31	290.41	228.27	191.23
10000	879.16	600.58	461.45	378.12	322.68	253.63	212.48
11000	967.08	660.63	507.60	415.93	354.94	278.99	233.72
12000	1055.00	720.69	553.74	453.74	387.21	304.36	254.97
13000	1142.91	780.75	599.89	491.55	419.48	329.72	276.22
14000	1230.83	840.80	646.03	529.36	451.75	355.08	297.46
15000	1318.74	900.86	692.18	567.18	484.01	380.44	318.71
16000	1406.66	960.92	738.32	604.99	516.28	405.81	339.96
17000	1494.58	1020.98	784.47	642.80	548.55	431.17	361.20
18000	1582.49	1081.03	830.61	680.61	580.81	456.53	382.45
19000	1670.41	1141.09	876.76	718.42	613.08	481.89	403.70
20000	1758.32	1201.15	922.90	756.23	645.35	507.26	424.95
21000	1846.24	1261.20	969.05	794.04	677.62	532.62	446.19
22000	1934.15	1321.26	1015.19	831.86	709.88	557.98	467.44
23000	2022.07	1381.32	1061.34	869.67	742.15	583.34	488.69
24000	2109.99	1441.37	1107.48	907.48	774.42	608.71	509.93
25000	2197.90	1501.43	1153.63	945.29	806.68	634.07	531.18
26000	2285.82	1561.49	1199.77	983.10	838.95	659.43	552.43
27000	2373.73	1621.55	1245.92	1020.91	871.22	684.79	573.68
28000	2461.65	1681.60	1292.06	1058.72	903.49	710.16	594.92
29000	2549.57	1741.66	1338.21	1096.54	935.75	735.52	616.17
30000	2637.48	1801.72	1384.35	1134.35	968.02	760.88	637.42
31000	2725.40	1861.77	1430.50	1172.16	1000.29	786.25	658.66
32000	2813.31	1921.83	1476.64	1209.97	1032.55	811.61	679.91
33000	2901.23	1981.89	1522.79	1247.78	1064.82	836.97	701.16
34000	2989.15	2041.95	1568.93	1285.59	1097.09	862.33	722.40
35000	3077.06	2102.00	1615.08	1323.40	1129.36	887.70	743.65
40000	3516.64	2402.29	1845.80	1512.46	1290.69	1014.51	849.89
45000	3956.22	2702.57	2076.53	1701.52	1452.03	1141.32	956.12
50000	4395.80	3002.86	2307.25	1890.58	1613.36	1268.13	1062.36
55000	4835.38	3303.14	2537.98	2079.63	1774.70	1394.95	1168.59
60000	5274.96	3603.43	2768.70	2268.69	1936.04	1521.76	1274.83
65000	5714.54	3903.72	2999.43	2457.75	2097.37	1648.57	1381.06
70000	6154.12	4204.00	3230.15	2646.80	2258.71	1775.39	1487.30
75000	6593.70	4504.29	3460.87	2835.86	2420.04	1902.20	1593.53
80000	7033.28	4804.57	3691.60	3024.92	2581.38	2029.01	1699.77
100000	8791.59	6005.71	4614.50	3781.15	3226.72	2536.26	2124.71

MONTHLY PAYMENT

Necessary to amortize a loan

10%

TERM AMOUNT	8 YEARS	10 YEARS	12 YEARS	15 YEARS	16 YEARS	17 YEARS	18 YEARS
$ 25	.38	.34	.30	.27	.27	.26	.25
50	.76	.67	.60	.54	.53	.52	.50
75	1.14	1.00	.90	.81	.79	.77	.75
100	1.52	1.33	1.20	1.08	1.05	1.03	1.00
200	3.04	2.65	2.40	2.15	2.10	2.05	2.00
300	4.56	3.97	3.59	3.23	3.14	3.07	3.00
400	6.07	5.29	4.79	4.30	4.19	4.09	4.00
500	7.59	6.61	5.98	5.38	5.23	5.11	5.00
600	9.11	7.93	7.18	6.45	6.28	6.13	6.00
700	10.63	9.26	8.37	7.53	7.33	7.15	7.00
800	12.14	10.58	9.57	8.60	8.37	8.17	8.00
900	13.66	11.90	10.76	9.68	9.42	9.20	9.00
1000	15.18	13.22	11.96	10.75	10.46	10.22	10.00
2000	30.35	26.44	23.91	21.50	20.92	20.43	20.00
3000	45.53	39.65	35.86	32.24	31.38	30.64	30.00
4000	60.70	52.87	47.81	42.99	41.84	40.85	40.00
5000	75.88	66.08	59.76	53.74	52.30	51.07	50.00
6000	91.05	79.30	71.71	64.48	62.76	61.28	60.00
7000	106.22	92.51	83.66	75.23	73.22	71.49	69.99
8000	121.40	105.73	95.61	85.97	83.68	81.70	79.99
9000	136.57	118.94	107.56	96.72	94.14	91.91	89.99
10000	151.75	132.16	119.51	107.47	104.60	102.13	99.99
11000	166.92	145.37	131.46	118.21	115.05	112.34	109.99
12000	182.09	158.59	143.41	128.96	125.51	122.55	119.99
13000	197.27	171.80	155.37	139.70	135.97	132.76	129.98
14000	212.44	185.02	167.32	150.45	146.43	142.97	139.98
15000	227.62	198.23	179.27	161.20	156.89	153.19	149.98
16000	242.79	211.45	191.22	171.94	167.35	163.40	159.98
17000	257.97	224.66	203.17	182.69	177.81	173.61	169.98
18000	273.14	237.88	215.12	193.43	188.27	183.82	179.98
19000	288.31	251.09	227.07	204.18	198.73	194.03	189.98
20000	303.49	264.31	239.02	214.93	209.19	204.25	199.97
21000	318.66	277.52	250.97	225.67	219.64	214.46	209.97
22000	333.84	290.74	262.92	236.42	230.10	224.67	219.97
23000	349.01	303.95	274.87	247.16	240.56	234.88	229.97
24000	364.18	317.17	286.82	257.91	251.02	245.10	239.97
25000	379.36	330.38	298.77	268.66	261.48	255.31	249.97
26000	394.53	343.60	310.73	279.40	271.94	265.52	259.96
27000	409.71	356.81	322.68	290.15	282.40	275.73	269.96
28000	424.88	370.03	334.63	300.89	292.86	285.94	279.96
29000	440.06	383.24	346.58	311.64	303.32	296.16	289.96
30000	455.23	396.46	358.53	322.39	313.78	306.37	299.96
31000	470.40	409.67	370.48	333.13	324.23	316.58	309.96
32000	485.58	422.89	382.43	343.88	334.69	326.79	319.95
33000	500.75	436.10	394.38	354.62	345.15	337.00	329.95
34000	515.93	449.32	406.33	365.37	355.61	347.22	339.95
35000	531.10	462.53	418.28	376.12	366.07	357.43	349.95
40000	606.97	528.61	478.04	429.85	418.37	408.49	399.94
45000	682.84	594.68	537.79	483.58	470.66	459.55	449.93
50000	758.71	660.76	597.54	537.31	522.96	510.61	499.93
55000	834.58	726.83	657.30	591.04	575.25	561.67	549.92
60000	910.45	792.91	717.05	644.77	627.55	612.73	599.91
65000	986.33	858.98	776.81	698.50	679.84	663.79	649.90
70000	1062.20	925.06	836.56	752.23	732.14	714.85	699.90
75000	1138.07	991.14	896.31	805.96	784.43	765.91	749.89
80000	1213.94	1057.21	956.07	859.69	836.73	816.97	799.88
100000	1517.42	1321.51	1195.08	1074.61	1045.91	1021.22	999.85

the same monthly payments? Not at all. You'll each have a tailor-made amortization schedule that fits your circumstances. Your monthly payments might be higher than those your neighbor pays because you might be reducing your principal faster. These principal reductions are not tax deductions, so you don't have any tax advantages; it's simply a matter of whether you can afford higher payments and whether your overall planning calls for reducing the debt on your property in a shorter time frame. That explains why your lender may say, "The rate of interest is 10 percent but your constant is 10.5 percent." Most people don't understand why there are two different interest rates.

The constant interest rate represents interest you're paying on the mortgage plus the amount of money you are paying toward amortization. Those two add up to the total amount of cash you are paying each month. This paydown of principal, plus the interest on the money you borrowed, will obviously be a higher percentage because it represents more money against the amount of money you borrowed.

It's possible to arrange another type of fixed mortgage with a somewhat confusing title: a changing fixed mortgage. Under this arrangement, you and the lender both agree to set the interest rate at a certain amount, but this rate isn't permanently etched in concrete. In the contract, you and the lender anticipate future changes in the defined interest rate. For example, you and the lender may agree to an interest rate of 10 percent for the first two years. For the next three years, the rate will be 10.5 percent; For the subsequent three-year period, the rate will be 11 percent.

Why would anyone agree to such a mortgage? This technique is used frequently when the property cannot sustain a current rate of interest; the investor might have a negative cash flow. Thus the lender is willing to accept a lesser degree of interest, possibly below market rate. By so doing, he is compensated in future years by contractually receiving what might be an above-market rate compared to today's standards. As an example, if today's market rate is 10 percent, the lender may agree to a rate starting at 8 percent—but after future changes, the rate might finish at 12 percent or higher, adjusting for the lender's loss of the use of money in the earlier years.

The amortization rate could also be changed contractually, but this is rarely done. The lender is mainly concerned about the interest rate.

Another type of fixed mortgage is the interest-only mortgage. You borrow a certain amount of money and your monthly payments cover interest only. Since you don't pay any principal, you aren't amortizing the mortgage. The low payments may seem like a boon at the outset, but in the future, when that mortgage matures, you'll be required to return the original amount of money.

Suppose you borrow $500,000 with an interest-only mortgage. When the note is due, you'll have to return the full $500,000 at one time. With an amortizing mortgage, since you've been paying off part of the principal each month, you will have to return less than $500,000 when the note is due. If a fully amortized mortgage is held to its conclusion, there will be no lump sum to pay. No part of the mortgage will remain unpaid.

We've discussed several types of fixed mortgages. Which is the best? There's no hard and fast answer. The mortgage you chose depends upon your answers to these questions:

- What do I want to do with the property?
- What type of mortgage can the property afford?
- What type of returns am I looking for?

You need to answer these questions for yourself. Only then will the conclusions direct you to the appropriate mortgage. *If you're not planning to hold the property to the conclusion of the mortgage, there's a chance that the mortgage may be a tool that can be used as an attraction for the next buyer.* This is a serious consideration when you mortgage property. We'll discuss this point in more detail later on.

Variable-Rate Mortgages

Variable-rate mortgages are the "new kid on the block." With these mortgages (also known as adjustable-rate mortgages), the interest rate fluctuates throughout the life of the mortgage. Why did they come about? Before the 1980s, interest rates on mortgages remained stable. A major change might have been one quarter of a percent. Lenders were able to attract money and pay their investors returns somewhat consistent with an established profitability based on the current and expected interest rates. But to protect themselves as interest rates became more volatile, lenders felt that mortgage rates should change in order to keep up with changes in the interest rates. Their thinking was: "Because we must attract investors to obtain funds to lend, we'll have to pay these investors higher rates. Thus we'll have to charge higher interest on mortgages." They also recognized the possibility that, if interest rates dropped, they would be lending the money for mortgages at lower interest rates. Thus, in the early 1980s, lending institutions introduced the variable rate mortgage.

What standards are these variable rates measured against? They can be based on any of a wide range of indexes. These include: the national consumer price index (CPI), the rate of inflation, Federal Reserve rates, government bond rates, or certain local rates. As a consumer, how can you evaluate the index used by a lender? These are the important considerations:

1. Look at the history of whatever index the interest rate is based on. How has it performed during times that mortgage rates have changed? As an example, in the early 1980s, the prime rate, which is a form of an index, had gone up as high as 21.5 percent. This obviously is an interest rate that is totally unacceptable to any real estate investment.

2. Whatever the variable rate is, put a cap on how high it can go. You might borrow today and have a variable rate of interest of 9 percent. In that case, during your negotiations, say to the lender, "Regardless of what happens to the index, the rate I pay can go up no further than 12 percent—which is three percentage points more."

Generally, the marketplace dictates what the cap is, but be aware of the need to negotiate a top to that rate in case the index continues to rise. When you set a maximum rate, you're assured that your interest rate cannot rise beyond that level. Thus you predetermine your costs, rather than leaving them open-ended. When times are stable, people tend to think the current situation will extrapolate into the future. That's not so. You're engaging in static analysis, not correct analysis. It's inevitable that changes will take place, and that they may go to extremes. *Be prepared for changes that will take place. Protect yourself accordingly.*

3. How fast can the variable rate be allowed to rise? If your index moves up 2 percentage points, you don't want to see your debt service increase that dramatically. It's unlikely the income you'll be receiving from your property will match that increase. Therefore, you'll want the mortgage contract to restrict the rate of increase. It might specify: "The interest rate cannot go up more than 1/2 percent per year." *Make sure you limit how far the interest rate can rise within a certain period of time.*

4. Beware of mortgages that carry the possibility of negative amortization. Under their terms, you might end up owing a principal amount *larger* than that you originally borrowed.

Which Should You Choose: Fixed or Variable?

Lenders like variable rates because they're protected in up markets. Even in down markets, variable mortgages enable them to make an acknowledged spread on their money, leading to profits for their organization. Borrowers don't like variable rates because of their uncertainty.

The availability of fixed versus variable mortgages is a function of the marketplace. Given a choice, try to obtain a fixed-rate mortgage, unless, as a strong inducement, the lender will offer interest rates on their variable mortgages that are considerably lower than the market rate.

As an example, the market rate for fixed mortgages may be 10 percent. A lender might offer a variable mortgage that starts at 8.5 percent. If you can achieve a rate that is substantially below market; then further cap it at a reasonable maximum; and, in addition, restrict its annual increase; then, from an interest standpoint, you could end up with a variable mortgage that is better than a fixed mortgage. Your awareness of all factors involved, plus your negotiating skills, can give you this financial advantage.

Just as new ice cream flavors are created constantly, new types of mortgages frequently appear. Currently, there's a hybrid adjustable-rate mortgage known as a convertible mortgage, which allows you to convert the mortgage to a fixed-rate mortgage within a specific period of time, without refinancing. Again, there's a trade-off. In return for this conversion privilege, the lender may require you to pay more points.

Taking Advantage of Interest Rate Changes

Once you mortgage property, don't go into mental retirement and forget about interest rates. You now have a vested interest in continuing to follow trends for mortgages on similar property. An awareness of interest rate changes can allow you to take care of special opportunites that arise at any time during your holding period. If interest rates drop significantly, you might want to replace your current mortgage with one that has lower rates. The process of replacing one mortgage with another is known as refinancing. A lower cost of service could allow you to place a much larger mortgage on the property for the same debt-service cost (monthly payment) that currently exists. Thus you pay off the first mortgage and obtain extra cash equivalent to the difference between the old and new mortgages.

For example, you might have a $500,000 mortgage with an annual cost of $50,000. If, as a result of lower interest rates, you can obtain a new mortgage on the property for $600,000 and still have a $50,000 cost, it's to your advantage to act. You take the $600,000, pay off the $500,000 mortgage, and put $100,000 in your pocket. This allows you to continue owning the property. Obviously, there are other conditions in the mortgage contract that may not allow you to do this. We'll discuss them shortly.

If you are a passive investor with someone managing your property, or if you're an investor through a limited partnership, talk to the responsible party to see if he is aware of the advantage of replacing one mortgage with another.

Impounds

Impounds are another important element in your carrying costs. This term refers to money the lender wants to set aside, either up front or along the way, to cover real estate taxes and insurance costs on the real estate. Because the lending agency wants to make sure that real estate taxes and insurance premiums are paid, it will add to your monthly cost the amortized rate for one or both of these (which might be 1/12 of the annual costs), in addition to your interest rate and amortization on the principal. Whether this money is paid up front or along the way, the big question is, do you want to pay it at your convenience or the lender's? You generally have the option to decide either way. Don't let the lender boss you. If it's more convenient, you can choose to pay the taxes and insurance premiums directly rather than going through the lender.

3. When Must the Mortgage Be Paid Back?

At the end of your mortgage's maturity, you must pay back all the money borrowed. If a lump sum is involved, that's known as a balloon payment. Or you might be reducing the mortgage through amortization, paying down the principal by a stipulated amount each month, so that nothing is due at maturity. If you have a 30-year amortization schedule and a 30-year mortgage, this involves no requirement to pay off any amount sooner. Thus your mortgage will be consistently reduced and the amount of principal will be lowered each year. At the end of 30 years, you'll owe nothing. Before the 1980s, borrowers were accustomed to this standard methodology; they liked having money out for the long term and were accustomed to very slight changes that took place in interest rates. Since interest rate movements have changed so dramatically in the 1980s, many lenders require balloon payments to be paid *before* the conclusion of the mortgage. *Even though a mortgage has a 30-year amortization schedule, it may have a balloon requirement stating that the amount of money remaining on the mortgage is due and fully payable in 15 years.*

There are also balloon payments that require a constant reduction of the mortgage, with specified amounts of money paid in five years, another amount five years later, and so on.

Don't be forced into taking a mortgage with a time frame and payment schedule that isn't consistent with your needs and goals. The key ingredient in determining optimum maturity is how long you intend to hold on to the particular piece of real estate. You shouldn't be put in the position of finding a new mortgage prior to the end of your planned holding period. If you want to hold the property for five years, don't accept a three-year mortgage; it might force you to take steps with the real estate that aren't consistent with your objectives over the planned holding period.

The maturity date of the mortgage should be at least 50 percent longer than your intended holding period. If your intended holding period is 10 years, the mortgage should be for 15 years. Ideally, the mortgage should be twice the length of time you intend to hold the real estate.

Unfortunately, we don't live in an ideal world. What should you do if banks make available mortgages with balloon payments that won't give you the length of time you wish to have, but will be consistent with other aspects of the real estate? Clearly, that isn't a good characteristic of a mortgage. You must look at all aspects of the mortgage and see how everything comes together. The possibility exists that, if there isn't enough money available for you to obtain the type of mortgage you need, and you can't buy for cash, you might not be able to buy the real estate. Don't buy the property if such conditions tell you not to buy it.

If you're confronted with the prospect of a balloon payment—particularly when it's due before your anticipated holding period is up—you're faced with the following question: How will you pay the mortgage back? It's dangerous to presume that you can find another mortgage. Don't count on that scenario. Higher interest rates may keep you from finding another mortgage. The amount that you can pay on debt service could dictate a considerably lesser mortgage. You need to look at the percentage of debt being put on the property. How realistic is it? Is the figure a conservative amount of debt as a percentage of debt to equity? Or is it too much? When you're faced with a balloon payment and the problem is further exacerbated by having an excessive amount of debt on the property, you've made the condition even worse. That's the total picture. When you think of maturity and the amount of money that needs to repaid, you must think through the type of plan that will allow you to accommodate that repayment. Make sure you're in control of your destiny and not forced to sell or take other action contrary to the sound investment planning going into your purchase.

4. Lock-in and Prepayment Considerations

Since a mortgage is held for a long time—anywhere from five to 30 years—we've discussed how you can take advantage of special opportunities if interest rates drop. But a bad mortgage might lock you in, leaving you unable to act.

The term "lock-in" means exactly what it implies. It's very punitive to borrowers. Under lock-in provisions, you cannot pay off the mortgage, or even reduce it. The only way you can change the mortgage is by offering the lender enough money to break the contract. As a borrower, you're powerless to break the contract on your own. Only the lender has that right. If the lending agency chooses, it can force the contract to remain binding.

You might want to refinance and put a considerable amount of cash in your pocket; but will the lender allow you to do this? When the lending agency parts with money, it is counting on a certain acceptable rate of return. They don't want that return violated, nor do they want to constantly turn the money over. The lender wants to make money on the amount of interest collected from you. Thus their thought process may be contrary to yours. You want to have a debt that is flexible, while they're counting on return from a fixed principle.

Suppose you want to pay off the debt, using money from any of several sources—whether it's from another mortgage or a stock market windfall. If you have a variable mortgage with an interest rate that is going up too high, you have another incentive to refinance. As we mentioned, you might be able to replace it with a mortgage with a lower interest rate. The important consideration is that mortgages are debts held for many years. During that period of time, there may be sound reasons why the borrower wants to pay off or reduce the mortgage. He or she should have that flexibility.

Look for the fine print in a mortgage contract. You may discover you have no option to pay the debt off earlier; or you might have to wait for a period of several years. Thus, if opportunities exist for refinancing, you cannot take advantage of them. You're locked in and cannot reduce or pay back that mortgage. Make sure you discuss lock-ins when you initially take out a mortgage.

A mortgage may have a lock-in for several years; beyond that point, you can pay back a portion or all of the mortgage. But even then, you're not home free. There may be another restriction—a prepayment penalty. This is a penalty for paying the mortgage sooner than the contractual arrangement calls for. In some instances, a mortgage may have a prepayment penalty clause without a lock-in restriction.

There are several types of prepayment penalties. In the most common form, we get back to that favorite term lenders love to use: points. In some instances, the prepayment penalty requires that you pay the lender a certain amount of points for the privilege of paying back their money. This may seem unfair, but the lending agency has loaned you money at a rate they wanted to maintain for a number of years. If that rate cannot be maintained, they want to be paid for the risk of having to go back into the marketplace and once again obtain an acceptable rate of return. So be sure to look at the cost of prepayment. The only guidelines are those of common sense.

A new type of prepayment penalty, primarily developed by insurance companies, is extremely unfair. This is called a yield maintenance penalty. By using present values of money, the insurance company wants to achieve the same value of money had the mortgage been held to its maturity. For example, if your mortgage rate is 9 percent, and you pay it back early because current rates are 7 percent, they would have to reissue a mortgage to another borrower for the 7 percent rate. To cover that perceived loss, the insurance company insists that you owe them 2 percent for the amount of mortgage that you prepay—for the remaining period of time, on a present value basis. This might double or triple the amount of money out of your pocket. *Do not accept a mortgage with that type of yield maintenance.* Once again, look at the entire package of all the mortgage ingredients we've been discussing; see how they come together in an entire package.

5. Assumption of a Mortgage

Since the lending agency has loaned you money with the real estate as security, it has a vested interest in your future actions. Will that organization permit you to allow someone to assume that mortgage if they continue to use the real estate as collateral? In most cases, the contract will say something like "assumption, or permission to assume mortgage, will not be unreasonably withheld." This means the lender has the right to determine who is going to be held accountable for the mortgage; but it also states that they cannot unreasonably withhold permission. For example, if a person has red hair, it would be unreasonable to withhold the assumption. But if a person has a history of avoiding responsibility for debt, and the lender can sufficiently prove that the risk would be considerably different from the one originally proposed when the money was lent to you, they may reasonably withhold permission for assumption.

Assumption is very important when you have a mortgage with good interest and maturity terms. A good mortgage is advantageous when you're ready to sell. It makes the sale of the property more fluid by allowing the next buyer to come in with less money and assume the current amount of debt.

Many people mistakenly feel that a piece of real estate is much more attractive when they pay off the mortgage and nothing is owed. The seller's returns may be higher, and this situation may satisfy certain needs for some investors; but paying off the mortgage may narrow your marketplace and make the real estate less liquid, because you're requiring a potential buyer to come in with a new mortgage. All the new costs and conditions which we've been describing are part and parcel of placing a new mortgage on a property.

Make sure you have an assumption clause. It makes your property more fluid and easier to sell by giving you a broader marketplace.

6. Can the Lender Attach Your Personal Assets?

If a property can no longer satisfy the interest and it goes into foreclosure because of nonpayment, where can the lender look for satisfaction? From a liability standpoint, there are two types of mortgages: non-recourse and recourse.

Non-recourse loans, currently more popular with lenders, allow the lender to look to the security of the real estate. They cannot attach the personal assets of the mortgage holder. Therefore, the borrower is in a protected position. The most he or she can lose is the real estate itself.

If a borrower has a recourse loan, upon the sale of the real estate, if the lender is not sufficiently satisfied as to the amount of money available to pay the mortgage, the agency can look to the mortgageholder's assets until the debt is satisfied. Fortunately for borrowers, this type of mortgage is less prevalent.

Always look for a non-recourse loan. Lack of one is the type of condition that would make you turn down a mortgage offer. Once again, you need to consider all factors. You'll notice in the economic valuation worksheet in Figure 11–1 that this ingredient is given the highest weight of all; it is absolutely the most serious factor in creating an economically feasible transaction.

7. How Committed Is the Lending Institution?

How valid is the lending institution's commitment? When the bank gives you a commitment to a loan you're satisfied with, you're going to start incurring costs in anticipation of ultimately obtaining the mortgage they've described. What are some of those expenses? You'll initiate inspection procedures, hiring people to evaluate the real estate. In addition, you'll use your own time and energies to evaluate the real estate in detail, using the Economic Valuation System.

Without a mortgage, you might not have a transaction, so you must sit down with the lender and qualify the type of commitment offered. How long will the mortgage offer be made available to you? What contingencies would allow the bank to declare that the mortgage commitment no longer exists? Point out that, based on their commitment, you're going to start spending money to evaluate the real estate. Obtain the commitment in writing.

BEWARE OF PARTICIPATION MORTGAGES

If the property appreciates in value during your holding period, you pocket the extra money when the real estate is sold. However, some mortgages have a new twist—one that hits you in the pocketbook.

Participation Mortgages. From time to time, the investors who provide money for the mortgage may require that the lender add extras to the mortgage, which the borrower will ultimately pay for. As an example, at some point the investors might say, "We want more than a specified yield because this is a risky period of time. If the real estate proves to be a good investment for the borrower, then we want to share in the benefits." Mortgages with this stipulation are called participation mortgages. Not only do you pay the lender the specified interest rates, but, in addition, you are going to share with that lender some extra money—perhaps the cash flow that you receive from the real estate along the way. You might also have to share some of the profits received upon the sale of your real estate.

Equity Participation Mortgages.   In this scenario, the lender is a partial owner as well as a lender to that real estate. Should you, as a real estate investor, agree to such terms? No! The next question might be: Is it necessary for you to agree to such terms in order to buy the property? Since you're putting your money at risk by buying the real estate, unless you feel you need a partner in the transaction, and that partner is also the lender, avoid such agreements. But, if you should want this type of arrangement, make sure the terms are satisfactory. If you don't want or need a partner, then you shouldn't be forced to take on one. Currently, as this book is being written, participation mortgages are in vogue.

We've covered the key ingredients that go into the makeup of a mortgage. As always, let common sense prevail. You *must* be aware of what is available in the marketplace.

CYMROT'S LAW NUMBER 10:

Shopping for a commodity called a mortgage is no different than shopping for an automobile. You need to shop, compare, and negotiate the best deal.

Many people assume that only a local banker can provide you with a mortgage. That's erroneous. You've spent years earning your money; don't throw it away. To complement all the time and effort you've expended in achieving your present net worth, you'll need to research the mortgage market. Read. Talk to people. Go to several mortgage sources and compare all the mortgage ingredients we've discussed. Add them up—and then take the best mortgage that satisfies your needs.

Since this is a complex chapter, our list of Tips to Remember is longer than usual.

TIPS TO REMEMBER

- A mortgage allows you to control more assets with less money.
- A good mortgage allows you to lower your costs initially and during the holding period.
- Borrow money as cheaply as possible and extend the pay-back period as far into the future as possible.
- To obtain the best mortgage, deal with a reputable mortgage broker *and* shop around on your own. Then compare the deals.
- Use the Economic Valuation System to compare the bottom-line cost, factoring in front-end costs plus those during the holding period.
- Avoid lock-in features that prevent you from paying off the mortgage faster.
- Make your property easier to sell by incorporating an assumption clause that allows a prospective buyer to assume your mortgage.
- Never accept a recourse mortgage. This would allow the lender to attach your personal assets.
- When a mortgage offer is made, be sure that the lender's commitment won't be withdrawn unreasonably.
- Evaluate the mortgage in terms of your goals with the real estate, your holding period, and the returns you hope to achieve.
- Never accept a mortgage that matures before your anticipated holding period is up.
- Before accepting a variable-rate mortgage, evaluate the index used, the rate at which the interest rate might rise, and the maximum interest rate.
- With a variable-rate mortgage, establish limits on how far the interest rate can rise within a certain period of time, and establish a top interest rate.
- Beware of mortgages that may saddle you with negative amortization.

- If given a choice, it's usually more advantageous to opt for a fixed-rate mortgage.
- Be aware of changing interest rates. Take advantage of opportunites to refinance if this action allows you to save money.
- If you're confronted with the prospect of balloon payments, make sure you can handle them when they're due.
- Read the fine print about prepayment penalties. Avoid yield maintenance prepayment penalties.
- Keep profits for yourself. Avoid mortgages that allow the lender to benefit from your property's appreciation.
- If you can't obtain a mortgage that's right for your needs, don't buy the real estate.

CHAPTER 12

LEVERAGE: GETTING THE
MOST FOR THE LEAST

In high school physics textbooks, you frequently see a drawing of someone raising a massive rock off the ground—not with his bare hands, but with the aid of a simple mechanical device called a lever. This individual is taking advantage of the extra power that mechanical leverage affords. Outside the realm of physics, leverage is also used as a boost in accomplishing certain goals. It provides the user with an increased advantage. In the financial world, the principles of leverage are universal. Even though we're going to discuss them in terms of purchasing real estate, you can apply them to other investments: stocks, commodities, and even government bonds. Now, let's start with basics. Exactly what does this word leverage mean?

For once, Webster's dictionary comes up with a definition we can use: "Leverage is the use of credit to enhance one's speculative capacity." When you make an investment using leverage, you buy more of the product because you're using someone else's money in addition to your own. The total purchase price is made up of your money plus borrowed money. In real estate, the purchase price (or the selling price) includes the down payment plus the mortgage. Leverage permits you to control larger amounts of assets with lesser amounts of money.

Webster says that when you use this credit (the mortgage), you've enhanced your speculative capacity. By borrowing, you incur an additional cost to the transaction—the interest charge and/or other charges that result from your using someone else's money. That money will have to be paid back in the future. So, why would anyone want to borrow? A street-smart investor once said, "The only way to make money is through the use of someone else's money." That's absolutely true.

CYMROT'S LAW NUMBER 11:

Buying for all-cash is for goals other than increasing net worth.

The Upside and Downside of Borrowed Money

The more leverage in an investment, the greater your returns. That fact justifies the mortgage you take out when purchasing real estate. The ability to control larger amounts of assets with lesser amounts of money constitutes the good-news side. But, there's a bad-news side.

The following illustration demonstrates the good-news/bad-news aspects. Joe Smith and Bob Drake both purchase property for $100. Each makes a down payment of $50 and thus starts out with $50 in equity. But then, their fortunes take a different turn. Joe's property increases in value while Bob's decreases. Let's see what that does to their investments:

Purchase price	$100
Down payment (equity)	50
Amount borrowed (mortgage)	50

Joe's investment of $100 appreciates by 25 percent to $125. His debt remains the same at $50, while his equity increases to $75.

New equity ($75) = Original equity ($50) + Appreciation ($25)

Joe's investment increased by 25 percent:

Purchase price (value): $100 $\rightarrow$ $125 = 25 percent increase

His return on investment has increased by 50 percent:

$$\frac{\text{Increase in equity}}{\text{Original equity}} = \frac{\$25}{\$50} = 50 \text{ percent increase}$$

Bob's story doesn't have such a happy ending. Instead of ap-preciating, his property decreases in value by $25; it is now worth only $75. His debt remains at $50 but his equity drops to $25. Thus, a 25 percent loss in investment value turns into a 50 percent loss in his equity. Leverage accelerates the downside momentum.

As these examples show, small changes in price or value are transformed into large changes in your equity. What does this mean to you? When using leverage, it's important to aim for perfect balance—the amount of leverage that exactly satisfies your specific needs. Before showing how to achieve this perfect balance, let's pause for a discussion of risk.

Risk

Every single form of investment incurs risk. You might believe that cash left under the mattress is safe, but it isn't. Let's assume that there's a moderate rate of inflation—2 or 3 percent annually. Even with that moderate rate, since your money is earning nothing, it is losing its ability to buy goods and services at the rate of 2 or 3 percent a year. Why? That money is only worth what it can buy in the form of goods and services. So, although the principal may be safe under the mattress, the negative yield of that money will reduce its value on a continuing basis. Over the past several hundred years, we have had constant inflation, with only a few brief periods of deflation when the ownership of greenbacks constituted good investments.

Isn't it safer to buy stocks for cash rather than on margin? If the stock market is going up, your investment is less safe than if you used leverage. In a bull market, leverage permits you to make greater profits. Before rushing to leverage your investment posi-tion, it's necessary to look at the cost of money and the time frame when that money is due.

ACHIEVING PERFECT BALANCE

Before you borrow money for investment purposes, look at the ramifications of this act. You want to achieve the degree of leverage that is comfortable for you. The perfect balance we mentioned above is made up of four ingredients; one is subjective, while the other three require objective evaluation.

1. Personal Soul-Searching

Personal soul-searching concerns your comfort level when borrowing money. Some people have been trained to borrow very little or nothing; others are very aggressive in this respect. To evaluate your own position, consider the following:

- In what stage of life are you? How many years of recuperative power do you have left relative to what you can lose?
- What are your investment objectives?
- What risk are you able and willing to take?

A discussion with your financial advisor can help clarify your thoughts.

Now we'll turn to elements of perfect balance that you can examine objectively.

2. Characteristics of the Real Estate Investment

Is the real estate investment solid or speculative? If an investment has a sound, in-place tenant roster with good leases, and it involves a structurally sound building as evaluated with the EVS, this investment can subscribe to more leverage. There's a higher degree of certainty that you can continue to service the debt.

The investment would be considered speculative if you're planning to change the entire tenant structure, hoping to successfully evict current tenants and lease to a new type of tenant that you've targeted. Or perhaps you're planning to make structural changes that might attract better tenants and increase your cash flow. In such speculative scenarios, you're hoping something is going to happen—as opposed to entering a solid, qualitative form of real estate investment. In contrast to the first example, you're speculating with the tenant structure and/or structural changes. The addition of more speculative elements needs to be looked at very seriously. The investment itself and what it is all about are important ingredients in achieving perfect balance.

3. What Size Debt Are You Considering?

After you have some idea as to the type of investment you're making, work out several "what-if" scenarios to determine their effect on your equity. What would the bottom line look like with a down payment of 20 percent? How would that differ from one of 30 percent, 40 percent, or 50 percent? You might even work up some figures for a down payment of 60 percent. Compare what happens—or what needs to happen—relative to the rents and expenses. You want to feel secure that you won't encounter problems about repayment. Studying these what-if scenarios helps you avoid excessive leverage that could trigger financial difficulties.

4. What Is the Cost of the Debt?

You usually pay debt costs on a monthly basis. To reach a point of perfect balance in leverage, you'll need to go through more what-if situations. The one situation you want to avoid is negative cash flow. Even a break-even situation leaves no margin for error.

You've probably heard of Murphy's Law—if something can go wrong, it will. Always assume that this law will torment you. Even though you think your goals are achievable, chances are that your objectives won't be met at first. Your income is likely to be less than anticipated. Thus, if you count on merely breaking even, things may actually be worse. By the time you've been an owner for nine months or so, you will probably have identified most of the things you didn't catch even after an extensive due diligence investigation.

To be in a secure position, evaluate the purchase, the amount of debt you're adding to it, and the cost of that debt. When you put these three ingredients together, you should have a comfortable cash flow—one that can protect you against any possible downside risks. The three objective ingredients we've discussed are a starting point. Now you need to examine borrowing costs in order to determine the extent of leverage to incur.

NEGATIVE AND POSITIVE BORROWING COSTS

To fine-tune your decision about leverage, you need to evaluate borrowing costs. These can be positive or negative. The real estate you're planning to buy has a certain return which is a function of the suggested purchase price and the net operating income.

Let's assume a capitalization rate of 8 percent. Thus, on an all-cash basis, the real estate is returning an 8 percent yield. We'll

FIGURE 12–1
Borrowing Costs On An Annual Basis

	All-Cash Transaction	Conservative Approach	Higher Leverage
Percent Down Payment	None	50%	25%
Down Payment	$50	$50	$50
Value of Real Estate	$50	$100	200
Debt	None	50	150
Cash Received (Annual Income)	4	8	16
Cost of Debt per Year	None	6	18
Return	$ 4	$ 2	$-2
Percent Return	8%	4%	-4%

presume that the mortgage you plan to obtain will cost 12 percent. You are giving up equity that is returning 8 percent while borrowing to buy more equity that will cost 12 percent. This is a negative cost to borrowing. What does it mean? The above three examples (Figure 12–1) serve as a demonstration. In each case, we will invest $50 in real estate yielding 8 percent, and we will borrow money at a cost of 12 percent.

Using the conservative approach, with 50 percent down, the $100 worth of real estate generates $8. The $50 worth of debt, at a rate of 12 percent, costs $6, leaving a real return of $2, or 4 percent on the $50 investment.

The conservative approach provides twice the amount of real estate as an all-cash investment, but the current yield is cut in half— 4 percent versus 8 percent.

In the high leverage example, the $50 down payment represents 25 percent of the purchase price. Therefore, the $200 worth of real estate has a debt of $150. With an 8 percent return, $16 is generated, but since the debt costs (at 12 percent) are $18, there is a negative return. If the real estate doesn't appreciate, in essence the equity has depreciated at 4 percent per year simply as a result of the debt cost.

How do these figures affect you? To understand their full impact, use your pencil, calculator or computer and start playing with numbers and percentages in a similar manner. Work with different combinations of your down payment, the cost of money, and the type of real estate. Ultimately, tie these numbers into your own personal objective.

Of course, taxes start to become a possible consideration when you look at potential losses, but this should not affect your initial purchase transaction. Tax legislation is bound to keep changing and thus won't determine the ultimate value; true cash flow will have the major effect.

When evaluating the degree of risk you wish to assume, simply look at the hard dollars of the transaction. What will the transaction cost? Does that make sense to you?

Are you considering the purchase of a home for your family? If so, you'll follow the same businesslike procedure outlined above. First, find a home you like. Even though the building won't generate income, you will do so as an individual. So consider the following:

1. What are my earnings?
2. What size mortgage will I incur?
3. What is the interest rate?

Based on the above, look at your personal profit and loss statement. From it, you can determine whether or not the leverage you're considering (from the proposed mortgage and interest rate) will generate a negative cash flow. This is not a position you want to be in. You want to run a profitable, successful business, and leverage should not take that privilege away.

What Leverage is Appropriate for You?

The graph in Figure 12–2 shows seven different combinations ranging from all cash to as little as a 10 percent down payment. It assumes an 8 percent capitalization rate from the real estate and a 12 percent cost of carrying the debt. As you can see, the range is from 8 percent return on investment to the cost of the debt representing a loss per annum of 28 percent of the principal, or your equity. This graph gives a sliding indication of the point at which the leverage might be appropriate for you. Of course, different assumptions of yield and cost of debt change the yield curve itself. The important lesson here is: Do not make a determination as to the extent of leverage without analyzing the yield curve and the type of investment we have in Figure 12–2.

FIGURE 12–2
Percent of Investment Returns Based on Percent of Down Payment

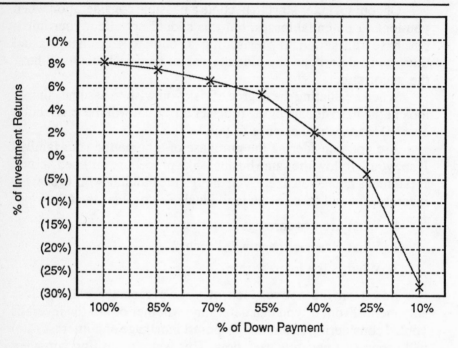

Income	$8	$8	$8	$8	$8	$8	$8
Down Payment (Investment)	100%	85%	70%	55%	40%	25%	10%
Debt	0	$15	$70	$45	$60	$75	$90
Cost of Debt	0	$1.80	$3.60	$5.40	$7.20	$9.00	$10.80
Net Cash	$8	$6.20	$4.40	$2.60	$80	-$1.00	-$2.30
% Return on Investment	8%	7.3%	6.9%	4.7%	2%	-4%	-28%

Special Buying Opportunities

Infrequently—but on certain fortituous occasions during a real estate cycle—an extraordinary buying opportunity develops. This situation exists when the return from the investment (the capitalization rate) exceeds the cost of borrowing. When this happens, the investment is paying for your cost of borrowing money. In other words, the cost of borrowing is free. In this happy situation, you're able to buy more real estate without incurring additional cost.

This opportunity is rare, but be aware of the possibility. *At such times, you can buy real estate that produces money in excess of the cost of borrowing. When these circumstances exist, consider committing large percentages of your assets into real estate. Such opportunities exist for brief periods of time. Take advantage of them.*

Suppose you purchased real estate for $100 at a 10 percent capitalization ratio, with an 8 percent cost of borrowing. On an all-cash purchase, you would incur no debt. Your return would be 10 percent.

The following example shows how leverage can increase your return dramatically. The purchase price, capitalization ratio, and cost of debt remain the same. Our only change is in the down payment. In this case, we put 50 percent down ($50).

With the conservative approach in Example B (Figure 12–3), the $50 down payment represents 50 percent in equity. It buys $100 worth of real estate. A 10 percent capitalization ratio would yield

FIGURE 12–3:
Dramatic Bargains

Example A: All-Cash Purchase
  Purchase Price = $100   Return = $10

Example B: 50 Percent Down Payment
  Purchase Price $100 = $10 Return
  Debt   50   −4 cost of debt
  Down Payment   50 $ 6 return = 12 Percent Actual Return

  The actual yield has gone up because we've leveraged the purchase. By putting 50 percent down you go from a 10 percent return to a 12 percent return.

$10. With $50 worth of debt at a cost of 8 percent, the debt service would be $4. Subtract that $4 cost of debt from the $10 return on the $100, and you have $6. That $6 from a $50 investment constitutes a 12 percent return. As you can see, by borrowing money, you increase the current return—on the assumption that the real estate doesn't appreciate from 10 percent to 12 percent. This situation, where you make money on the spread between debt costs and yield, represents positive leverage.

When working with positive leverage, the more debt you incur, the higher your current return becomes. The cost of your debt is lower relative to the income produced by the real estate.

Even when confronted with the unique buying opportunities outlined above, you still need to look at the amount of leverage and the investment itself. In a positive leveraged position, you would be willing to incur greater leverage than in a situation with negative leverage. *But you still need to decide how much leverage you can live with. The more leverage you incur, the greater the risk. When the principal moves (up or down), it is magnified that much more, as we've seen.*

Avoid Overextending Yourself

Occasionally, overzealous real estate brokers encourage investors to purchase second homes as rentals. What's their justification? Here's their pitch: "You can make a small down payment and gain tax benefits by utilizing deductions of interest payments and negative cash flow." With those tantalizing benefits looming, many people purchased duplexes, four-plexes, and larger units with minimal down payments. They were able to deduct interest on the debt service, often producing a negative cash flow as a result of some of the illustrations above. These people felt that their purchases were justified because they controlled more assets for such a small outlay. They expected a higher return on their investment. *This is a valid assumption only as long as prices go up and nothing else changes (such as tax laws).* But investments don't work that way. Investments sometimes decline in value; in addition, legislative changes can impact real estate adversely. Many people bought real estate based on values that were created from deductibility of tax benefits—but now their property is worth considerably less because legislative changes have decreased or actually removed that deductibility. Even the threat of such changes has an adverse impact.

It might be tempting to operate on the premise that the more assets you control, the greater your return will be. This is a misleading, false assumption. The extent of debt you assume should not be driven by the amount of assets you can control to the maximum limit. *Do not attempt to control as much assets as you possibly can unless you have given serious consideration to the four ingredients mentioned above.* To achieve perfect balance, the four ingredients we've discussed—and *only* those four—should affect the extent of leverage you take on. Don't factor in tax considerations. Although it may feel comfortable ego-wise to control a larger amount of assets, it could be very uncomfortable equity-wise.

Keeping Leverage Flexible

It's important to keep leverage flexible. As times change, you may want to increase or decrease your leverage. An all-cash buyer always has the option to put on a mortgage after purchasing the property.

When you go into a leverage position from the beginning by taking out a mortgage, avoid the possibility of strict lock-ins. These force you to maintain that leverage or suffer very punitive measures if you make changes. Insurance companies insist on lock-ins and are strict in the early years, imposing punitive measures if changes are made. Savings and loan associations are far more liberal. Variable loans allow you to do whatever you want relative to paying off the mortgage; but they, too, have their risks, as you have seen in our discussion of mortgages.

Whenever possible, maintain flexibility. When you purchase property, leave yourself options regarding leverage. The four ingredients we've discussed that help you determine the best level of leverage for yourself are not a one-time judgment. Review them continually. At certain times, it may make sense to leverage more. Make sure that option is available to you.

Increasing Your Leverage

When would you want to increase your leverage? Here are several situations:

1. Your tenants have stabilized.

2. The area has grown stronger.

3. You can look forward to considerably greater rental increases.

4. Your expenses are lower.

5. You have a higher return.

6. You want to take out some cash.

As a result of taking out cash (increasing your leverage), you will incur more debt. To determine the extent of this debt, you should carefully analyze the factors discussed above (capitalization rate and cost of debt). This will help you determine the extent of leverage that is affordable.

Decreasing Your Leverage

There may be a period when it's beneficial to decrease your leverage. This opportunity presents itself as a result of the following:

1. The yield on the real estate may be sufficiently lower.

2. You have sufficient returns from other forms of investment.

3. You want to reduce the mortgage so the real estate will have less debt to service.

Final Thoughts on Leverage

Leverage is not a one-time decision. To give your investment the best opportunity to succeed, consider leverage as a series of continuing decisions. Make sure you retain the right to change the degree of leverage when necessary.

The minimum acceptable score utilizing Fig. 12–4 is 6.

After mastering the principles of optimum leverage in real estate, you can examine and evaluate borrowing with other forms of investment. Although we've discussed leveraging in terms of income-generating real estate and mortgages, the same principles apply to your own home, a margin account for stocks or commodities, and to government bonds. The principles of buying on leverage are universal and apply to all these purchases.

FIGURE 12–4
Leverage Worksheet

PROPERTY NAME _____

TYPE OF PROPERTY _____

ADDRESS _____

SELLER _____

NUMBER OF UNITS _____

TOTAL NUMBER OF SQUARE FEET _____

PURCHASE PRICE _____

CASH DOWN PAYMENT _____

MORTGAGE DESCRIPTION _____

LEVERAGE - DESCRIPTION

_____

_____

_____

_____

LEVERAGE - PROPERTY VALUATION

		Rating			
Condition	Subject	Bad	Avg	Good	TOTAL SCORE
NEG	1. Negative Cash Flow	(1)	2	3	
B/E, 3, 2, 1 Year	2. Break Even	(3)	4	5	
CF, 1, 2, 3 Year	3. Cash Flow	(3)	4	5	
0-2%, 2-4%, 4%+	4. 6 Year Cash Projection				
Versus Actual					
Investment		4	5	6	
	TOTAL	(3)	15	19	

It's particularly important to understand leverage with regard to real estate. The other investments mentioned above provide liquidity for a quick sale; thus you can change your leverage by reducing the size of the investment. It's easy to sell a portion of your stock holdings, part of a commodity contract, or some of the bonds you own. Real estate precludes that action. First, it is very difficult to sell real estate rapidly. Second, it is even more difficult to sell a portion of your real estate.

Thus we return to our theme with regard to real estate investing: research, research, research. The good news is that well-researched real estate will return substantially above average. Leverage plays a very distinct role in real estate investing—and works only when done correctly.

TIPS TO REMEMBER

- Leverage permits you to control more assets with less money. You make use of other people's funds.
- Leverage paves the way for greater returns—or greater losses.
- Strive to balance your personal comfort level with the real estate investment, the size of the debt, and its cost to you.
- Evaluate current income and expenses so you can make valid projections of future yield.
- Keep options open to increase or decrease leverage as your situation changes.

CHAPTER 13

MANAGEMENT: ANOTHER HAT TO WEAR

By now, you've progressed a considerable distance from "square one." While traveling along the path to real estate ownership, you've learned how to evaluate the physical and financial aspects of property. Then comes the leap of faith—the actual purchase. At this point—when you and your lawyer are looking over the final papers, prior to signing them—you might be asking, "What next?" If this is the first time you've raised that question, your timing is bad. You should ask yourself that question—and answer it—*before* signing the escrow papers. Only when you have a clear picture of what lies ahead will you be ready to own and manage property wisely. Good management is the execution of a prior plan.

Inept management kills profits faster than a sonic boom breaks windows. Many people perceive that property management is irrelevant and/or easy. That misconception makes so many real estate investments turn bad. The following conversation took place with several businessmen who planned to pool their money—totalling one million dollars—and buy real estate.

CYMROT:

Why have you chosen to invest in real estate?

BUSINESS SPOKESPERSON:

It's a good investment.

CYMROT:

I understand. But why don't you invest in an airplane factory?

BUSINESS SPOKESPERSON:

We don't know anything about an airplane factory.

CYMROT:

What do you know about real estate?

Members of the business group looked at one another blankly. It became apparent that their presumption was that "real estate is something you hopefully buy correctly, and, from that point on, it kind of takes care of itself."

As we've emphasized throughout this book, real estate is a business. Management of a real estate business requires experience, professionalism, expertise, dedication, and all the other attributes that make *any* individual business succeed.

Expertise in property management never comes overnight. You'll find dozens of books devoted to just this subject. Some schools give courses on this topic. You might even find one-day seminars on property management. Obviously, this single chapter won't make you an expert—but it *can* enlighten you to the point where you recognize the importance, and complexities, of property management. We'll also help you make basic decisions about whether you or someone else should manage the property. You'll learn what to look for in the property management organization you hire.

Let's get back to basics. What is property management? What is the manager or management team supposed to do? Generally, property managers assume responsibility for the net operating income of the real estate. They're accountable for all activities that go into the income and expense side. To refresh your memory:

$$\text{Net operating income} = \text{Income} - \text{Expenses}.$$

Other activities, such as obtaining or refinancing a mortgage, paydowns on a mortgage, and capital expenditures, are not concerns of a property managing company. This isn't to say that property management companies never handle these projects—but their most important function, from your viewpoint, is the daily involvement in achieving the net operating income you expect.

What ingredients make up the income of your real estate? Rent collections come to mind immediately. As the owner of commercial property, you would also be concerned with consumer price index collections, and/or common-area maintenance collections. If a tenant doesn't pay on time, the property management must follow up on these delays. Property managers make bank deposits and keep records of these activities. In addition to setting up a procedure for such tasks, you, as the owner, must have legal knowledge of the local laws pertaining to all of the above. Other activities include leasing, and making rental surveys to find out how you stand in the marketplace. You can't operate in a vacuum; you must know what other real estate businesses are charging for their square feet. Your real estate business also requires an advertising program, promotion programs, and perhaps referral contests, and mailings to potential prospects. Footwork is required, too. You or the property manager may find it necessary to visit companies in the local area to encourage them to become clients in your real estate business. All of these represent activities and tools for the orchestration of a successful marketing plan.

The above-mentioned activities tie into your anticipated revenue. Based on your expectations, a marketing plan will be designed that utilizes all of the above tools, and any others you deem necessary. But who designs this master plan? Much depends upon who is managing the property, who owns it, and who has specific responsibilities. We'll examine two scenarios.

The Buck Stops with You

We'll start with you. Suppose you don't have an on-site manager or a property manager. That leaves you with the responsibility of handling all income-oriented activities. That's a big job to fill, and you must do it well in order to protect your substantial real estate investment. Did you expect this responsibility when you signed on the dotted line? Or did you just presume that tenants pay rent regularly, and when they leave, someone else comes to the apartment almost automatically? If you own commercial property, when a lessee walks out, do you expect some other store owner to conveniently come in and take his place? Obviously, things don't happen this easily. Real estate is no different from any other commodity. Nothing happens until something is sold. All the ingredients that go into making a sale (to get people to use your square feet) are no different from the effort that goes into other businesses trying to sell stereos or tennis shoes.

The Buck Stops With Your Property Manager

The exact opposite happens when your real estate has a property management company and on-site personnel. With your approval, the property management company designs a marketing plan and a budget and supervises their execution by on-site management personnel. They use all the tools we've described above.

In between these two extremes, you can set up any combination of responsibilities. Much depends upon the extent you want to involve yourself in the management of your property.

GENERATING INCOME

Generating income isn't easy. Keep uppermost in mind the fact that your tenant or lessee is a client in your real estate business. That client is one of the most important ingredients in any business. He or she is the source of your income. Other owners of similar real estate compete against you for these clients—all the time. The better the client, the more intense the competition.

As an apartment owner, how do you convince people to come to see your building? Once prospective tenants visit, how do you convince them to lease your square feet—recognizing that other apartment owners are trying their hardest to sign up these same clients? Your competitors are offering attractive benefits similar to those you're dangling before potential clients. If you succeed in signing someone up, how do you convince that tenant to stay in your apartment building once the lease is up? You need to use all the advertising and promotional tools mentioned above.

Commercial space is even more difficult to lease. The businesses you seek to attract are more identifiable, and there are fewer potential tenants. In addition, your efforts to persuade business owners are counterbalanced by professional real estate brokers who are actively involved in leasing other commercial space. How can you succeed against this competition? Work harder and use common sense. Passive management—whether by you, the broker, or your property management firm—won't work.

Every single business needs a budget, a marketing plan, and a business plan. These are critical. A budget is a financial projection. A marketing plan is a tool designed to efficiently increase the income of a business by effectively selling its product. A business plan allows you to achieve your budget by incorporating the marketing plan in the overall strategy. *These three are key factors in the success of any business, anywhere, anyplace—especially real estate.*

Long before a real estate investor purchases property, he or she should design a business plan that seems achievable. That business plan consists of a budget plus a game plan that offers guidance in achieving that budget. On the income side, your business plan will have projections of revenues and methodology for achieving the level of income you seek. Your thinking should be, "These are my income projections, my tools, and my method for achieving goals."

An essential part of your marketing plan is a careful study of comparisons, zeroing in on the same type of real estate in your area. You and your competitors are targeting the same clients in that community, so it's essential to know what other real estate owners are doing (see Figure 13–1). How do your rents compare with theirs? What about your common-area maintenance requests? What consumer price index do they use? Whatever the income you're trying to achieve per square foot, you must be aware of the "going rate" in that area. How does your offering rank in the marketplace? Your rent survey must include the following:

- Comparable square feet.
- Comparable amenities.
- Comparable locations.
- Comparable types of clients that may be available.

Whether you're the owner of residential or commercial property, an important document in your income planning is a record of when leases expire. Long before a tenant's lease expires, you must prepare to take the initiative and convince this client to sign a new lease.

It's not enough to collect data. The next step is to analyze it. Another significant document, particularly in residential real estate, is a form that allows management to analyze the traffic coming to that particular project. You'll want to collect information about the

FIGURE 13-1
Rental Rate Survey

RENTAL RATE SURVEY

SUBJECT PROPERTY: _____
DATE: _____

PROPERTY	STUDIOS	JR. 1 BR	STD. 1 BR	DELUXE 1 BR	1 BR W/DEN	2 BR 1 BA	DELUXE 2 BR 1 BA	2 BR 1½ BA	2 BR 2 BA	3 BR	PROPERTY SQ. FT.	APT. AMENITIES	REC. AMENITIES	VACANCY STATUS/ PROMOS

number of prospective tenants who show up as "shoppers," those who are seriously interested in your square feet, and those who actually sign leases. What is the potential traffic in each of these categories? How did you attract that traffic? Was it through advertising, referrals, or other methods? Which methods work best for you? How much of that traffic resulted in new leases? Keep records so you can see what sort of income per square foot that traffic generated. You could also figure out the income per person resulting from the traffic. These numbers can help you estimate conversion percentages relating to future clients of your real estate.

As your real estate collects revenues from rental fees, it's important to have appropriate controls in place for processing the checks received. Try to eliminate handling cash, except for small amounts of petty cash. That's part of money control.

When the checks are collected at the beginning of the month, arrangements should be made to deposit them every single day. A business must balance its books on a daily basis. If they don't balance on a particular day, that only leaves one day to track the trail back.

You should receive instant bank credit for these deposits to make sure your cash flow receives the appropriate interest. In addition, any people handling cash should be bonded for an adequate amount of money, depending upon much money they handle. Accurate records need to be maintained for any delinquency of rent. In case you turn over any delinquencies to your attorney for further collection, it's essential to have proper documentation indicating that you've followed local laws exactly.

Monthly profit and loss statements should be prepared, either by your management firm or on your own.

EXPENSES: KEEPING THEM UNDER CONTROL

Expenses are more controllable than income; but they also need to be managed more intensely on an everyday basis. Here are some of the categories that go into the expense side of your profit and loss statement:

1. Personnel. You can have anywhere from 1 to 99 people employed by a particular piece of real estate. Examples include manager, one or more assistant managers, maintenance people, maids for cleaning, leasing agents, gardeners, painters, security personnel, and more. The size and needs of the property dictate the size of your staff. Regardless of number of people employed, you will have payroll expenses, Social Security payments, possibly major medical benefits, and, in some cases, profit-sharing benefits. All of these are a function of the competitiveness in your marketplace. What does the competition offer comparable personnel?

There are some strong arguments about whether certain types of job functions, such as maintenance and gardening, should be handled by employees of the real estate or assumed by outside vendors with contracts for performing those functions. Each case must be analyzed individually. There isn't a single right or wrong way. Be aware of your options and determine what makes the most sense for your particular piece of real estate.

2. Real Estate Taxes and Insurance.   Look at these constantly. Never accept the current level of payments as a sum etched in concrete. If you feel that your taxes are too high, file an appeal with the proper board, substantiating the reasons why you believe your taxes should be reduced.

Insurance bills, too, shouldn't be paid automatically. Check with other agents occasionally to see whether your current policy is competitive with theirs in terms of coverage and cost.

3. Utility Costs.   This may seem like a minor cost, but volumes have been written about ways to reduce utility costs. Some of the questions you should ask are: Which is preferable, fluorescent or incandescent lighting? When I have vacant space, should it be kept heated in the winter and air-conditioned in the summer? Should the lights be kept on? During what hours? What about hallway lights? Which is the most efficient HVAC system for my building? If the real estate is large and complicated you might consider hiring a professional engineer. This could prove to be a very cheap investment.

4. Expenses for Advertising, Mailing, Promotion, Brokerage, Referrals.   These budgeted items are part of your marketing plan. Watch and monitor them carefully. Simply because you have allocated funds for each of these items doesn't necessarily mean you must spend that money. Is a particular approach working? If it isn't effective, and you can't remedy the situation, why spend more money on that tactic? On the other hand, if your monitoring reveals that one of these techniques is working very well, spend more money on that approach. Go with the winner!

5. Maintenance.   The type and size of your property will dictate the number of items you list under the category of maintenance. Major items include painting, gardening, carpeting, carpet repairs, roof repairs, trash pickup, resurfacing, plus purchase of tools and equipment.

Experts frequently say that property management is a nickel-and-dime business—and those coins add up to millions of dollars. That's especially true when applied to maintenance expenses. This is one of the easiest areas to get out of hand. People who take the path of least resistance do the following:

- Buy items hapazardly from local stores.
- Neglect to look for quantity discounts.
- Buy even though the purchase isn't necessary.
- Don't spend time to find out about the most efficient materials.

They take the "easy" way out with piecemeal buying, assuming that each purchase is small and not of sufficient consequence. Don't make this mistake. Pay attention to maintenance expenses more intensely and consistently than expenses for other areas.

The profit and loss statement shown in Figure 13–2 provides a fairly comprehensive list of subjects involved in managing apartment units.

For people like the group of potential investors we mentioned at the beginning of the chapter, a P&L statement like this is a revelation. Its detail may seem overwhelming, yet this chart is representative of the items that will appear on your P&L statement. People who presume they can buy real estate and then casually watch it themselves have entered into an impossible situation. If they're gainfully employed, they can't put adequate effort into the management of real estate simply because they never anticipated all those items in a P&L statement. Yet staying on top of all these

FIGURE 13–2

Operating Statement (December 1987)

	DECEMBER	DEC BUDGET	VARIANCE	Y-T-D/Y-T-D BUDGET	VARIANCE
INCOME					
Rent Income					
Returned Checks (Net)					
Cleaning & Damages					
Vending Machines					
Laundry Machines					
Interest					
Late & Returned Check Charges					
Furniture Rental					
Credit Reports					
Miscellaneous Income					
Security Deposits Received					
Security Deposits Refunded					
Security Deposits Forfeited					
TOTAL INCOME					
EXPENSES					
RENTAL EXPENSE:					
Advertising					
Promotion					
Rent Concessions					
Credit Reports					
Furniture Rent & Storage					
Shopper Fees					
Signs					
Miscellaneous Rental					
TOTAL RENTAL EXPENSE					
ADMINISTRATIVE EXPENSE:					
Bad Debts					
Association Dues					
Audit					
Interest					
Legal					
Management Fee					
Managers Payroll					
Staff Units					
Office Payroll					
Office Supplies					
Payroll Taxes					
Health Insurance					
Telephone					
Business License					
Auto Allowance					
Miscellaneous Administrative					
TOTAL ADMINISTRATIVE EXPENSE					
UTILITIES:					
Electricity					
Gas					
Water					
Sewer Services					
Cable Television					
Miscellaneous Utilities					
TOTAL UTILITIES					

FIGURE 13–2

(Concluded)

	DECEMBER	DEC BUDGET	VARIANCE	Y-T-D/Y-T-D BUDGET	VARIANCE
BUILDING MAINTENANCE:					
Air Conditioning/ Heating					
Appliance Repairs					
Cleaning Payroll					
Cleaning Service					
Cleaning Supplies					
Communications					
Drapery/Carpet Cleaning					
Drapery Purchase					
Electrical					
Elevator					
Exterior Painting					
Extermination					
Fire Extinguishers					
Grounds Contract					
Grounds Payroll					
Grounds Supplies					
Lighting					
Maintenance Payroll					
Painting Payroll					
Painting Contract					
Painting Supplies					
Plumbing					
Pool/Jacuzzi					
Refuse					
Rental Equipment					
Repairs Contract					
Repairs Supplies					
Roof Repairs					
Security Payroll					
Security Supplies					
Security Services					
Smoke Alarms					
Miscellaenous Maintenance					
TOTAL BUILDING MAINTENANCE					
TAXES & INSURANCE:					
Property Insurance					
Mortgage Insurance					
Income Taxes					
Property Taxes					
TOTAL TAXES & INSURANCE					
TOTAL OPERATING EXPENSE					
NET OPERATING INCOME					
FINANCIAL EXPENSE:					
Payment on First Mortgage					
Payment on Second Mortgage					
Other Mortgages					
Miscellaneous Financial					
TOTAL FINANCIAL EXPENSE					
NET INCOME					

items is absolutely necessary if the real estate investment is to be successful.

So when do you manage, and how do you manage? If you're employed full-time, involvement in any type of active real estate management is very difficult. It works only under very unique circumstances, such as a commercial triple net lease, wherein tenants are responsible for all of the activities on that piece of real estate. It's even simpler if there is just one major tenant. In that case, you wouldn't need any management team. You would merely deposit the monthly rent and visit the property occasionally to make sure that the lessee is maintaining your asset responsibly. But this is a unique situation. Most readers of this book won't be involved in a triple net lease. That is more of an institutional type of purchase because it provides a yield with very minimal upside potential. It represents more of a credit arrangement which is determined by the quality of the lessee. The value of the real estate would diminish dramatically if the lessee were to close down his business, or move out.

In all other types of real estate investments, you'll need to set up a much more active form of property management. Your first determination should be: Can the real estate afford an on-site management person? The following guidelines are rough because many variables go into that decision. If you own apartments or commercial real estate, and you start to deal with more than 15 tenants or lessees, you will probably need—and be able to afford—an on-site management person.

There is no hard and fast rule of thumb, though. An apartment building with 15 tenants might not support an on-site manager; on the other hand, an apartment building with fewer tenants might support an on-site manager. What makes the difference? You need to determine how much income each tenant generates. What is the size of each apartment unit? Fifteen studio apartments are different from 15 three-bedroom units.

If you own commercial property, the income from 15 lessees occupying 500 square feet each is a lot different than that generated by 15 lessees operating 2,000 or 5,000 square feet each. So the amount of income generated per square foot can serve as a starting point. With this as a common denominator you now convert expenses and debt service accordingly. An analysis of these numbers will give you a clearer picture of management availability.

The outside management help you hire can vary. You might have an on-site manager who reports to you directly or who is supervised by a property management company. You could also have a property management company with or without an on-site manager. It's not necessary to have an on-site manager before hiring a property management company. That company can send its own people to visit the property from time to time, perform all the necessary maintenance, and handle leasing. The company will report back to you and keep you informed about what is going on.

Should you hire a property management company? It depends on your desires plus the ability of the real estate to absorb those expenses. Property management costs money. Yet good property management is probably one of the cheapest investments an owner can make. Property management will cost from 3 to 7 percent of the revenues collected. That could wipe out an entire return, putting the real estate into a negative cash flow position. Only you, the owner—using good, common business sense—can determine whether a property managment firm is a good investment.

SELECTION OF A PROPERTY MANAGEMENT COMPANY

The property management company you hire has a great impact on the success of your real estate investment. What are some of the characteristics you should look for?

1. Nothing substitutes for experience—*particularly in the type of real estate you own, and in your particular geographical area.*

2. How successful has the firm been with other owners? Obtain the names of others who use the firm and ask those individuals for references.

3. Visit buildings the firm manages. Look for physical proof that they've been successful in operating other real estate businesses similar to yours, and in the same area.

4. Provide the company with your business plan. Ask them to prepare a budget of income and expenses.

5. Evaluate their budget in relation to your plan to see how well they understand the potential of your property. Ask questions about how they will go about implementing your plan. If the answers satisfy you, then you can feel comfortable about hiring the company.

6. Visit the company's offices to see if they have the facilities to create all of the reports you request and that they are operating a successful company.

All property management firms assign a specific person to oversee one or more properties. When you interview a property management company, they put their best foot forward, setting up a meeting with the senior personnel. In addition, ask to see the person who will be responsible for your property—the individual your on-site manager will report to. Spend time with that individual since he or she will actually be supervising your property.

Check with several property management companies to find out the going rates for property like yours. Don't decide solely on the basis of price. Generally you get what you pay for. Be aware of how much good property management firms charge, and how much poor ones charge.

Most property management contracts are reasonably standard. Insist upon a 30-day cancellation clause within the contract. You don't want to be contractually locked in with a person or company that you find unsatisfactory. The company will commit considerable resources for the success of your real estate, so they don't want to be thrown out with one day's notice. But they aren't entitled to more than 30 days notice before you replace them with another firm.

The property management company should report to you on a monthly basis at minimum, with monthly profit and loss statements that list all income and all expenses. Compare these figures with the budget that you previously agreed to. In some categories, you're likely to find variances between the budget and actual figures. The property management company should provide you with an explanation.

PROPERTY MANAGEMENT:
PEOPLE VS. THINGS

A recurring problem with property management firms, whether they handle residential or commercial property, is the balance between dealing with people and dealing with things. Property management is made up of two ingredients:

1. Attracting clients.
2. Maintaining the real estate.

The clients of your real estate could be substantial companies or individuals. Satisfying them requires a certain dialogue and capability. On the other side of the coin, maintenance sometimes requires wearing overalls and getting into the trenches of the real estate. It covers everything from crawling underneath the building to picking up pieces of paper strewn about. This is part of the nickel-and-dime business we mentioned earlier.

The property management firm must achieve a balance between the two extremes just mentioned. You may be trying to lease space valued at several million dollars for the length of the lease. At the same time, you're concerned about taking care of shrubs and trees outside, and making sure the sidewalks are cleaned and swept.

Whether you have a property management firm or an on-site manager, chances are that the person in charge emphasizes one of the categories above to the exclusion of the other. Because of his or her experience and background, the manager may tend to work in the area which is most comfortable, thus shortchanging the other aspects of management. People tend to pay most attention to the area they have the most experience in. The result is that they become less proficient in the other area.

You may come across buildings that look beautiful but aren't leased up to the standards they deserve, with the rents they should be generating. On the other hand, some buildings that aren't as attractive as they should be always seem to be leased up.

The management company you hire *must* balance the delicate task of leasing with the nuts and bolts of regular maintenance. Obviously, the ideal you're aiming for is a good-looking building leased up with the appropriate tenants. You need the right balance of people to achieve this—people who will concern themselves with the seriousness of each area.

Marketing is probably the most difficult of these two areas. The success of marketing is always built around the prospect of being turned down. If your managers don't take the risk of being turned down, they're reducing your chances of clients signing or renewing a lease. Managers who find it much more comfortable to walk around and pick up trash are doing only half the job you require.

To keep on top of trends, join one or more of the management associations listed in the appendix and read a sampling of the trade publications listed.

TIPS TO REMEMBER

- Buying real estate wisely is just the first step in generating profits. The quality of management can make or break your investment. Your goal is to maximize net operating income.

- Good management requires a plan for generating income and controlling expenses. Work on this plan and clarify your goals before purchasing real estate.

- Survey similar property in the area to make sure your property is competitive.

- Before hiring a property manager, decide whether your real estate can generate enough income to pay the fees.

- Choose a property management company carefully, based on their experience and track record.

- Make sure your property manager balances marketing with maintenance.

CHAPTER 14

TIME TO SELL: REACHING THE END OF THE RAINBOW

When should you sell your real estate? You can apply the same principles to real estate that you do to any investment. Start your decision-making process with the question, Would I buy this particular investment now?

If the answer is no, then the next question is, Why not? When you answer the second question, you'll have a list of reasons why you wouldn't buy the investment you now own. Logic dictates that if you won't buy what you own, then why should you keep it?

Another frequently asked question is, Are all the reasons still in place to justify my original investment? If you purchased the real estate for a series of reasons and these are still intact, then the appreciation you expect is still viable. In other words, hold on to the investment.

While these two approaches help your decision-making process, there are other criteria that are unique to real estate. These are the ones to concentrate on:

1. Is the income plateauing?
2. Are capital expenditures going to increase?
3. Any combination of the above two criteria.

Let's examine these in detail.

Income Stops Growing

Has the income of your real estate business reached such a level that you don't believe you'll be able to increase it in the future?

In any business, if you think your income is plateauing, you're ultimately looking at a future reduction of profit margin. This lessening of profits affects the value of your investment. The rise in value may slow down or reach a plateau.

Rising Capital Expenditures

As a real estate owner, you'll be faced with a lengthy list of expenditures at some point in time. We can present an analogy with ownership of a car. At 50,000 miles, it's time to change the tires and put significant money into the engine. Now, you ask, "Is it worth this expenditure?" If you think you can still get a return on your money, you'll go ahead with the repairs. The same holds true for a real estate investment.

When your real estate approaches the ten-year mark, you may face major capital expenditures such as replacement of a roof, driveways, and heating systems. Is it worthwhile to go ahead and spend the money?

ANTICIPATING THE TURNING POINT

When it becomes obvious that the income is plateauing and/or capital expenditures will drain profits, the time to sell at an optimum price may have passed. At this point, when you ask, "Would I buy my real estate at the current market value?" and the answer is negative, you may already have set yourself up for a lower selling price. *As a street-smart real estate investor, you need to look for early warning signals in order to maximize the potential sale price.*

Let's remember our EVS system. That's what got you into real estate, and it can also get you out profitably. All the EVS ingredients don't vanish upon purchase. Some of them can help you choose the most appropriate time to sell. Of the seven keys (area, location, structural integrity, amenities, capitalization ratio, mortgage, and leverage), four remain alive throughout your holding period for the purpose of analyzing a sale. The other elements— amenities, mortgage, and leverage—need to be analyzed during the holding period for reasons discussed in Chapter 11. While you need to keep abreast of these three considerations, they're not as crucial as area, location, structural integrity, and capitalization ratio when you're thinking about selling.

Sometimes these four elements may stay the same, but they're more likely to get better or worse as time goes on. Ultimately, the area, location, and structure will have a significant impact on the capitalization ratio—the makeup of the income and expenses of that real estate.

Focus your attention on area, location, structural integrity, and capitalization ratio. They're the watchdogs that allow you to determine when to sell the real estate—before it hits its peak and starts to decline.

Let's look at each of these factors individually.

Area

The essence of our discussion of area in Chapter 6 encompassed the following: Is the area economically healthy? Does it have all the facilities that would support a mini-society—an employment base, housing, shopping, recreation, and cultural support? Is the trend of these activities accelerating upward? On a comparable basis, is their acceleration faster than the national average? Is the area growing faster than others nearby?

The subtopics of housing, culture, and employment included considerations such as measurement of per capita income, per capita saving income, per capita retail spending, employment percentages, the quality of the roads (including their ingress and egress), the quality of museums, and many more factors. Follow each of these throughout your holding period.

What's the key factor? *Keep your eye on the employment base.* Watch for all factors that might affect this. From employment figures, you will become aware of the other items just mentioned. How can you stay on top of trends? It's easy. Read the newspaper to see whether stores and plants are opening or closing. One of the most effective ways to feel the economic pulse is to drive through an area. When you see empty stores for lease, deterioration of shopping centers, and vacant space in office buildings, you're not just looking at empty space—you're looking at present and/or future employment problems.

FIGURE 14–1
Signals to Sell

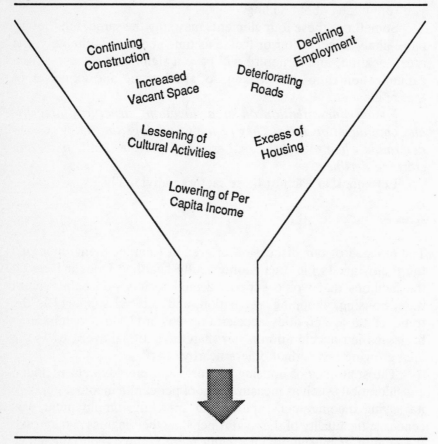

Ask your banker and people at the Chamber of Commerce about the health of local businesses. Read local business publications. This combination of field work, reading, and talking to knowledgable people will enable you to see trends. You'll know whether new businesses are coming in and boosting employment, or whether conditions are deteriorating.

Changes in your area are the first ingredient to watch. The sooner you catch these early warning signals, the sooner you'll be aware of other signals that follow one another like a series of ocean waves. A watchdog stance gives you the opportunity to take advantage of a potential decline in an area as soon as possible.

Location

You must be aware of what's happening in the area immediately surrounding your real estate. For example, if there is vacant land adjacent to it, find out as soon as possible about any changes other than the intended use. Then evaluate these changes. Remember—all the ingredients involved in the EVS don't end on purchase.

Possible changes include a business closing, an apartment house nearby experiencing high vacancies, or a school being closed down. There are numerous potential changes in the immediate surrounding land and/or buildings. One of the best ways to keep abreast of changes is to know the owners of all property in the surrounding area and stay in touch with them. If you can't get straight answers from those sources, your local bank generally has a good idea of what's happening. If they can't help, get in touch with the local planning board. *Stay in touch with everything going on in your immediate area.*

Obviously, you want to see a continuation of upscale development that will have a positive impact on your own real estate. For example, if you owned an apartment house, it would be helpful if someone built a luxurious apartment complex next door, upgrading the area, and upgrading potential rents. If you owned a store, it would be an encouraging sign to have a substantial, well-known chain open next door (with non-competing merchandise) that would bring more traffic to the area. Be constantly aware of what's going on immediately adjacent to your real estate.

Structural Integrity

In order to keep your property from "going to the dogs" you need a three-point program.

1. Every piece of real estate should have an ongoing preventive maintenance program. Our EVS checklist in Chapter 8 can serve as a guide, keeping you in touch with all aspects of the structure.

2. Develop a high awareness of your lessees' complaints.

3. Visit the real estate frequently for a visual inspection.

These three processes provide clues about what's happening to your real estate. Through visual inspections, you'll see changes in the real estate—the kinds of subtle changes that take place in structures as they grow older. You'll notice parts of the real estate buckle. Walls may lose their 90-degree angles. Some of the real estate will no longer be as efficient as before. The roof may allow some water in. Wind may come in through cracks around windows. Your parking lot may develop cracks or puddles. Your awareness of these problems—and constant maintenance—can prolong the lives of mechanical systems, walls, window fittings, and parking lot. But you can only prolong them so far. It's like our analogy of a car. By driving carefully, you may help the car's tires last longer than the average driver does. But sooner or later, they are going to wear out. A building is no different.

Your awareness of present and future deterioration can give you an edge. By watching the trend, you can put your building on the market before a particular part breaks down. The law dictates that you hide nothing from the seller. The old days of caveat emptor (buyer beware) are gone. A seller is obligated to make the potential buyer aware of any significant problems. You can't hide them. You may have to charge a lower price if the roof needs immediate repairs; but the price you receive could be higher if roof repairs won't be necessary for a few years. As a seller, you'll be in a more advantageous position if the parking lot is intact now, with some minor cracks, versus a parking lot that needs replacing immediately after purchase. By keeping a careful eye on trends through the three techniques outlined above, you'll be in an advantageous position.

Capitalization Ratio

From this discussion, you can practically predict the sequence that leads to problems with the capitalization ratio. First, there's a problem with the area's employment base. Then location is impacted. Structural integrity may not be affected by these situations, but, after a certain period of time, the capitalization ratio will feel the pinch. At this point, you're reaching the later stages. As we said earlier, problems with area, location, and structural integrity should have alerted you to action *before* they affect your capitalization ratio. By the time your capitalization ratio is affected, your income and expenses have also been affected. Increased expenses rapidly begin to take away from the potential value of your building's resale.

Always presume that the potential buyer of your building is a professional. He or she is going to ask intelligent questions. Fully anticipate that the buyer will carry out a careful due diligence examination of your building.

The potential buyer will notice a decline in income, vacancies, a lack of rental increases, and deliquencies from bad tenants. When he compares the record of your current income stream with that of increases in prior years and observes the slowdown of income, he will want this reflected in the purchase price. He *knows* that your business income is no longer accelerating.

This situation is similar to the stock market. When is the best time to sell stock? Bail out when the earnings *start* to slow down. If earnings have already slowed down, that fact is already reflected in the stock's price. You want to anticipate—and sell—long before the lackluster earnings reduce your sale price. Real estate is no different. Once the income has started to slow down and the problems of delinquencies and vacancies start to rise, you've missed the boat. At this point, any professional buyer will recognize these problems and will ask for a lower purchase price and/or a change in terms.

STEPS IN SELLING

Let's presume you've taken all the right steps. You've monitored the area and location; you've watched the structure very closely; you haven't experienced any change in the income pattern of your real estate. And you've made a decision. These trends indicate that this is a good time to sell. The next question is: What price should I ask?

Here's how to determine the value of your real estate. First, select a brokerage firm. Visit a company that has been in your area for a considerable length of time. Speak to the manager, discussing your needs and wants. Then he can match your needs and personality with the most appropriate broker. If, for any reason, the relationship between you and the broker doesn't work out, you have recourse to the manager. At this point, he or she can give you another broker, or you can terminate your relationship with that firm.

Deal with representatives from at least two different real estate brokerage firms. Have each one come in at separate times to evalute your real estate. Indicate to each one that you're thinking of giving him or her the opportunity to sell your real estate. Ask each one to estimate a fair price for the property. There's nothing wrong with dealing with two or more people at this time. You are examining the possibility of a relationship and would like to see how the broker handles the evaluation of your real estate. Each individual will come up with a price and terms. Put this in a file for the moment.

Simultaneously, you should be reading the real estate section of your local newspaper. Look for offerings of real estate comparable to yours, and for statistics on recent sales of similar property. What are the prices? Follow up on ads for real estate similar to yours. If an address is given, drive by, look at the property, and compare it to yours. In addition, assume the role of a prospective buyer and send away for information. Study the information and see how the other property relates to yours. Look for common denominators. For example, since the amount of square feet in commercial buildings (office buildings and shopping centers) may not be exactly the same, reduce their figures to prices on a per-square-foot basis. With apartment houses, figure out the price per unit—but make sure there's a comparison of the number of bedrooms and all amenities. The comparison analysis chart in Figure 13–1 shows the information you'll need to compare apartments.

Gather information on all of the comparables that exist in the immediate area. Compare data on price and terms with your real estate. Try to be as objective as possible. Everyone believes that his or her real estate is unique and better than the rest. Let the facts talk for you.

Base your choice of brokerage firm and broker on their experience with your type of real estate, how familiar they are with the area, and what their track record is for similar sales. If you decide to use a broker, keep in mind that his or her ambition is to have you sign a contract to list the property as long as possible. The broker will want exclusive rights for the sale of the building and will insist that he or she must be in absolute control for a long period of time in order to do the best job for you. A broker's motivation for selling is based entirely on the size of the commission. However, it isn't in your best interest to tie up the building for an extended period of time with one firm or individual. That person's interests may become sidelined to another activity; or the person may not live up to your expectations. There's a certain chemistry necessary between broker and seller. If that doesn't develop, you're at a disadvantage. Remember, that broker is becoming your employee.

From your standpoint, it's best to sign for the shortest listing. That might be 30 or 60 days, and certainly not more than 90 days. If the broker is doing a satisfactory job—bringing in many people and talking to them about the building—you can extend the listing. But the option should always be yours. It's more advantageous to extend a shorter exclusive listing than to lock up the agreement for an extended period of time. The argument is simple: If the broker does a good job, then your extensions will result in a long-term agreement. If that person feels the need for the security of a long-term contract, maybe he has doubts about his ability to do a good job.

If you want to sign an exclusive listing, that's fine. But, before you sign, consider whether you have potential leads of your own, or might develop any. It would be a shame to pay a broker a commission for a sale that results from your effort. Therefore, before signing an exclusive listing, include in the agreement a stipulation that if the real estate is sold to one of your leads, the broker will not receive a commission. The broker will probably want those leads specified—and that's fair.

Another advantage to having a short-term contract and renewing it is the flexibility you gain. If you develop a new relationship with some individual, on renewal of the contract you can include that individual into the list of potential buyers whose purchase would eliminate the need to pay the broker a commission.

Setting a Price and Terms

Price is easier to set than terms. Earlier in this book, we discussed price and terms in our discussion of buying real estate. Now we're interested in the other end of the transaction. Incidentally, when purchasing real estate, try to negotiate the price based on today's income and tomorrow's expenses. When you're selling, try to establish a price based on tomorrow's income and today's expenses.

How much cash will you receive from the sale? How much will you take back in the form of notes, if any? Will you receive enough money to pay off all your mortgages, your tax liability, and an additional amount that you had planned to use for some other purchase? You'll need to answer these important questions when setting up the terms as well as the potential sales price of your real estate. If you think you can get a more attractive price by taking notes, when will you need the additional cash? The answer determines the length of the second note or second mortage that you may take back in addition to the cash on sale.

What elements should you consider before deciding to take back a note? Do you need the income that will be provided from either the cash or the note? That dictates to a large degree what type of interest rate you will have. There are many ways to put together a combination of cash and notes to help make a transaction. *But, first and foremost, determine your own needs. Let them be a guideline for setting the three key ingredients of a note: length of time, amount, and interest rate.* These three considerations are important—and the only ones that go into your decision about a second note.

Determine what you're going to do with the sale proceeds and check with your accountant before you set the terms and receive the money. This helps make sure that you don't incur any additional tax liability.

Don't try to squeeze every last penny out of the buyer. Aim for a reasonable price that satisfies you.

Cleaning Up Your Act

Let's assume you purchased the real estate at the right time and the right price. Now you've determined that this is the appropriate time to sell. You've decided what constitutes a fair price and terms. What's next on the list? Put everything in order. In other words, clean your real estate. Professionals call the result of this activity "improved curb appeal."

If you were to drive past the real estate and pull up alongside the curb, what kind of feeling would that property project? Neatness and cleanliness project a good, favorable feeling. Everything looks solid and intact, without cracks. Trees are trimmed. Lawns look neat. Windows are clean. There's no debris on walkways. Freshly painted doors beckon. Hardware on them looks in tip-top condition. People feel good about neat, clean-looking real estate. It encourages them to enter negotiations for a sensible price.

Your investment in cleaning real estate—getting it ready for sale—pays off. The time and money you spend is cheap compared to the potential results in terms of additional dollars in your pocket. It usually isn't necessary to undertake structural changes at this time. A prospective buyer looking at an apartment house with curb appeal feels comfortable; the building conveys an aura that good tenants live there. A retail store with curb appeal looks like an attractive place to shop, and that means money in the bank for the real estate owner. When everything is in order, your real estate projects a comfort level that's translated back into significant dollars and better terms for you in the sales price.

There's no special trick to achieving this comfort level. Just use common sense. Walk through your building and grounds, making a list of everything that needs to be cleaned. If you can do it yourself, fine. If you need to hire and direct maintenance people, handle the job that way.

Marketing Your Real Estate

Now that you've prepared your real estate for sale, how do you market it? One of the most important determinations for successful marketing is the one that zeros in on exactly what type of real estate you have. It's not enough to say, "I'm selling an apartment house," or "I own a shopping center." Exactly what type of real estate do you own? This may seem like a very simple question, but asking it sets the stage for the success you'll achieve when selling the real estate.

For example, are you selling a private home, an apartment house, a shopping center or an office building? The second important question is: What are the special characteristics of that real estate? If you're selling a private home, is it an expensive one? Is it a unique type of home? In what way? Is there something special about your apartment house? Does it cater to families or single people? Does your office building have a single tenant, or is it divided into many small offices that cater to small business professionals?

Why do we emphasize the importance of determining the type of real estate and focusing on its idiosyncrasies? Potential buyers will follow traditional methods of finding out about real estate for sale. For example, certain publications offer homes for the wealthy. Others help promote the sale of retail space and/or office space with unique characteristics. Some brokerage firms specialize in apartment buildings. Others handle commercial space. There are brokerage firms that specialize in suburban real estate; others concentrate on urban real estate. There are support publications for all of these activities. Thus, it's very important that the following steps take place:

1. Choose an experienced broker who has potential buyers for the type of real estate you're selling.
2. Make sure that your type of real estate is advertised in the appropriate publications.

Another technique for boosting sales possibilities consists of traditional, old-fashioned signs directing people to your property. This alerts people who may be driving in the area that your property is for sale. Signage must be attractive; it is symbolic of an attractive building. The printing should be clear and include a phone number for contacting the broker.

While You're Waiting for a Buyer

Be patient. Don't expect to sell your real estate on the first day. Before you can make a sale, it takes the right person for the right piece of real estate. Listen to the comments people make when examining your real estate. Their remarks may clue you in to the necessity for making refinements. As the selling process goes on, carefully monitor it. This helps confirm that you've taken all of the right steps. People's remarks will also reveal whether you've targeted the correct potential buyers. Make sure your broker is involved in this monitoring process. It's your real estate, but the broker should give you feedback and recommendations. If your broker mentions that nobody is coming to look at the real estate, that's an important bit of news. It signifies several possibilities:

1. Your advertising is poor.
2. The broker didn't show the property to other brokers.
3. The signage is poor.
4. Your broker isn't accustomed to selling this type of real estate.

If monitoring confirms that you're attracting traffic, and people are asking reasonable questions, then be patient. Sooner or later you're going to have a buyer willing to sign a contract at the terms and price that will assure you of a successful sale.

What Next?

It's happened. You've found a buyer who has examined the real estate, given a deposit, and arranged for his financing. That deposit now becomes what is known in the trade as "hard money." This means it's non-refundable. The closing date is set and you're ready to be notified by the title company. Despite all this good news, you can't afford to be passive now.

Figure 14–3 shows a typical proration statement you'll receive at the closing of escrow for an apartment house.

You, or someone representing you, should be present at the title company to review all the documentation and mathematics. First, you should have a copy of the purchase agreement or contract with you. Don't trust your memory. Review this document to make sure the title company has complied with the agreement. Bring along a calculator. Be prepared to calculate *all* totals and prorations. Review all supporting documentation to get to the totals. As an example, review the rent roll to verify occupancy and income.

Because of the tremendous volume of numbers that go into the computation of a transaction, it's common for errors to creep

FIGURE 14–2
Sample Closing Pro-Ration Sheet

TITLE COMPANY

PROPERTY:	CHARGES	CREDITS
Consideration of Sale Price	$ 1,085,000.00	$
Paid Outside of Escrow		
Deposits		190,000.00
By First Deed of Trust		
By Second Deed of Trust		
all inclusive trust deed to seller		1,005,000.00
Pro-Rations Made as of: 12/4/87		
taxes for half year $13,413.55, paid to 7/1/87		11,401.51
rent at $8,254.00 per month, paid to 1/1/87 (49 units)		7,428.51
rent at $150.00 per month, paid to 12/22/87 (1 unit)		90.00
Rent at $3,753.00 per month, paid to 12/15/87 (21 units)		1,376.10
Security Deposits		4,268.00
Commission Paid to:		
Policy of Title Insurance additional title & escrow fee	100.00	
Transfer Tax Stamps		
Recording Deed	2.80	
Recording Trust Deed	4.40	
Recording certificate of limited partnership	6.80	
pay first and second half taxes	26,827.10	
Reconveyance Fee		
Escrow Fee		
Drawing Deed		
Drawing Trust Deed		
charge buyer, credit seller prepaid interest on all	100,000.00	
inclusive trust deed		
change of records fee – Mortgage Company	40.00	
credit buyer, charge seller in lieu of termite repairs		8,500.00
Balance Due	16,083.02	
Balance Due You for Which Our Check is Enclosed		
TOTALS	$ 1,228,064.12	$ 1,228,064.12

in. Most real estate professionals will tell you that they almost always detect errors that *might* not have been corrected later on if they hadn't reviewed the numbers at that time. There's no guarantee that anyone representing you would have the initiative or patience to question every number on the title sheet for your benefit. You must make sure that every credit and debit is correct.

TIPS TO REMEMBER

- Sell when the income from your real estate indicates the beginning of a plateau, or capital expenditures start to increase, or a combination of both occurs.
- Don't wait until you experience a turndown in profits. Anticipate problems and sell before this happens.
- Maintain your property well throughout the holding period. You'll have less to clean up in order to generate curb appeal.
- Constantly monitor these four elements of the Economic Valuation System: area, location, structural integrity, and capitalization ratio.
- Set a fair price. Professional buyers *know* when a price is excessive and they'll shun your property.
- Choose a broker experienced in your type of real estate.
- Choose a broker experienced in the area where your real estate is located.
- Sign your contract with a broker for the shortest term.
- Arrange for terms that minimize your tax liability.
- Zero in on potential buyers most likely to puchase your property. Monitor the selling process.
- Review all escrow papers carefully.

CHAPTER 15

KNOWING WHERE YOU ARE

In this chapter, you'll learn one final secret of street-smart real estate investors: timing. There's no "bad" time to buy; the secret is to adapt your strategy to the current market, whatever phase of a cycle it is in. Are you at the top? The bottom? Is the market turning around? Knowing where you are in a real estate cycle holds the key to greater profits; it also can impact the length of time you will hold the real estate. By buying at the wrong part of the cycle your holding period could be extended for many more years.

You've learned how to dramatically increase the probability of good returns by using the Economic Valuation Process. When you combine that knowledge with a plan for action that incorporates optimum timing, you will have a winning game plan. If you believe the real estate market is topping out, you can still achieve good returns, but you don't have to be as aggressive in your buying. Conversely, if you believe you are at the bottom of a cycle, you can afford to buy more aggressively. Your holding period for the real estate will be shorter, and your yield will be dramatically greater. How can you judge where you are in a cycle? First, you need to understand all factors that impact the real estate market.

Although the principles in this book will be as useful fifty years from now as they are today, we need a starting point in our discussion. Since this book is being written in the autumn of 1987, it's appropriate to start with the current situation. Right now, the general public believes that four factors are impacting the real estate market: inflation, deflation, taxes, and bankruptcies. These factors are rarely understood.

Where Are We Today?

We're currently in a period of very low inflation. Inflation rates are approximately 2 percent to 3 percent. In some respects, a case could be made to support the position that we're in a deflationary market. This occurs when prices are going up at a slower rate than earnings, making money more valuable.

Many people believe that taxes have a great impact on the value of real estate. In October 1986, Congress passed the single most significant tax reform bill in the history of this country. This bill removed many of the tax advantages real estate previously enjoyed.

General partnerships are experiencing an extraordinarily high rate of bankruptcies. Savings and loan associations are impacted by mortgages having negative values as a result of there being no equity in certain real estate. A great deal of real estate is valued at less than the debt on it.

These scenarios are all happening at once. Do they signify the top of the market? The bottom? Or are there tops and bottoms occuring simultaneously in multiple markets?

Let's go back to the beginning by looking at four myths that distort the average person's conception of timing.

Inflation

Many people believe that real estate is an inflation hedge—and that you must have inflation in order to invest in real estate successfully. They'll tell you, "Property values increase when we're in a period of inflation. Don't invest in real estate unless you have inflation." These statements are all false.

Later in this chapter, we'll demonstrate that inflation has no impact on the particular market cycle you're in. Only two types of real estate might be affected by inflation: (1) a private home and (2) commercial real estate with leases tied to indices that reflect the rate of inflation.

A private home is the purest form of real estate. All things being equal, if the neighborhood doesn't change dramatically and there aren't any changes in sociological values in the area, replacement cost becomes the ultimate driving force behind creating the value. There are no profit and loss statements, and no cash flow. Thus the replacement cost is the benchmark. As costs to build comparable homes escalate, the price of a home will increase.

As far as commercial real estate with leases tied to inflation indices is concerned, the inflationary rate will affect values in some respects, but not entirely. We'll discuss this in more detail later in the chapter.

Deflation

Some doomsayers believe that deflation is the kiss of death. They'll declare, "In a deflationary period, don't invest in real estate. Run from it. Liquidate your holdings and avoid owning any real estate." Nonsense. That couldn't be further from the truth. Deflation does not have an impact on the overall return on real estate.

Tax Reform

Here's another myth: Real estate by itself doesn't provide sufficient returns; it isn't an attractive investment unless there are tax advantages. The truth is that tax returns and good real estate are not necessarily synonymous. If they happen to come together, it's purely by accident.

Bankruptcies

We're living in an era of bankruptcies triggered by real estate problems. Does this mean that if you invest in real estate, you'll go bankrupt? No.

To sum up, inflation is not necessary for a successful real estate investment. Neither inflation or deflation will impact or detract from a successful real estate investment. You don't need tax benefits to make profits in real estate. And, even though some people are having problems that force them into bankruptcy, that should not affect your real estate investing. These four ingredients we've discussed, which are the overriding considerations on today's market, may impact the decision-making process of some investors. But, in reality, these factors have little or no impact on what happens in the real estate market. The best way to prove this is to discuss inflation in more detail.

THE MYTH OF INFLATION

You do *not* need inflation to make a real estate investment work out. Frequently, when a real estate consultant predicts that rents in a particular building will increase, novice investors ask, "What rate of inflation did you factor in?" They assume that if the inflation rate is 5 percent, rental increases will also be 5 percent—or if the rate of inflation is 10 percent, then the rental increases will also be 10 percent. Not so! Rental increases have nothing to do with inflation.

What *does* affect real estate? In earlier chapters we've emphasized that profits create value in real estate. The ability to operate at a profit, generating a strong bottom line, creates value. You help create that profit by being able to increase the income— by the ability to increase rents. Following this cause-and-effect scenario, keep in mind the point we've been emphasizing all along: real estate is a business; a business that buys, sells, and leases square feet. The ability to succeed in this business rests upon your ability to charge more for those square feet, while you control expenses. This develops an ever-widening profit margin, thereby increasing your profits, and subsequently increasing the value of your real estate.

When does a landlord increase the rent? He or she can do so when the building is full, totally disregarding whether or not inflation exists. If a building is full and there is no inflation, the landlord will increase rent. If the building is half full and the rate of inflation is high, the landlord *cannot* increase the rent.

What is the driving force behind the ability to increase the income and, subsequently, the profitability of real estate? The driving force is *supply and demand*. This is no different from any other business. Your product is square feet. When there's an excess of square feet, you have vacancies—unusable square feet—competition increases dramatically, and you are unable to increase your income. When there is a shortage of square feet, occupancy is high—more clients are competing for those square feet. As a landlord, you can then increase the cost of those square feet by increasing the rent. If you investigate conditions in various parts of the country, you'll find that a lack of rental increases is the result of vacancies which are a function of excess capacity.

REAL ESTATE CYCLES

Real estate is a cyclical industry. Like other cyclical industries, it creates excesses and shortages. Look at the historical pattern. Even in Roman times, shortages alternated with excesses. Why is real estate cyclical? One explanation is that real estate development has always been in the hands of the entrepreneur; it has never been corporatized. In instances where corporations have become involved in real estate development, their flirtation with it has been short-lived. Bethelehem Steel, ITT, U.S. Steel, and many other major corporations have attempted to get into real estate. But the rhythm of the real estate development business is entrepreneurial by nature. It just doesn't lend itself to the type of rhythm that exists in corporations. Corporations move by committees, manuals, and procedures which are fairly rigid. Changes in decisions are generally slow to take place. The entrepreneur forces a faster decision-making process and is generally more adaptable to change. Neither one is wrong—they just operate differently.

By virtue of its entrepreneurial nature, real estate development is not long-term in its planning. Entrepreneurs have historically tended to construct real estate with total disregard for its demand. If credit and money are available, developers will build. This pattern, repeated through the years, results in an excess of real estate from time to time. Later in this chapter, we'll discuss these trends and how they lead to real estate cycles.

One Size Doesn't Fit All

The one-size-fits-all concept may work with stretch socks, but, in terms of economics, it falls short. Diverse geographical regions don't fit into a single mold. Thus it's essential to know what cycle you're in, relative to where you live. As our country has matured, it no longer moves with any degree of uniformity. In the past, if unemployment was 6 percent in New York, it reached almost identical levels in the South, Midwest, and West. When a recession developed, the entire country suffered. A period of inflation affected all parts of the country. An economic recovery was felt in all geographic areas. Today, one region may be experiencing a boom while another struggles with high unemployment.

Many years ago, business people often quoted the saying, "As General Motors goes, so goes the country." This is no longer true. The United States is no longer a manufacturing nation; it is built around many different industries, including service, finance, and manufacturing. As a result, the country has become very fractionalized economically. Different sections of the nation are in different parts of the economic cycle. Carrying this thought further, different regions are in different parts of *the real estate cycle.*

Some sections of the country are at the bottom of the real estate cycle; some are at the top. This means that some regions are overbuilt and others are underbuilt. Thus, while prices in certain parts of the country are very high, in other regions prices might be very low. *Before buying real estate in your area, determine what point of the cycle exists there.*

Furthermore, not only do you have different sections of the country in different parts of a cycle—you also discover that *different types of real estate will be in different parts of a cycle.* Each behaves in a unique manner, within a defined part of the cycle.

For example, in the region where you live, office buildings may be at the bottom part of the market cycle, shopping centers in the middle part, and apartments at the top of the cycle. Thus it's conceivable that office buildings could have a 15 percent vacancy, shopping centers a 10 percent vacancy, and apartments no vacancies. These cycles, created by local supply and demand, will have an impact on the type of real estate you choose to buy. They will also affect your selling decisions.

The Four Phases of a Real Estate Cycle

The ups and downs of real estate can be divided into four parts. Figure 15–1 shows them graphically.

One phase of the cycle represents the bottom of the real estate market for a certain period of time. This is followed by a period

FIGURE 15–1
The A, B, C, and D of a Real Estate Cycle

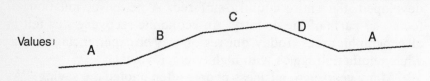

of time in which real estate values break away from the bottom and head in an upward direction. Next comes the top phase of the cycle, which remains at a high level for some time. Then comes the downturn, ultimately connecting with the bottom of the market. In Figure 15–1, these are designated B, C, D, and A.

Averages aren't etched in concrete—but as a point of reference, since World War II, each phase of a cycle has lasted an average of two years. Thus, if you bought at the beginning of a cycle bottom and sold at the beginning or middle of the following top, you would be holding that real estate for approximately five or six years. If you decided to hold on through another complete cycle, you would eventually sell for a higher price. But there's a tradeoff. By purchasing real estate at the bottom of a cycle and selling at the first top, you achieve the maximum profits in the shortest period of time. This presumes you are in an area of the country that is average.

Now comes the hard part. How can you tell which phase of a cycle you're currently in? Presently, we'll list the characteristics which will help you identify those phases. The most difficult part comes when you attempt to analyze how long that phase will last. As an example, let's look at the current real estate situation in the Southwest, particularly in energy-and farm-related areas.

Economic problems, combined with overbuilding in Houston, indicate that the bottom phase could last much longer than two years. It may last five or six years, and even longer in some cases. You may recall that certain parts of the country suffered from effects of overbuilding between 1974 and approximately 1981. Florida, which suffered extensively, required five years to fully recover. So even though we've indicated that each phase of a real estate cycle is approximately two years, this depends upon several factors. Areas that receive the largest amount of publicity—Florida, for example—generally have the most extensive overbuilding.

FIGURE 15–2
Criteria for Real Estate Cycles

	A	B	C	D	A
VALUES	Depressed	Increasing	Increasing	Declining	Depressed
RENTS	Low	Increasing	Increasing	Declining	Low
NEW CONSTRUCTION	V. little	Increasing	Booming	Slowing	V. little
OCCUPANCY LEVEL	Low	Increasing	High	Decreasing	Low
VACANCY LEVEL	High	Beginning to Decrease	Low	Increasing	High
INVESTOR CONFIDENCE	Low	Negative to neutral	Positive	Sl. negative	Low
PROFIT MARGINS	Low	Improving	Widest	Decline	Low
ACTION	Buy	Second best time to buy	Sell	Be cautious	Buy

They're perceived as growth areas and their boom atmosphere attracts developers who can build more easily without restrictions. This fuels the boom and the overbuilding. It also leads to a longer recovery time.

Houston is currently at the bottom of a cycle, and it's difficult to predict how long it will stay at that level. The northeastern part of the country, particularly Boston, is at the top of a cycle.

How aggressive should your buying and selling be? Your plan for action depends upon the phase of the real estate cycle. The first step calls for identifying that phase. Let's begin our discussion with the bottom phase, the A in Figure 15–1 and Figure 15–2.

The Market Bottom
Take a look at the horizon in your city. During the A phase, you won't notice any building cranes silhouetted against the skyline. If

you don't see those cranes, no construction is taking place. No additional square feet are being created. Thus the natural absorption forces are taking place.

Since you have reached the bottom of the cycle, what's happening to the real estate? Occupancy levels are very low—or, to put it differently, vacancy rates are high. You see many "For Lease" signs. You notice empty commercial buildings. Apartment owners are offering all sorts of special concessions in order to attract tenants.

In the newspaper, you'll come across an abundance of negative articles on real estate. You'll read about many foreclosures resulting from the vacant, excess space that had previously been created in the marketplace. Business writers may comment on the dramatic increase in tenant improvements in commercial real estate, and how this adds to the landlord's expenses in processing new leases. Incentives relating to tenant improvements and concessions add to the landlord's costs and bring about deteriorating profit margins. The scenario continues to darken. These deteriorating profit margins, and decreased (or zero) profits, result in negative cash flow and, often, bankruptcy.

When too many square feet have been created, the above-mentioned conditions prevail. At this bottom point, developers cease to create additional square feet. Street-smart real estate investors regard this scenario as the accumulation stage. This is not a theory of contra-investing; it is the recognition of the economic conditions and opportunities that exist when there is an excess of square feet in the marketplace.

The Beginnings of an Upward Move

What indicates a turnaround? Don't look for signals from an increase in rents or the emergence of inflation. Those happen later on. Instead, during Phase B, look for the number of vacancies to start decreasing. You'll see articles about apartment vacancies dropping from 8 percent to 6 percent. Commercial space that had a vacancy rate of 10 percent may now have a rate of 8 percent. As these vacancies start to decline (because new construction has been slowed or halted), you'll know that you are now into Phase B. There's an air of neutrality. You won't see encouraging signs such as rents increasing; but neither will you see discouraging signs such as constant talk of people losing money, and of bankruptcies. Because vacancies are starting to decline, investor perception is somewhat encouraged; the downtrend is over. At this stage, street-smart real estate investors increase the accumulation of real estate.

Approaching the Summit

During Phase C, you begin to approach the top of the market. Vacancies have gone down and landlords have increased rents. Investor confidence approaches its peak. Newspapers proclaim that it's a wonderful time to invest because rents are going up. But these same newspapers don't understand that this "wonderful time" is already reflected in the prices of real estate. The disappearance of vacancies and increase in rents mirror the fact that shortages have been developing. This is a boon to builders for two reasons:

1. They can lobby the government for incentives to create additional real estate in response to shortages—in housing, office buildings, and shopping centers. Traditionally, the government responds with some sort of subsidy through tax advantages.

2. As rents increase, they will reach levels that ultimately make it economically justifiable to begin a new wave of construction.

In Phase A, rents were decreasing, not increasing. Landlords gave away concessions. As the rents were being reduced, the cost of manufacturing real estate continued to increase. Throughout Phase A and Phase B, developers were squeezed and unlikely to make profits. Thus construction slowed down and money became unavailable to them. During Phase C, money becomes available to developers and they gear up for action. With total disregard for demand, they continue to build until excesses are created in the marketplace. By then, development no longer makes sense economically. This shuts off the supply of capital that makes construction possible. The government takes one step back and says, "Wait. We're subsidizing the creation of vacant real estate, and the market is already glutted. That doesn't make sense. We can direct our incentives to other sociological needs." The goverment then cuts off their incentives. This may not happen to all real estate, since, as we have seen, all types of real estate don't move in tandem.

You must examine each piece of real estate within your marketplace to see which phase of the cycle each is in.

When the news is good, it signifies that rents are being increased and values are moving up. These are the times when additional development takes place. As this development surges, what happens? Rental increases begin to slow down and ultimately stop. You begin to notice increasing vacancies. You have now entered Phase D, the downturn.

The Downturn

Phase C and Phase D are the most unattractive times to invest. You can still have a successful investment if you follow the Economic Valuation System, but you will have to wait a longer time. You'll have to pass through C, B, A, D, and Phase C once again in order to maximize your return. Thus *the aggressiveness with which you approach your buying and selling activities depends a great deal on an understanding of which phase of the cycle you are in with regard to your particular type of real estate and its geographical location.*

A Brief Look at History

A glimpse at the period from approximately 1967 to 1987 offers an interesting illustration of real estate cycles. During that time, capital came from several different sources and we've had four reasonably predictable cycles. In the late 1960s, money was available through very low-cost debt. The debt cost was generally at rates that were less than the rate of inflation. As a result, for a period of approximately ten years, investors had a positive spread between their borrowing costs and the rate of inflation.

During the following five years, commercial banks fronted for the REITs through Wall Street and raised a considerable amount of money—in excess of $25 billion. This created a tremendous amount of overbuilding. Finally, in the early 1980s, taxes became the driving force behind the creation of capital. The 1980 tax act created the concept of 15-year depreciation and the ability to design real estate deals with a very high degree of deductibility. Too many people stopped analyzing real estate in terms of intrinsic value; they simply looked at it as a tax vehicle—a way to get money back from the government, and, in fact, pay no taxes.

These three different sources of capital—low cost debt, Wall Street, and, finally, tax benefits that the government gave and then took away—show how creative developers can be when trying to obtain money for development.

Cycles and Profit Margins

At the top of a real estate cycle, you will see many building cranes in action. This is a tipoff that developers are busy creating a considerable amount of square feet. They're also creating a tug-of-war that signifies the beginning of a deteriorating profit margin. Since profits are the ultimate guide to the success of an investment, the greater your profits, the more your investment will appreciate. Added to that, the ability to manage your investment, controlling income over expenses, means a widening profit margin and further appreciation.

The four phases of a real estate cycle are a study of the four phases of the profit margin in real estate. At the bottom of the cycle, in Phase A, your profit margins are the narrowest, because your vacancies are at their highest level and you're forced to make concessions to tenants. As this condition starts to improve, through Phase B, vacancies now disappear for the most part. Rents increase and concessions decrease to the point that they no longer exist. You are now entering an era of widening profit margins. Construction has not materially increased so very little new square footage enters the marketplace.

As you reach Phase C, you are now at the widest part of your profit margin, generating the highest amount of profits because the small amount of square footage under construction is not significant. At this point, where your profit margin is the widest, you will be able to attract buyers and achieve the highest price and best terms when you sell.

As development gears up, your profit margin begins its downturn. Your potential sales price and good terms also start to decline.

Final Thoughts

When you buy real estate, don't look for a home run. You can increase your net worth with bunts, singles, and doubles. Some of these hits may turn into a home run, but you won't know the outcome when you purchase the real estate. You simply want to have a good batting average. Remember our earlier discussion on the difficulty of recovering from a loss. Looking for home runs involves an unnecessary degree of high risk. When you buy real estate, don't presume to steal it. Don't think you'll walk away with an extraordinary value. That's not how you buy real estate. Presume that the seller is just as smart as you are; he knows what the real estate is worth. What you want to do is simply pay a fair value for that real estate. Where does your skill come in? You want to see the future more clearly than the seller. That's the potential home run. But expect to pay a fair value.

The following true story offers a revealing glimpse of fair value in the marketplace. A group of very successful businessmen had just purchased an attractive apartment house and paid a price which was considerably less than the replacement cost for a new building with similar amenities. They paid a price amounting to $15,000 per apartment unit and considered this purchase a "steal."

CYMROT:

What is the occupancy?

BUSINESSMAN:

It's approximately 40 percent.

CYMROT:

I understand you own a another business. Is it successful?

BUSINESSMAN:

Yes.

CYMROT:

Would it be worth much less if you were to lose 60 percent of your clients?

BUSINESSMAN:

Of course.

CYMROT:

Why is the real estate any different? With the present occupancy rate, 60 percent of your clients are non-existent.

We've said this earlier, but it's important to emphasize— the most difficult cost to estimate in real estate, and the one that is always significantly more than you ever thought it would be, is the lease-up cost. This businessman thought he had "stolen" something; yet he paid only what that real estate was worth. He'll experience a considerable amount of negative cash flow until he gets that property back to a fully occupied status. Considering the amount of money he'll need to spend, his final cost won't be much different from the price that the real estate would have been worth if he had bought it at a fair market value when it was fully occupied. There's no reason to take chances like this. Be prepared to pay a fair value for good real estate.

Never be forced into buying a piece of real estate you aren't comfortable with because it is the "last opportunity." There is no last opportunity in real estate. Be patient and you'll find another excellent opportunity.

Entering into a partnership might pave the way for you to buy larger pieces of real estate. But don't team up with people with dissimilar objectives. It's wiser to buy smaller properties with fewer partners who have similar interests.

Buy real estate that generates a positive cash flow now. Make sure that cash flow comes from the real estate itself and not from some financial guaranties provided by the seller.

Be familiar with all costs in the transaction. Don't find yourself short of cash because of title insurance costs, legal fees, and insurance expenses. When you sell real estate, understand the cost of transferring deposits over to the new owner, including pro rata costs that would be incurred for part of the insurance and real estate taxes. Discuss all procedures and potential costs with the real estate broker or the title company. When you sell, be aware of your expected proceeds.

TIPS TO REMEMBER

- The driving force behind your ability to raise rents is supply and demand, not inflation.
- Real estate cycles are not uniform throughout the country. Determine the phase of the real estate cycle in your geo-

graphic area, and for the type of real estate you own or plan to purchase.

- If you use the Economic Valuation System, the success of your real estate investment doesn't depend upon real estate cycles. However, by observing cycles, you can shorten the holding period and make profits faster.

- At the bottom of a real estate cycle, profit margins are the narrowest.

- You can recognize that an uptrend is starting when vacancies begin to decline. This is the optimum time to accumulate real estate.

- An understanding of real estate cycles helps improve your timing in making buying and selling decisions.

EPILOGUE

While learning about the techniques of street-smart real estate investing, I hope you have been provoked. Many people never move off that line of least resistance known as the "easy way." They defer action, waiting for a vague tomorrow that never materializes.

Learning alone doesn't generate results. Utilization of knowledge brings about accomplishments. I want to provoke you to take action—to move away from the steady stream of average people and join the upper quartile of individuals who enjoy a higher quality of life.

Knowledge without action remains abstract. Action without knowledge can have disastrous results. By synchronizing knowledge and action, you'll use the principles of successful real estate investing in many transactions. As you build your net worth, you can take extended vacations, send your children to college, enjoy the lifestyle you deserve, and perhaps retire early.

Thank you for reading this book. By showing you how to increase your net worth, I hope I've added some meaning to the quality of your life and to that of your loved ones.

ALLEN CYMROT

APPENDIX

REAL ESTATE-RELATED ASSOCIATIONS

1. Department of Housing & Urban Development
   Multifamily Housing Division
   451 Seventh Street, S.W.
   Washington, D.C. 20410
   202/755–6495

2. Manufactured Housing Institute
   1745 Jefferson Davis Highway, #611
   Arlington, Virginia 22202
   703/979–6620

3. Mortgage Bankers Association
   1125 15th Street, N.W.
   Washington, D.C. 20005
   202/861–6500

4. National Apartment Association
   1111 14th Street, N.W., #900
   Washington, D.C. 20005
   202/842–4050
   Publications:
      Multi-Housing Advocate (monthly)
      Units (quarterly advertiser)

5. National Association of Home Builders
   15th & M Streets, N.W.
   Washington, D.C. 20005
   202/822–0200
   Publications:
      NAHB News (weekly)
      Builder (monthly advertiser)

6. National Association of Housing and Redevelopment Officials
   1320 18th Street, N.W.
   Washington, D.C. 20036
   202/429–2960
   Publications:
   Journal of Housing (monthly)
   NAHRO Monitor (semimonthly)

7. National Association of Neighborhoods
   1651 Fuller Street, N.W.
   Washington, D.C. 20009
   202/332–7766
   Publication:
   NAN Bulletin (monthly)

8. National Association of Real Estate Editors
   P.O. Box 129
   Burlingame, California 94011
   415/344–2600

9. National Association of Real Estate Investment Trusts
   1101 17th Street, N.W., #700
   Washington, D.C. 20036
   202/785–8717

10. National Association of Realtors
    777 14th Street, N.W.
    Washington, D.C. 20005
    202/383–1000

11. National Conference of States on Building Codes and Standards
    481 Carlisle Drive
    Herndon, VA 22070
    703/437–0100
    Publications:
    Bulletin (bi-monthly)
    Newsletter (bi-monthly)

12. National Institute of Real Estate Management
    430 N. Michigan Avenue
    Chicago, Illinois 60611
    312/661–1930

13. National Leased Housing
2300 M Street, N.W.
Washington, D.C. 20037
202/785-8888
Publication:
  NLHA Bulletin (monthly)

14. National Multi Housing Council
1250 Connecticut Avenue, N.W., #620
Washington, D.C. 20036
202/659–3381
Publications:
  Newsletter (quarterly)
  Washington Watch (weekly)

15. National Realty Committee
1250 Connecticut Avenue, N.W., #630
Washington, D.C. 20036
202/785-0808
  Newsletter (monthly)

16. National Rehab Association
1726 18th Street, N.W.
Washington, D.C. 20009
202/328–9171

17. Real Estate Educators Association
Suite 100
230 N. Michigan Avenue
Chicago, Illinois 60611
312/372–9800
Publication:
  REE Action (quarterly)

18. Real Estate Securities and Syndications Institute
430 N. Michigan Avenue
Chicago, Illinois 60611
Publications:
  Real Estate Securities Journal
  RESSI Review

19. Realtors National Marketing Institute
    430 N. Michigan Avenue
    Chicago, Illinois 60611
    312/670–3780
    Publications:
    CCIM Chapter Briefs
    Commercial Investment Journal (quarterly)
    CRB News Brief
    Real Estate Business (bi-monthly)
    Real Estate Perspectives

REAL ESTATE-RELATED PUBLICATIONS

1. *Community Development Digest*
   CD Publications
   100 Summit Building
   8555 16th Street
   Silver Spring, MD 20910
   301/588–6380
   $199/year—monthly

2. *Data User*
   U.S. Department of Commerce
   Bureau of the Census
   Washington, D.C. 20233
   301/783–3238

3. *Evans-Novak Tax Report*
   1750 Pennsylvania Avenue, N.W., #1312
   Washington, D.C. 20006
   202/393–4340
   $200/year—biweekly

4. *Housing Affairs Letter*
   CD Publications
   $199/year—monthly

5. *Housing & Development Reporter*
   Bureau of National Affairs, Inc.
   1231 25th Street, N.W.
   Washington, D.C. 20037
   202/452–4200
   Weekly

6. *Housing Law Bulletin*
   National Housing Law Project
   1950 Addison Street
   Berkeley, CA 94704
   415/548–9400
   $35/year—6 times a year

7. *Housing Market Report*
   CD Publications
   $187/year—24 issues

8. *Landlord Tenant Law Bulletin*
   Quinlan Publishing Co., Inc.
   131 Beverly Street
   Boston, MA 02114
   617/542–0048
   $39.50/year—monthly

9. *Landlord-Tenant Relations Report*
   CD Publications
   $97/year—monthly

10. *Managing Housing*
    CD Publications
    $79/year—monthly

11. *Multi-Housing News*
    1515 Broadway
    New York, New York 10036
    212/869–1300
    Monthly—free

12. *The Real Estate Finance Journal*
    Warren, Gorham & Lamont, Inc.
    One Penn Plaza
    New York, New York 10119
    212/971–5000
    Quarterly

13. *Real Estate Investing Letter*
    Management Resources, Inc.
    96 Morton Street
    New York, NY 10014
    212/620–3131
    $96/year—monthly

14. *Real Estate Investment Digest*
    2111 National Press Building
    Washington, D.C. 20045
    $96/year—monthly

15. *Real Estate Review*
    Warren, Gorham & Lamont, Inc.
    One Penn Plaza
    New York, New York 10119
    212/971–5000
    Quarterly

16. *U.S. Housing Markets*
    404 Penobscot Building
    Detroit, MI 48226
    313/963–9441
    #130/year—monthly plus quarterly forecasts

ADDRESSES OF FINANCIAL PUBLICATIONS:

Barron's
300 North Zeeb Road
Ann Arbor, Michigan 48106

Changing Times
Subscription Center
Editor's Park, MD 20782

Financial Planning Magazine
Institute for Business Planning
2 Concourse Parkway #800
Atlanta, Georgia 30328

Forbes
60 Fifth Ave.
New York, NY 10011

Fortune
1271 Ave. of the Americas
Rockefeller Center
New York, NY 10020

Money Magazine
Subscription Department
P.O. Box 54429
Boulder, Colorado 80322-4429

Registered Representative Magazine
Plaza Publishing Co, Inc.
4300 Campus Drive
Campus Plaza
Newport Beach, CA 92660

Wall Street Journal
Subscription Service Division
P.O. Box 820
Chicopee, MA 01021-9985

LOCATION OF FEDERAL RESERVE BANKS IN THE UNITED STATES

Atlanta
104 Marietta St. NW
Atlanta, GA 30303-2702
404-586-8500

Boston
600 Atlantic Ave.
Boston, MA 02210-2211
617-973-3000

Chicago
230 S. LaSalle St.
Chicago, IL 60604-1413
312-322-5322

Cleveland
E. Sixth St. & Superior Ave.
Cleveland, OH 44114-2597
216-579-2000

Dallas
400 S. Akard
Dallas, TX 75202-5304
214-651-6111

Kansas City
925 Grand Ave.
Kansas City, MO 64106-2008
816-881-2000

Minneapolis
250 Marquette Ave.
Minneapolis, MN 55401-2117
612-340-2345

New York
33 Liberty St.
New York, NY 10005-1011
212-791-5000

Philadelphia
100 N. Sixth St.
Philadelphia, PA 19106-1516
215-574-8000

Richmond
701 Byrd St.
Richmond, VA 23219-4528
804-843-1250

St. Louis
Box 442
St. Louis, MO 63166-0942
314-444-8444

San Francisco
400 Sansome St.
San Francisco, CA 94111-3305
415-544-2000

GLOSSARY OF REAL ESTATE TERMS

amenities Support facilities that attract and keep the type of client you seek.

amortized loan A loan in which the principal as well as the interest are payable in monthly or other periodic installments over the term of the loan.

area A piece of geography that includes living, employment, shopping, and entertainment within a 20-minute boundary.

balance sheet A financial statement showing the assets and liabilities of a person or a business at a particular point in time. The bottom line indicates net worth—what you would have left if you liquidated all assets.

balloon payment The payment of a mortgage loan that is considerably larger than the required periodic payments because the loan amount was not fully amortized.

capitalization rate The rate of return a property will produce on the owner's investment. It shows your return assuming no mortgage or tax benefits are available.

capitalization ratio Net operating income divided by purchase price.

cash flow The net spendable income from an investment, determined by deducting all operating and fixed expenses (including debt service) from the gross income. If expenses exceed income, the result is a negative cash flow.

Economic Valuation System An orderly approach to real estate buying. It enables you to maximize investment results by providing criteria for evaluating physical and financial aspects of any real estate purchase.

equity The interest or value which an owner has in his or her property over and above any mortgage indebtedness.

escrow The closing of a transaction through a third party called an escrow agent, who receives certain funds and documents to be delivered upon the performance of specific conditions outlined in the escrow agreement, as dictated by the purchase agreement.

fixed-rate mortgage A mortgage in which the interest rate remains the same throughout the life of the mortgage.

gross rent multiplier A figure representing the relationship of the annual collection of rent to the purchase price. Purchase price divided by the gross rental income equals the gross rent multiplier.

interest A charge made by a lender for the use of money.

lease An agreement between a landlord (lessor) and a tenant (the lessee), transferring the right to exclusive possession and use of the landlord's real property to the lessee for a specified period of time, with certain conditions and for a stated rent.

leverage The use of credit to purchase real estate.

market price The actual selling price of a property.

master limited partnerships (MLPs) Pools of limited partnerships, legally similar to real estate limited partnerships.

mortgage A debt on property or land. The borrower (mortgagor) borrows money from the lender (mortgagee) and uses either land or improvements on the land, or both, as the collateral to secure such borrowing. This is non-recourse borrowing.

net lease A lease requiring a tenant to pay not only rent, but also all costs incurred in maintaining the property, including taxes, insurance, utilities, and repairs. It usually excludes capital improvements.

net operating income (NOI) Gross income minus operating expenses.

option An agreement to keep open for a set period an offer to sell or purchase property.

percentage lease A lease commonly used for commercial property, such as a shopping center. The rental is based on the tenant's gross sales at the premises. This type of lease generally stipulates a base monthly rental plus a percentage of any gross sales above a specified amount.

profit and loss statement An accounting record that shows net profit or loss over a cumulative period of time. It consists of two parts: income and expenses.

profit margin A ratio representing money left after paying expenses, divided by the sales or income taken in.

profits from a sale Sales price − (cost + expenses) = profits.

prospectus   A statement outlining the main features of a business enterprise when it is being sold as a security. It follows a format required by the Securities and Exchange Commission.

purchase price   Down payment plus mortgage.

real estate investment trusts (REITs)   Trusts that invest in diversified real estate, mortgage portfolios, land, or some combination of them. Their stock is usually publicly traded on exchanges or over the counter.

real estate limited partnerships (RELPs)   A public or private (as defined by S.E.C. regulations) offering of real estate purchased and managed by general partners. The funds of investors (limited partners) are pooled.

structural integrity   The approval or qualification of all mechanical and structural improvements, as well as the supporting land.

syndicate   A combination of persons or firms to accomplish a joint venture of mutual interest.

tax rate   The rate at which real property is taxed in a particular tax district or county. For example, in a certain county the tax rate on real property might be .065 cents per dollar of assessed valuation.

time is of the essence   A phrase in a contract that requires the performance of a certain act within a stated period of time.

variable-rate mortgage   A mortgage in which the interest rate can vary during the term of the mortgage. Also known as adjustable-rate mortgage.

yield   Net operating income or cash flow if a mortgage exists divided by purchase price, multiplied by 100.

INDEX

A

Active investing
  duties involved, 28–30
  initial investment, 30
Amenities
  Amenities Worksheet, 138–139
  definition, 132
  effects of, 133–136
  evaluation of, 137–145
Amortization; *see* mortgages
Apartments
  advantages for new investors, 41
  disadvantages, 42
  need for hiring a manager, 42
Area
  Area Valuation Worksheet, 88–89
  changes in, 221–223
  chart, 86
  competition within, 94, 95
  criteria for judging, 88–98
  definition, 85
  effect of real estate cycles, 238–239
  employment base, 85–86
  sources of information, 86–87

B

Balance sheet
  business, 7
  definition, 7
  personal, 8, 13, 14
  significance, 9, 10

Brokers
  purchase transactions, 44
  sales transactions, 225–227, 230–231, 233

C

Capital appreciation
  increases net worth, 33, 37
Capitalization Rate
  and leverage, 151–152
  Capitalization Rate Worksheet, 162
  definition, 148
  effect on value and price, 150–153
Capitalization ratio
  definition, 35
  effect on price, 152–153
  effect on property value, 35–36, 149–155,
  monitoring for changes, 224–225
  qualitative study, 154–160
  quantitative study, 150–154
Cash flow
  balance sheet, 7
  effect of repairs on, 114–115
  profit and loss statement, 6
Competition
  and marketing plan, 207–208
  within an area, 94–95
Contracts
  protection for buyer, 79
  relationship to Economic Valuation
    System, 79–82